100 Years
of African
Missions

Essays in Honor of
Wendell Broom

100 Years of African Missions: Essays in Honor of Wendell Broom

A·C·U
PRESS

ACU Box 29138
Abilene, TX 79699
www.acu.edu/acupress

Cover Design and Typesetting by Sarah Bales

Stanley E. Granberg, editor

Printed in the United States of America

ISBN 0-915547-68-6

Library of Congress Card Number: 2001092766

1,2,3,4,5

Table of Contents

Section III
Mission Strategies and Issues

Section IV
Concluding Thoughts

Introduction

My first introduction to Wendell Broom was in 1982 during the Summer Seminar in Missions at Abilene Christian University. Wendell taught the church growth class that our Meru mission team took as we prepared for the Kenyan mission field. I was entranced with the way Wendell infused the course material with life, not only from his experiences on the mission field in Nigeria, but with his passion and knowledge of God's activity in the world. Wendell urged us to look beyond the methods, the numbers, the ideas of planting germinal churches towards the energizing work of God and His Spirit. Wendell transformed the way I saw the world, and the way I would later approach my mission work in Kenya.

It was at the evening devotionals, our mission vespers, however, where Wendell made his deepest impact on me. Night after night he led us to explore the depth of God's love for the world and its people in ways that I had not experienced before. He reached into my heart and plucked cords which had as yet never sounded–and made them sing. Wendell is, for me, the most adept devotional master I have ever encountered. It was during those heady days of preparation for the field that the thought first struck me that here was a man whose life for God deserved a special celebration.

Through the years since then, Wendell and Betty Broom continued to influence me and so many other missionaries. The Brooms came through Kenya several times, sharing their encouragement with everyone they met. On furloughs we would pass through Abilene and share a visit or phone conversation with them. After my family returned to the States, the annual World Mission Workshop became a reunion time where Wendell and I could grab a corner table to dream the dreams of God together. Wendell continually encouraged me as I pursued first the Th.M. in church leadership and then the Ph.D. as I studied African church leaders. When I at last finished that final degree it seemed time to honor Wendell with a book. Knowing how many people Wendell has influenced, the task begged for the involvement of others. It was truly a joy to see how the contributing authors gladly, enthusiastically, accepted and carried out their assignments. We can think of no better way to express our appreciation for this man who has influenced us in so ways then to tell the story of God's missionary work in Africa through the Churches of Christ. One hundred and a few years they now total, and what marvelous years they have been.

As you, the reader, make your way through these pages there are a few thoughts I would ask you to keep in mind. First, take time to develop an overall view of this one hundred years of mission work. I believe you will be amazed at the breadth of the work in Africa, breadth of time, geography and in the many forms these ministries have taken. Second, despite the variety of works represented here there is a consistency which underlies the different storylines. While each author writes with his own style and perspective, all the authors share a similar passion for what God has called them to do. It is clearly evident that these authors have not just done their research on these chapters, they have lived what these chapters portray.

Finally, remember that this volume is, at best, only a partial account of this part God's mission in Africa. There are other voices which lie behind those of the authors, and even the author's subjects, whose contributions are, in some ways, even more vital than those of the people about whom you will read. Particularly I refer to our African brothers and sisters and to missionary wives and women. Listen for their voices behind these written words, for they are there; often subtle and at times overshadowed, but present nevertheless. Perhaps the day will come when another volume will be written to celebrate their contributions.

This book is organized into four major sections. Section I introduces Wendell Broom. The first chapter is Wendell's biography, which lets you see the way God has both developed and used Wendell as his missionary servant. In chapter 2 Wendell reflects on the history of Africa, the amazing Christianization of this continent in less than 150 years, and the 100 years of mission work of the Churches of Christ in Africa. In chapter 3 Gailyn Van Rheenen reviews the missionary metaphors, some quixotic and others sublime, which have marked Wendell's writings and teaching.

Section II is "God's Call to a Continent: People and Places." This series of seven chapters provides an overview of the history and major elements of the African mission work of the Churches of Christ. Chapters 4, 5, and 6 survey the three primary geographic divisions of Africa south of the Sahara desert: Southern Africa, West Africa and East Africa. These chapters orient to these geographic regions of Africa, then provide brief surveys of many of the works of the Churches of Christ in each country. These surveys are not exhaustive, but they do try to give as complete a picture as possible of the mission personnel, important events and places within each country's mission history. Finally, these survey chapters provide a snapshot of the current state of the church in each country, how many Churches of Christ, church members, on-going efforts, and key national Christians.

The remaining chapters in Section II review specific types of mission efforts which have been important to the work of the Churches of Christ in Africa. Tex Williams, director of World Bible School, provides a history of World Bible School and demonstrates how this simple tool has effectively penetrated Africa and brought a significant harvest of believers into the kingdom of God. Sam Shewmaker, lifelong missionary, describes the "Africans Claiming Africa" conferences which have gathered together African brethren from across the continent to discuss how they will carry on the evangelizing work of the church. Glenn Boyd, president emeritus of International Health Care Foundation, discusses the historical transitions in mission-based health care from its beginnings as informal "treatment on the road" to the establishment of mission hospitals and clinics staffed by professional health care workers and evangelists. The final chapter in Section II is a collection on Christian education in Africa written by Henry Huffard, president of African Christian Schools Foundation, William Searcy, chairman and registrar of the Nairobi Great Commission School, and Roger Dickson, director of the International School of Biblical Studies. These men demonstrate that Christian education, in its multitude of forms, continues to be a powerful influence for the advancement and stability of the African church.

Section IV: "Mission Strategies and Issues" presents a series of more formal chapters which will be of particular interest to field missionaries and missiologists. These chapters, drawn primarily from doctoral research, discuss foundational concepts for understanding leadership in East Africa, the formation and training of mission teams, the issues involved in phasing out foreign missionaries in ongoing works, humanitarian relief, and development works and, ends with a look into the African worldview in the chapter "The Gospel and the Spirits." There is a wealth of helpful material in these chapters on topics critical to the long-term success of the African church and the missionary enterprise.

The final section shares some concluding thoughts on the

future of African missions and the African church. Sam Shewmaker in "The Future of Missions in Africa," probes for new strategies, evangelistic resources and roles for the western church and African Christians as we head into the next century. The final content chapter is a speech given by Wendell Broom in 1997 to 178 Nigerian evangelists and church leaders which challenged them (and us) to fill in the unevangelized gaps of Africa with a deliberate church-planting strategy to join the churches of West and East Africa by "meeting in the middle." The book concludes with an extensive bibliography of books, research, and articles on African missions by missionaries and authors associated with the Churches of Christ.

SECTION I

Wendell Broom: A Man for Missions

CHAPTER 1

Wendell Broom: A Biography

Stanley E. Granberg

Stanley Granberg served as a missionary in Meru, Kenya from 1983-1993. He holds the Ph.D from the Open University: Oxford Centre for Mission Studies. He taught as missionary-in-residence at Lubbock Christian University and is currently associate professor of Bible and Missions at Cascade College, Portland, Oregon. stanleygranberg@cs.com

There are few heroes these days; at least that is what we hear people say. But still, when one takes the time to look, there are heroes around us–quiet, unassuming people–who go about their lives with integrity of heart and steadfastness of faith. Heroes are people whom we look up to, people after whom we can model our lives, people who by dint of expertise, accomplishment or character seem to live beyond the rest of us. But most of all, heroes are people who give us hope. Wendell Broom is such a person. My prayer is that in the following few pages your life will be enriched as you see in Wendell's life the pattern of God's hand molding, preparing, guiding for His purposes and glory. And perhaps, you will gain a new hero too.

Early Years as an Oklahoma Sooner, 1923-1940

Wendell Broom was born to Benjamin Rufus Broom and

Gladys Elizabeth Wright Broom on April 6, 1923 in Oklahoma City, Oklahoma, followed by a brother, Charles. Wendell and the state of Oklahoma grew up together, the former Indian Territory having gained statehood only sixteen years earlier. Wendell's father was a native born Georgian who went west with the emerging oil industry. Rufus worked for Magnolia Petroleum managing a filling station in Oklahoma City for forty-two years. Wendell's mother, Gladys, was born and raised in Arkansas.

Rufus and Gladys carried out a frontier courtship. They first met in Georgia where Gladys had traveled to visit relatives. The following year, after a season of paper courting through letters, Rufus made a trip to Arkansas to visit Gladys and her family. That trip must have gone well, because Rufus followed it with a third visit when he married Gladys and took her back with him to his new home in Oklahoma.

Growing up in a pioneer setting made its imprint on Wendell. At that time most Oklahoma residents were transplants from the older states to the east. The Brooms, like many of the people around them, were a practical family with a fiscally conservative streak which kept the family fed and clothed through the depression years. Hardships were not going to dislodge this family. Rufus sold gas at his Magnolia Petroleum filling station for ten cents a gallon, taking home a penny profit for each gallon sold, while Gladys stretched out the family's food budget with beans and cornbread. Boarders in the Broom home provided some extra some extra income. Gladys' sister spent most of the 1920s living with the Broom family, and other boarders came and went. Physical hardships were not feared in the Broom home; perseverance was a trait which grew in Wendell as he grew up in the Sooner state.

Wendell's spiritual formation centered around the 10th and Francis Church of Christ, the first church of Christ in Oklahoma

City. Even though Rufus Broom was raised Presbyterian, Gladys' heritage in the churches of Christ was the primary religious force in the Broom household. Wendell garnered a strong pulpit education in the Bible from the preachers who occupied the 10th and Francis pulpit: C. A. Norred, A. O. Colley, C. E. McGaughey, Yater Tant, Jack Meyer and others. Foy Wallace was a regular "meeting" preacher at the congregation in those years. By 1942 the 10th and Francis congregation was the largest in the state with over 1,200 members.

Two people in particular influenced Wendell's spiritual growth during his early years. The first was his mother. While Gladys was never obvious with her desires, Wendell now sees his mother as being guided by a dream for him to preach. When Wendell was eight years old Gladys arranged for him to take private "expression" lessons at twenty-five cents an hour. Wendell learned poetry for recitation and was taught skills in pronunciation and annunciation.

When Wendell was in high school his mom found another way to hone Wendell's public speaking skills. Wendell became active in the Boy Scouts of America. In his junior year Wendell ran for state governor in the Scout program. Gladys drove Wendell to two or three speaking engagements a week barnstorming Scout troops with campaign speeches. Wendell lost the election, but he learned how to speak his mind in a directive, persuasive manner. Wendell now feels more strongly than ever that his mother had a plan she was quietly promoting for preparing her son for service in the Kingdom of God.

Finally, when Wendell left for college at Freed-Hardeman Gladys began buying a book for Wendell's personal library at each birthday. These were well chosen books to meet the needs of a preacher. Her first purchase was *Young's Analytical Concordance.* Each new volume Gladys sent reflected the considered opinion of a practicing pulpit man whose advice Gladys had sought out so she could buy a useful gift for her son. The influence of a faithful mother was a gentle, constant source of persuasion in the formation of Wendell's spiritual life.

The second formative person influencing Wendell's career path at the 10th and Francis congregation was Lewis Fisher. Brother Fisher was an American Indian and he had a passion for training boys to preach. Each year he would round up all the sixteen or seventeen year olds he could find and take them to preach in the smaller country churches surrounding Oklahoma City. Brother Fisher relentlessly pursued Wendell (at least that is how Wendell remembers it) to get him on the preaching team. In Wendell's junior year he became one of fifteen or so young men on Fisher's preaching team, ten of whom became preachers.

The elders wanted to support these efforts, so that summer they arranged for John P. Lewis, the Bible chair director at Oklahoma University in Norman, to drive in on Tuesday evenings to teach these young men. The first class had only two boys in attendance. Sunday morning the elders read off a list of boys they wanted to meet with after services; Wendell's name was among them. The boys knew what was in store. As they sat on the front pew the elders started at one end and asked each boy why he had not been present Tuesday evening for the training class. Wendell sat at the farthest end of the bench. As each boy gave his answer Wendell searched his mind for some straw of a remark that might save him. At that time Wendell was just five merit badges away from making Eagle Scout. Scouting was an important part of Wendell's life, but the Scout troop meetings were on Tuesday evenings. When the elders put their question to Wendell he gave up scouting and joined the preaching class. The active, directive force of the elders in his church, the informal ministry of Lewis Fisher, and the influence of

6

his godly mother laid the groundwork and prepared Wendell to decide on his career–he was going to preach.

College Years: 1941-1945

Wendell was the first in his family to graduate from college. With his career decision firmly in mind the only choice was what college to attend. The preachers his family consulted were firm in recommending the A.A. degree granting Freed-Hardeman college in Henderson, Tennessee so that Wendell could study under N. B. Hardeman, "a great pulpit man" as they put it. That summer, 1941, Foy Wallace helped Wendell to register for the draft as a ministerial student, a status he held through his graduation from Abilene Christian College in 1945, two weeks after the German surrender. Wendell sees God's hand in keeping him from earthly war. Because of this Wendell feels an incredible debt for the kingdom and has never refused an invitation for ministry anywhere in the world. God needed a man to prepare for kingdom duty, not war duty.

God used Wendell's two years at Freed-Hardeman College to add further to his preparation. The most significant event was meeting his future wife, Betty Billingsley, whom Wendell married upon his graduation from ACC in 1945. Like Wendell, Betty had grown up in Oklahoma where her father had practiced frontier medicine when Oklahoma was Indian Territory. A second important personal event was baptizing his father during his first summer home in 1942, the first person Wendell baptized. Educationally, the most lasting contribution Wendell gained from Freed-Hardeman came through W. C. Hall who taught English composition, spoken English and Old Testament classes. Brother Hall's aim in life was to teach men sound speech habits for the pulpit. Students thought him a vicious teacher who would end their speeches at the first grammatical error or the second "um" or mispronunciation. While Hall's

7

reputation among the students brought forth anger, Wendell recalls that "furious students remember their lessons."

Since Freed-Hardeman College was a two year school Wendell planned to go elsewhere for his bachelor's degree. From early on Wendell's dream had been to graduate from Abilene Christian College (ACC) in Abilene, Texas. At age six or seven, while visiting a relative in Arkansas, he happened upon a 1923 ACC yearbook in a bedroom closet. That yearbook belonging to his cousins, all four graduates of ACC, set the idea in Wendell's heart that he too would graduate from ACC. ACC introduced Wendell to scholarly biblical studies through a strong Bible program and opened Wendell to a wider world and a more diverse brotherhood of the churches of Christ. Wendell was a leader on campus, serving as president of the junior class, of the Acapella chorus, and of the student association his senior year. These positions challenged him to sharpen his leadership and public speaking skills.

Two instructors were standouts for Wendell at ACC. One was Charles Roberson, professor of New Testament Greek. This course was not taught at Freed-Hardeman College, so Wendell took his first year of Greek as a junior and his second and third years simultaneously as a senior. Wendell remembers Roberson as a master pedagogical instructor, an equal to W. C. Hall at Freed-Hardeman.

The other faculty influence was Howard Schug, ACC language instructor who taught Latin, Spanish and French. Schug was passionate about God's mission in the world. He co-authored *The Harvest Field*, the first published book on missions in the churches of Christ, with ACC president Jesse P. Sewell. Schug was also the faculty sponsor of the ACC missions club, which met Wednesday evenings in the break between supper and the Wednesday prayer meeting. The mission club was a loosely organized coterie of students with a like-mind for missions. Among this group of students and mission pioneers were Otis Gatewood (missionary to Germany and the Soviet Union), Cline Paden (missionary to Italy and founder of Sunset International Bible Institute), Richard Walker (missionary to Germany) and J. Harold Thomas (missionary to the northeast United States). These students were looking for a place in the kingdom. Their speakers were any missionary (few in number at that time) who would share with them "crumbs from the rich man's table." But, like Jesus with the loaves and fishes, God used those crumbs to spawn the post-WWII burst of missions by the churches of Christ. This charged atmosphere of expectation buried a seed deep in Wendell's heart, a seed that began its growth in the northeast United States, grew strong in Nigeria, and finally came full circle back at ACU.

The Mission Fields: Delaware, Nigeria, Hawaii

True to his pioneer upbringing, upon graduating from ACC in 1945 with a degree in Bible Wendell and his new bride, Betty Billingsley Broom, moved to Delaware for their first preaching ministry. In those years the northeastern United States was a true mission field for the largely southern Churches of Christ. In 1938 there were only two full-time preachers of the Churches of Christ north of Washington D. C. The Brooms left Abilene with all their possessions loaded into the backseat and trunk of their 1936 Chevy and headed to Wilmington, Delaware to substitute preach for the small Elsmere congregation for six weeks while their regular preacher visited Arizona. He did not return, so the Brooms took up full-time residence in Wilmington working under the oversight of the elders of the Old Hickory Church of Christ in Nashville, Tennessee. The Old Hickory congregation supported Wendell in Delaware for seven years.

Delaware and Pennsylvania, 1945-1955

The Elsmere congregation had just twenty-eight members in 1945. But it was a work which challenged Wendell to communicate God's Word to them and to lead these members to greater maturity and growth. Wendell gained valuable teaching experience and preparation in the Word preaching at the Wilmington church. The success was remarkable with the membership growing from twenty-eight in 1945 to 130 in 1952. Those years also gave Wendell a taste of church-planting as he started two other congregations in southern Delaware and attempted two more church plants in New Jersey and Annapolis. Wendell also took the opportunity to continue his academic growth, taking classes at Faith Theological Seminary and Temple University Divinity School. In 1952 the Brooms moved to Philadelphia to work with the 56th and Warrington Church of Christ. In 1955, with ten years of preaching experience, stability in their marriage relationship, and three children in the nest (Wendell Jr., 1947; Mary Beth, 1950; David, 1953), God had brought this family to the point of readiness for a call to foreign missions.

Nigeria, 1955-1960

In the aftermath of WWII the churches of Christ were waking up to God's call to foreign missions. George Gurganus followed in the footsteps of J. M. McCaleb to post-war Japan. Otis Gatewood blazed the trail into post-war Europe, particularly Germany. Cline Paden began work in Italy. The church was bursting with new missions activity, but, for the most part, the home churches were ill-prepared. Our brotherhood schools also were just beginning to see the need for missions preparation. But God was already at work in Nigeria, through a man named C. A. O. Essien, a Nigerian policeman. Essien, like many of his friends, was a drinker, and a womanizer. He often used his official position for purposes of graft and greed. In 1948 Essien awoke from a disturbing dream in the cold sweat of fear. In his dream he had died and gone to the judgment bar of heaven–there Essien realized he was lost. When he awoke, Essien repented before God in his heart and began to search for salvation. Essien studied the Bible through a correspondence course by the Churches of Christ which came by way of Germany, but had originated in Tennessee. Drawing upon the teachings from this course and his meager background with the Presbyterian church, Essien converted some friends; and together they planted sixty-five small churches over the next few years. Eldred Echols[1] has referred to Essien as "the Alexander Campbell of Africa." He was a powerful preacher, a strong leader of men who could call others to allegiance in the kingdom of God and follow him in the kind of service to God to which he gave his heart, his soul and his passion. The impact of God on one man has untold potential. From this small beginning, a great planting of the church in Africa would arise.

Howard Horton and Jimmy Johnson, the first American missionaries of the Churches of Christ to reside in Nigeria, arrived in 1952 to follow up on Essien's work. These men had no training in missions and no plans to speak of, except to preach and teach wherever and as often as they could. Their first two years were survival years spent in building adequate housing and learning how to live in equatorial Africa. Horton knew, however, that what they needed was more help, so he made a list of men whom he knew and wrote them about the needs of this new work in Nigeria. One person on Horton's list was Wendell Broom; the two had worked together briefly in the Northeast. When Horton's letter arrived Wendell had become a successful church-planter and located preacher in

---

[1] Eldred Echols himself was a pioneer in opening up the work in Nigeria. You may read his story in *Wings of the Morning- The Saga of an African Pilgrim.*

Philadelphia, a mission field in itself. Wendell had many family obligations at the time. Wendell Jr. was seven years old, Mary Beth was five, David two and Betty was pregnant with Margaret. Betty's mother had cancer, and Wendell and Betty could see a care-giving task on the horizon. They could not possibly answer this call. Wendell wrote a letter to Horton identifying all the reasons why they could not be the ones to come, and then threw the letter away. Wendell wrote five more letters explaining why he and Betty could not come to Nigeria. None made it any farther than the wastebasket. As so often happens with people of missionary heart, Wendell knew that while the reasons they could not go might be fitting for paper, they would not be adequate answers before the throne of God. The only letter he mailed to Howard Horton was their acceptance letter.

How do you prepare to leave family, home, and the only life you know to move halfway around the world to a place which would not even have registered as a third world country at that time? Reflecting on his preparation, Wendell calls it "one notch above zero." There was no program, plan, or place where someone could go to prepare for mission work. Wendell was able to spend six weeks traveling with Howard Horton in the United States, speaking to congregations and questioning Horton about Nigeria. This was missions on the frontier—a place where God would again use Wendell and Betty's pioneer spirit. For three months the Broom family lived with Wendell's parents and did fund-raising. The 10th and Francis congregation agreed to pay them $5,000 a year for a two-year commitment, with supplemental funds coming from individual supporters. It was not much, but it was enough to meet the family's needs. In February 1955 Margaret was born and in July 1955 Wendell, Betty and their four young children boarded a plane for Africa; they would not see Betty's mother alive again.

Equatorial Africa is not an easy place to live. It is always hot, and humid most of the time. The Churches of Christ were then located only in the southeast corner of Nigeria, mostly among the Ibibio people. There was no electricity, no running water, no indoor plumbing, not any of the conveniences of home. Water for cooking, bathing and cleaning was hauled from the river. Cooking was done on a wood-burning stove. This was bush living, the kind that consumes your time with surviving and drains away your strength. Wendell and Betty were not alone, though, in dealing with these rigors. Other missionary families, many of them Freed-Hardeman schoolmates, would follow: Bill Nicks, James Finney, Elvis Huffard, Sewell Hall, Rees Bryant, Burney Bawcom, Gene Peden, E. Lucien Palmer, and others.

The immediate work demand was to continue feeding the sixty-five small churches begun by C. A. O. Essien and friends. This meant extensive travel on jungle roads to the small villages scattered across the countryside. It also meant accepting the invitations to preach at new villages to begin new congregations. Sundays were given over to preaching at the older churches. The men often visited three to five congregations on a single Sunday; on one typical preaching trip they taught fourteen different groups in four days. Weekday mornings, from eight to twelve, were spent teaching in the new Bible training school Howard Horton had begun in 1954. The first forty students were in their second year when Wendell arrived. The Americans taught in English in the Bible School, because all the students were English speakers. The Bible School followed a two-year program of classes, taking in forty new men every year. That small school, later named Nigerian Christian Bible College, continues to graduate about forty preachers a year and has done so every year since 1954, except for the three years of the Biafran war. Certainly there are many factors which contributed to the growth of

2,500 Churches of Christ in Nigeria with over 200,000 members; Nigerian Christian Bible College was one.

Missiology, the study of how to do missions, was in its infancy in 1955. The missionaries experienced mistakes along with the triumphs. One of the underlying causes of many difficulties Wendell and his co-workers experienced was their blindness to the cross-cultural issues of being an American working in Africa. What is eternal and what is temporal? How do you raise Nigerian Christians when all you know is how to be an American Christian? This was a constant question for Wendell in those years. Not knowing the answers made the introduction of chrome-plated communion trays, bull horns for preaching and other innovations seem natural. But such American exports seldom gave back in benefits more than they produced in trouble. One lesson which powerfully shaped Wendell's mission philosophy came from the decision to put outstanding graduates of the Bible training school on American support.

What do you do with forty brand new graduates from your first class of preachers? From the American point of view the practical, logical answer was to find a way for these men to make their full-time living as preachers. But the local churches were not ready to do that. Wendell's Feb. 1, 1956 newsletter indicates their problem and their solution,

> WHAT NOW? Denominational-trained churches expect to be forced to pay their preachers: we will not do this, for scriptural reasons. The result is that churches are in a slump between denominational "pressure-giving" and maturity in Christian giving. Combine with this their poverty (wages average from 30 to 50 cents per day) and the result is that we have 200 churches that need teaching and 40 well-trained preachers–but due to the financial situation, the men are being forced to return to secular work to keep from starving.

...for $20 American a month (for each preacher)...we propose to send two men to each district to work among the churches (with 60 churches in some districts, two men are not enough, but it's better than nothing). These men will visit among the churches, teach three month training courses (four days a week, four classes a day) for elders, deacons, Bible teachers, etc.

All the men in the first graduating class received this support. Men in the next class got similar support. But what would be done with the third class, and the fourth, fifth and so on? How far could this be replicated?

Just two years later their solution had become the problem. Wendell wrote in his Jan. 4, 1958 newsletter,

For about two years, some American brethren and churches have been supporting and helping to support some of the Nigerian evangelists. This was done in an effort to get the teaching before the churches until they could grow and progress enough to support their own men. Now, however, we find that our American help is having the opposite effect—the churches are wanting more and more American help rather than less and less. Instead of helping them move toward independence and self-support, it has been causing them to lean more and more upon the American brethren.

Wendell relates that the American-supported preachers were not seen by their fellow Nigerians as people with answers to life's struggles; these men were paid American employees. As a result, these preachers lost their credibility as independent witnesses of the gospel of Jesus Christ. Some of the churches with salaried preachers stopped growing at thirty to forty members while non-salaried churches would grow to be much larger. Also, the good relationships between the American missionaries and the salaried, national preachers began to sour.

Facing the unexpected consequences of paying national evangelists, the missionaries reversed their policy. They began to reduce the amount of salary each preacher received twenty-five percent every six months until all support was gone. The Americans traveled to every congregation they could reach to tell them the plan and to encourage those Christians to begin paying their own workers. It was a difficult task but forty-five years later the situation appears to support their wisdom and courage.

When Wendell and Betty's two-year commitment was about to end, they knew it was not yet time to return to the States. Wendell put their thoughts to paper in the April 14, 1957 newsletter,

> As the time passed the half way mark of our work over here, we began to think of the future. Tenth and Francis church had promised to support us for 2 years, which they have carried out in a most excellent way. I thought two years would be enough of a contribution for us to make to this work. But I have asked the elders of Tenth and Francis church to continue their fellowship with us in this work, and make it possible for us to return for another two years work.
>
> Why do this? There are many good reasons why a man ought not to bring his family back again. For one thing, there is separation from loved ones. While we've been here, Betty's mother passed away (as did Billy Nick's father, sister Johnson's mother, brother Finney's father, sister Finney's brother-in-law) and it is a heavy feeling to be so far away at such times. There are problems with the schooling. There is the expense of the trip again, and the necessary raising of travel and operational funds, which is essential if we return (it makes me shudder to face the prospect again of running about seeking for the necessary funds). I guess all these can be pretty formidable reasons for not coming—especially to those who add to them the dangers of "African life" which they judge . . . formidable enough to keep many good and capable preachers from such a vital work as this.
>
> And that is just the reason we feel we must return.

This work must be done, and there just aren't enough men to do it. We would personally prefer to return to the Northeastern US, resume local work, and enjoy the mission work in that needy section among our own people. but who will do the work here?

Betty and Wendell renewed their commitment for another two and a half years, as did the 10th and Francis church, and the work continued. New and exciting opportunities arose. In 1958 Benny Lee Fudge was corresponding with a Ghanaian friend. Later that year Sewell Hall and Wendell traveled to Ghana to find this man. He was a member of the Salvation Army and just a few years away from retiring. Based on his new commitment to Jesus in baptism, during this visit the man resigned his post and began to preach with the churches of Christ. Today there are 700 congregations in Ghana with 56,000 members. Wendell was also involved in beginning the work in Cameroun where he and his party of seven Nigerian preachers planted three churches during a three week trip. Cameroun now has 127 congregations with 3,150 members.

The church in Nigeria has matured into a church with outstanding leaders, men and women, who have excelled in faithfulness. Among them are several holding doctoral degrees as well as dozens holding master's degrees. These men lead Bible training schools, administer hospitals, organize mission work into other parts of Nigeria and surrounding countries. The Nigerian Christians know that the doctrinal and leadership decisions of God's people in Nigeria rest with them and they accept those responsibilities in the presence of God with commitment and dedication.

The Broom family returned to the States in 1960. The fatigue factor of working long hours in tropical conditions, driving jungle roads, and preaching and teaching daily had taken their toll. There was also the emotional impact of living in constant contact with extreme poverty, illness and death. It was time to return to the States for renewal and to finish raising their five children, Kathryn having been born in Nigeria in 1958. It was also a time God needed to prepare Wendell for his next major contribution to missions.

THE ROAD TO ABILENE CHRISTIAN COLLEGE

Delaware and Hawaii, 1960-1968

Returning to the States from the foreign mission field is often a disorienting process, but the Brooms made their re-entry with minimal difficulties and adjustments. Returning to Elsmere, Delaware, a place familiar to them, eased the Broom's transition. The church loved Wendell and Betty, recognizing them as a couple returning with hard-earned experience. Wendell and Betty worked with the Elsmere congregation from 1960-1965. The church was over two hundred strong, but in 1960 it still had need to grow. First and foremost on Wendell's mind was to challenge the church to work beyond their congregational borders. Within twelve months the congregation was supporting Jerry Reynolds to work with Dwayne Davenport in Ghana. Wendell and the church were also involved in the start of Northeastern Christian College where Wendell served on the board of directors. The Elsmere congregation appointed elders for the first time and built a new building during this second five years Wendell and Betty worked with them. It was a satisfying return to stateside preaching. The last of the Broom children, Jonathan, was born there in 1962.

God's missionary call to Wendell was not, however, a part time or even a part of a life-time call. Years earlier Wendell had commented to Betty that a perfect career would be to preach, to work on the mission field, and to teach missions at a Christian college. It

18

was in pursuit of that dream that Wendell moved his family to Honolulu, Hawaii in 1965. Wendell's intention was to enter the doctoral program in anthropology at the University of Hawaii. God had other plans. The anthropology department rejected Wendell's application for admittance when they learned his purpose for studying anthropology was to learn better how to do cross-cultural mission work. So from 1965-68 Wendell preached for the Keeaumoku St. Church of Christ and waited for the Lord's door of opportunity to open.

God's door came in the guise of George Gurganus. Gurganus was the pioneer missions educator in the Churches of Christ. He did mission work in Japan in the 1950s, an experience which convinced him of the need for training in mission work. Following up on this recognition Gurganus studied at Pennsylvania State University, becoming the first person in the churches of Christ to receive an advanced degree in a missions related field. In 1963 Gurganus created the Summer Seminar in Missions at Harding Graduate School of Religion in Memphis, Tennessee to provide missions training. He invited Wendell to teach at that first summer missions seminar. In 1968 Gurganus moved the Summer Seminar in Missions to Abilene Christian College. His goal was to develop the first missions department in Church of Christ schools. To accomplish this goal he needed another full-time missions professor on faculty and Wendell was his man. ACC extended an invitation to Wendell but with the stipulation that he complete a missions degree at Fuller Theological Seminary's School of World Mission in Pasadena, California.

Fuller Theological Seminary/School of World Mission, 1969-1970

Fuller's School of World Mission is one of the largest and most influential missions training programs in the world. The School of

World Missions was founded by Donald McGavran, father of the Church Growth Movement. McGavran shared a heritage in the Restoration Movement. He was also the man with the ideas which captured Wendell's attention as offering insights and answers to many of the events he had experienced in Nigeria. Wendell elected to study under McGavran, making church growth his area of research[2].

For the eighteen months they were in Pasadena, California Wendell and Betty had no regular income. Their faith was challenged, but God provided what they needed, blessing the Broom family in ways Wendell says even now they do not fully understand. They were also surprised by the difficult social adjustment they experienced, moving out of pulpit ministry into a ministry of education. For their entire career their lives and friendships had been wrapped up in the church wherever they were ministering. Now those relationships were gone. They found the world outside pulpit ministry to be a hard, cold world for them. Wendell acquired a new set of relationships revolving around missions, and God provided them with fellow students and with his mentor, Donald McGavran.

McGavran was well acquainted with the Churches of Christ. He knew Gurganus, had spoken twice at Harding Graduate School and was familiar with ACC as well. In a rare invitation to a master's level student McGavran offered Wendell the opportunity to attend the faculty meetings of the School of World Missions. McGavran knew that the education Wendell needed to take with him to ACC was not just book learning; he would also need understanding and skills to work within the system of an institution. Wendell needed to know what faculty did, how they made decisions, and how

---

[2] Broom, Wendell (1970). *Growth of Churches of Christ among the Ibibio of Nigeria.* Unpublished master's thesis, Fuller Theological Seminary, School of World Mission.

programs fit into the overall functioning of a school. McGavran graciously and effectively mentored Wendell in these areas as well as in his academic studies. Wendell graduated with the M.A. in church growth from Fuller in 1970. With renewed strength in God's providing character and a godly mentor it was time to head to Abilene.

Abilene Christian University, 1970-1992

In 1968 George Gurganus moved to ACC, which became Abilene Christian University (ACU) in 1976, with the dream of creating the first missions department among schools of the Churches of Christ. George was an intense program builder, and he worked diligently to bring that dream to fruition from 1968 to 1980. Wendell came to ACU as Gurganus' right-hand man, complementing George's experience in Japan with his own experience in Africa and tempering George's fiery style with his calm consideration. The two men made a powerful team, and under their direction a nascent missions department began to emerge.

The centerpiece of ACU's missions program was the academic study of missions and preparation of missionaries. Wendell taught courses on missions such as *Introduction to Church Growth, Missionary Anthropology, Mission and Expansion of the Church, World Christians, Introduction to Communism,* and *Special Studies in Africa.* Wendell brought his academic expertise into the classroom, but what most students remember about his classes is the heart of the missionary they saw as Wendell shared stories and experiences from the mission field.

Gurganus and Wendell continued to build the missions program, adding a two-year apprenticeship program called MARK and a missionary-in-residence program which has attracted numerous field missionaries to teach Bible classes and recruit mission teams.

They also initiated the annual Teachers of Mission Workshop in the 1970's, a program which ACU continues to host.

The Summer Seminar in Missions continued to grow as well. Here again is a place where Wendell demonstrated his heart for God and missions. For many years Wendell coordinated the evening devotions at the Summer Seminar. Wendell did not just coordinate the speakers or topics, but he coordinated our hearts with God's heart as well. Sometimes he did that with a short lesson, at other times it was with a few words of instruction or encouragement. But more than in any other way, Wendell led us into the heart of God through his prayers. As he prayed for us, for missionaries around the world, for victories in the kingdom he roused in our hearts the same passion for missions and the world which he felt so keenly and which so surely infuses God's heart too.

When Gurganus retired from ACU in 1980 the missions program was still operating within the Bible department. Ed Mathews followed Gurganus as director of the missions group. Ed and Wendell continued to develop the missions program, moving it towards departmental status. They added new courses to the curriculum, strengthened the missionary in residence program, and added a master's degree component. The two men worked diligently to accomplish their goal for the missions program, receiving departmental status within ACU in 1984.

Wendell's involvement with missions at ACU was the fulfillment of a personal dream. Looking back it also seems evident that ACU was part of the pattern of God's involvement in Wendell's life. Teaching at ACU allowed Wendell the opportunity to influence Christian men and women for missions, to seed the mission programs which now exist at most of our brotherhood schools, and to continue his direct involvement in missions.

Retirement Years, 1993 to Present

Retirement for the Brooms has not meant retirement from work, but more time to work in the mission field! For the past several decades Wendell has filled the role of church statistician for Africa for the Churches of Christ. His Fuller thesis was the first church growth research thesis in the Churches of Christ. Wendell has continued that project, conducting a church growth survey of Nigeria every decade since. His continued involvement in Nigeria has let him influence some of the grandchildren of those men and women he taught in the 1950s. He has worked to encourage the Nigerian churches to be more trans-tribal and international in their vision for the kingdom. During his retirement years Wendell expanded his record keeping to all of Africa. During the third *Africans Claiming Africa* conference, held in South Africa in May, 2000, Wendell announced that for the first time there are more congregations of the Churches of Christ in Africa than there are in the United States and there will soon be more members as well.

Wendell has also continued to grow as an African generalist and world missiologist during his retirement years. Wendell and Betty have brought their influence, expertise and encouragement to missionaries and mission works by spending significant periods of time in Nigeria, Kenya, Ethiopia, Uganda, South Africa and Ghana. They lived in Papua New Guinea for several months while Wendell did consulting work with Pioneer Bible Translators. He also did thirteen months of mission work in Siberia and a semester's study in Jerusalem.

Looking to the Future

The mark that Wendell and Betty Broom have made on missions study at ACU, on missions in the Churches of Christ and on the world is of legendary proportions. The lessons they learned at God's hand in fifty years of kingdom service give guidance and insight for present and future missions tasks. Here are Wendell's views, in his words, on the most important missions tasks facing the churches of Christ in the next fifty years:

> The first major task is facing those of us who are involved with the African church. We must re-examine the relationship between Africa and America. The radical growth of the church in Africa calls us to redefine what we think Africans are capable of doing, then we must urge them to do it. We must confess the serious flaw of the lack of evangelism in the American church and recognize the fantastic way the African church is evangelizing. We must identify new functions which recognize the strengths of our respective churches and maintain our relationships with regard to those new functions.
>
> Second, we need to take advantage of the tremendous people and financial resources of the boomer generation as they begin to come into retirement. Many boomers are retiring with the physical and financial capacity to do fifteen or twenty years of mission work. Boomers need to be challenged and trained to make use of these gifts in the mission field for the glory of God.
>
> The third major task facing us is China. When the Iron Curtain fell in 1990 the Christian world was confronted with a tremendous openness of the people and the possibility for church planting. Despite years of semi-clandestine literature work in the Soviet Union by the Churches of Christ we were unprepared for the new opportunities and we made numerous mistakes before finding our evangelizing, church-planting feet. Right now we ought to be examining the evolutionary process by which Marxism came to the moral, political and financial bankruptcy which led to the wall's fall, with an eye towards predicting the time when similar events will open China to evangelism. Simultaneously we need to be preparing front-line people, preferably Chinese converts from the Chinese diaspora, and supporting churches who

will be ready for intense Chinese evangelism. Even at this point there is abundant evidence that the underground church in China is growing well. How much more could we add to that if we are well prepared for China's opening?

Finally, the American church is facing serious battles at home with both secularization and a nostalgic longing for a golden past. Secularization lures us with a siren's call to be more like the world in order to be able to reach the world, a curiously powerful piece of circular reasoning. Our nostalgic longing for the glory days of the Restoration Movement brings a petrifying process to the church which is deadly. These two forces can be countered. One way is through a vigorous worship renewal, a renewal which scares some of us to death, but also provides new life to churches with wise leaders who offer appropriate avenues to achieve worship renewal. The other avenue we must pursue is to recover a lively, New Testament doctrine of the church. The 21st century church must be able to meet the challenges of a changing world based on a Holy Spirit mentality. Missions can take a leading role in reviving our churches in this way (Broom interview, June, 2000).

This renewal of a vibrant church which brings new life to the world calls forth the blessing Wendell would bequeath to the church. "The early church suffered under a cruel boot of Roman persecution, yet it thrived and brought transforming power to bear on its society. The American dream of our time and place is not cruel to the church; it simply ignores us in favor of the economies and politics of the world" (Broom interview, June 2000). Wendell's blessing to us, the present and future church, is this, that the church in America, with the uncountable blessings God has bestowed on us, would insist with greater vigor that the American dream give way to the dream of the kingdom of God in the hearts of our young people, that our sons and daughters be godly men and women who clearly see the lostness of the major continents of the world and know how the divine person of Jesus speaks to the cultural currents of our time (Broom interview, June 2000).

Maranatha—Lord Jesus come.

CHAPTER 2

Reflections on the 20th Century in African Missions

Wendell Broom, Sr.

Wendell Broom is professor emeritus at Abilene Christian University. Wendell, with Betty as his companion, has served the Lord's church as preacher, missionary, and teacher for over fifty years.

A Century of Change

The end of the 20th century and the beginning of the 21st is an ideal time for reflection on the Kingdom of God. When David became king it was noted that "… the men of Issachar…understood the times and knew what Israel should do…" (I Chronicles 12:32). Queen Esther's husband depended on "…wise men who understood the times…" (Esther 1:13). So we, at the turn of the century , are well advised to seek out the men who understand the times and know what the missionary forces of our time ought to be about.

One scholar has written that "… the figures …of statistics are signs made by God…" (Heijke 1966, p. 36). It is one thing to acknowledge the presence and the working of God in our world, but it is something quite more important to trace out the detailed steps of God by knowing what he has done and is doing. Knowing this we shall be much better prepared to know what we can do to work in support of his plans.

The beginning place must be with the population of our planet. From the days of Adam until 1900 the human race had grown to only 1.6 billion. That number doubled in the next 70 years to 3.7 billion, and almost doubled again to 6 billion by 2000. In this one hundred years the rise of metro-cities (100,000 or more) has grown from 300 to 4,100 cities. The mega-cities (1 million or more) have increased from 20 to 410. The wisdom needed to make good decisions can be imagined by the prediction that in fifteen years (by 2015), Lagos, Nigeria will have become the third largest city in the world with a population of 23.2 million citizens (Brockerhoff, 2000, p. 10). Municipal planners in Lagos had better "understand the times" to know what streets, water, sewage, power, schools and police will be needed by 2015, not to mention what leaders of the churches and senders of missionaries ought to be planning.

Planners for the year 2050 need to be aware of the trends Barrett identifies in the following world statistics:

	1900	1970	2000
Population of the world	1.6 billion	3.7 billion	6.05 billion
Christian believers	558 million	1,136 billion	2 billion
Christian believers as % of world population	34.4%	33.4%	33.0%
Christian martyrs (per year)	35,600	230,000	165,000
Christians in N. America	59.5 million	169 million	212 million
Christians in Africa	8.7 million	117 million	255.6 million
Christian books per year	3,500	25,000	35,000
Bibles distributed	5 million	25 million	70 million
Christian radio stations	0	1,230	4,000
Christian radio monthly listeners	0	150 million	600 million
Evangelism—hours per year	10 billion	99 billion	480 billion
Unevangelized as % of world population	50%	44%	25%

Table 1. World statistics for 2000 AD (Barrett, 2000, p. 25).

To see the increase of believers from 558 million to 2,000 million (2 billion) may seem incredible if we do not consider the number of Christian books printed, of Bibles distributed, of radio stations on the air, and the four fold increase of evangelism hours. This, of course, is a reflection of the technological changes of the century, including travel time (from horses to mach one air travel) communications, medical advances and the prolongation of human life, agriculture, education, etc. Only God knows what further technological progress may enable his servants to further reduce the percentages of the unevangelized of earth by the end of the next century.

Who could have guessed in 1885, when the European nation states sliced up the continent of Africa with the Berlin Treaty, that their colonial empires (spawned by technologies that demanded raw materials far beyond what Europe could provide) would last only two generations and by 1970 would be totally dissolved. The colonial dreams of Queen Victoria and the fabled British Empire (upon which the sun never set) in fact remained only a memory after only three generations. The resulting new independent nations of Africa were ushered into the world amidst political demands for which they were ill prepared. In the African Congo, for instance, it was reported that there were less than two dozen academically trained lawyers and engineers ready to assume the political and industrial leadership of the nation as it formed in 1960.

Had we "...understood the times... and...known what Israel should do..." the continent might be much different from its present turmoil and chaos.

The Onward March of Change

The waves of change have washed over the beaches of African Christianity for twenty centuries. During Christianity's early years North Africa held a place of leadership, especially out of Alexandria,

29

producing many influential leaders in the period of the Church Fathers. As unhealthy change occurred in the 3rd and 4th centuries, fertilized by temporal power and corruption, North Africa gave birth to the early monasticism and spiritual retreats into solitude as the answer to the spiritual degeneration of the majority-popular Christianity. During the torpidity of the dark ages Africa gave birth to Islam. By the 8th century the impotent Christianity of North Africa had surrendered to the militant evangelism of the Moslem hordes and armies. Later, while the surges of the Renaissance swept over Europe and the reforms of Luther were trumpeted by the new printing press, these changes missed Africa, partly due to the insulating blanket of Islam north of the Sahara. Finally, in the 1700s and 1800s, the old Roman church and the new Protestant churches navigated their explorers and missionaries around the coast of Africa, mapping, trading, and building coastal outposts of Christianity. As Livingston, Speke, and others explored the Dark Continent's interior answering the questions, "Who lives in there? Where do the rivers come from? What is life like in the DARK CONTINENT?," the Spirit of God sent the impulses of divine mercy, grace, and Jesus' Messiahship deep into the interior. Thus, even as the missionaries of the colonizers planted their denominations and overstayed their ministries, the Spirit of God was planting lively seeds of resurrection power in responsive hearts. Finally, in the last century of the millennium, the renewal of the African church by schism gave birth to 20,000 denominations, unique to Africa, bearing the cultural patterns of a world which remains largely alien to the peoples of the West.

And so, in our generation, we see the virility of an African-owned church, bearing the cultural imprints of their rich heritage, exhibiting the irrepressible joys and celebrations of the triumph of Jesus King of kings, surging into the twenty-first century. The

30

homelands of the missionaries–Europe and the US–still retain the "dark continent" impressions of a previous century. We deny the sterility left on the mother churches by the ravages of two World Wars, the greedy history of capitalism, the deadly ravages of atheistic socialism and communism, the dictatorship of the new technology, and the obsessive appetites of materialism. While pragmatic historians label Europe as post-Christian and North America as pluralistic materialism, Christianity is invigorating its new homeland. Winston Churchill said to his generation, "Africa is a lion still sleeping; be careful lest you awaken her to your dismay." Today, the Christian lion that is Africa is awakening.

African Christianity in the 20th Century

Christianity in 1900 was centered in the "West," meaning Europe and North America. It was easy to expect that it would remain so ad infinitum, or even more optimistically, that the goal of the Christian West would be "The evangelization of the world in this generation."

> The 20th century itself, however, has proved to be startlingly different from these expectations. Certainly the total of Christians has grown enormously, from 558 millions in 1900 to 1,433 millions by 1980. Certainly also, since 1900 Christianity has become massively accepted as the religion of developing countries in the so-called Third World, Africa in particular. But no one expected the massive defections from Christianity that subsequently took place in Western Europe due to secularism in Russia and later Eastern Europe due to Communism, and in the Americas due to materialism" (Barrett, 1982, p. 3).

In this 20th century there arose a whole new segment of Christianity, termed by Barrett (1982) the "non-white indigenous bloc," whose growth is given in the following table:

1900	7.2 million
1970	49 million
1985	76 million
200	124 million

Table 2. Population of the non-white indigenous bloc (Barrett, 1982, p. 6).

This newly recognized bloc of world Christianity arose primarily in Africa, growing out of a base of traditional, animistic and ancestral religions, along with some inroads among those of the Islamic faith south of the Sahara. This new Christian bloc is of such immensity and significance that Barrett sees Africa as the new "center of World Christianity " in the 21st century.

Churches of Christ in Africa in the 20th Century

The earliest fore-runners of the American Churches of Christ were two dramatic pioneers. One was Alexander Cross, an ex-slave, sent to Liberia as a missionary in 1856; he died within months, leaving no permanent fruit of his ministry. In 1897 a New Zealand preacher, John Sherriff, went to South Africa, supporting himself by his skills as a stone mason. By apprenticing South Africans, he trained them to evangelize, and thereby laid the foundations for future plantings of many congregations. Early missionaries who followed John Sherriff were the following:

William N. Short	1921
George M. Scott	1926
Dow Merritt	1926
Wm. Leslie Brown	1929
A. B. Reese	1929
S. D. Garrett	1930

Alvin Hobby	1938
Myrtle Rowe	1939
J. C. Shewmaker	1939
Henry Ewing	1941
Eldred Echols	1943
Foy Short	1947
J. A. Brittell	1947
Ken Elder	1949
Guy Caskey	1949
J. C. Reed	1949
Henry Pierce	1950

Table 3. List of African missionaries of the Churches of Christ, 1900-1950 (Shewmaker, 1970, p.170).

After 1950 a wave of missionaries swept over the continent. A rough estimate of a thousand families moved into resident ministries in various colonial nations. In Nigeria detailed records show that 188 missionaries (mostly married couples with their families and some unmarried individuals) resided in Nigeria between 1952 and 2000. Of those 188 individuals, 58% of them were working in evangelism and church planting (including evangelist training and Bible Schools), 28% were in medical missions, and 15% were assisting in village primary and secondary education. Hundreds more went on short term "campaigns" (a few days or up to several weeks) doing medical missions, evangelism, or humanitarian relief projects. Growing out of these activities the records show the Nigerian Churches of Christ growing steadily (Table 4):

Year	Congregations
1950	65
1960	125
1970	335
1980	705
1990	1805
2000	3500-4000 (estimated)

Table 4. Number of congregations of churches of Christ in Nigeria (Broom, 2000).

Missionaries across the continent, like those in Nigeria, made their mark upon sub-Sahara Africa. By 1989 records were being kept of all these sub-Saharan countries. Table 5 shows the results of their ministries under the power of God:

	Churches	Members
1989	6,222	419,207
1992	6,959	409,924
1994	7,406	428,908
1997	9,401	685,532
2000	12,753	799,870

Table 5. Numbers of churches and members of the Churches of Christ in Africa, 1989-2000 (ACA, 2000).

By 1992 these workers had planted churches in twenty nations. By 2000 their work had spread into 35 nations, leaving just 8 African nations yet without a congregation of the Churches of Christ.

Why has the response to Jesus been so enormous in Africa compared to other sectors of the world? The following have been components of the African receptivity.

God's Providence

By the grace of God's power and providence, a certain receptivity has emerged. Out of a natural, cultural kind of responsiveness to deities and gods, the heralding of the Messiah has met with recognition of the supremacy of Jesus, as deep calls unto deep. Again and again the new recipients of the Kingdom have told of dreams, expectations, a kind of "kairos", expressed by phrases like "We have known someone like you would come" or "Why did it take you so long to get here". The legendary work of the prophet Harris and his evangelistic march across West Africa (1913–1915) is one of many such evidences of a God-prepared receptivity (Haliburton, 1973).

Preaching and Teaching

The first wave of expatriate messengers used multiple means and agencies to spread the Seed. Public preaching and teaching in markets, town squares, private homes and the "in-season out of season" kind of ministry of the book of Acts prevailed. Bible schools and leadership training proliferated, some of which were accredited and others not; some large, some small; some academic and others in hands-on experience, but all insisting on "teaching faithful men who will teach others also" (2 Tim. 2:2). The Paul-Timothy style of older men discipling and mentoring younger men was a frequent pattern.

The African missionaries also set a tone of vigorous evangelism which equated believing and spreading the faith. As one missionary stated it, "the act of baptism was at the same time the ordination to ministry." The use of correspondence courses (such as the World Bible School lessons) connected American Bible teachers with African students/seekers in every nook and cranny of African society, from social outcasts to ambassadors of their nations. As well, great efforts were made to translate the Bible into the major languages of many nations. In Nigeria translations into the 55 tribal languages began as early as the 1850s.

Indigenous Ownership

The African churches often developed a sense of "indigenous ownership" of the churches which led to what Roland Allen (1962) called "the spontaneous expansion of the church". The Divine Force which originated the receptivity and pervaded the ministry (both expatriate and indigenous) also bestowed a sense of "ownership" of the church. This ownership created a boldness for evangelism. It also instilled and gave expression to the grateful joy which believers felt at their first freedom from the fears of animism and ancestor worship and made them bold to speak openly and frequently of the "fire in their bones" (Jer.20:9). This work of the Spirit of God which was promised came upon the church, empowering the believers for kingdom work on earth.

Obstructions to Growth

While all these components listed above promoted the growth of the African church, there also were deterrents to the flow of the Divine in the history of church planting. David Barrett wrote of this in *Schism and Renewal in Africa* (1968). Barrett documents well the obstructions which arise when missionaries claim the "ownership of the churches" as their own right and heritage, creating a prolonged adolescence of believers whose rights to full maturity as sons and daughters of God are denied by unbiblical insistence upon the controlling power being retained in the hands of the early introducers of faith. Barrett also describes the resulting unshackling process quite precisely, even giving numerical predictors as to where and when the schismatic force of foreign ownership will erupt, demanding an indigenous right of renewal. This demand of young (second or third generation) believers for spiritual self-determination has proven to be the irresistible force which casts off the repressive cultural baggage and asserts the rights of "freedom in Christ."

The Century Ahead: 2000 to 2100

If you are reading this you will probably not be alive to see what the church will be like in 2100, or what Africa or America will be. The history of times past is our heritage, and much easier to understand than the future. But the future is our destiny, so let's look at the future.

Social and Economic Trends

Two social trends will dominate Africa in the coming century: population growth and urbanization. Africa will steadily outstrip the other continents in population and will become more and more urbanized. In the year 2000 only 29% of the people of sub-Saharan Africa were living in cities compared with 74% in Latin America and 83% in Northern Europe (Brockerhoff, 2000, p. 10). By the year 2025, 49% of the people in sub Saharan Africa will live in its cities (as compared with 11% in 1950). American Churches of Christ between 1820 and 2000 have moved very slowly out of the rural patterns of their early years, finding it hard to make the transition to urban church styles and habits. With 89% of Africa's people being rural in 1950 it was relatively easy for Churches of Christ to root. It will not be as easy to grow amidst the people of the burgeoning cities of the future. Church leaders will have to learn appropriately relevant patterns of ministry and "being" urban churches, or see their churches die out in the African metro and mega-cities of 2025. If the 60 Churches of Christ in Lagos, Nigeria learn how to make the urban ministry shift they will experience booming growth patterns by 2015 when Lagos reaches its predicted 23.2 million population.

If the African church leaders are not aware of this trend, their American co-workers will need to update them with the annual statistics published in the *Occasional Bulletin* or in the *Population Reference Bureau.*

Despite the current pessimistic attitude toward business and development (both on the part of America and Nigeria), there are glimmers of hope.

> This year, Texas-based SBC Communications bought a 30 percent stake in Telekom South Africa, the state owned Telephone Company, for $1.26 billion. It was not just the size of the investment that made global analysts sit up and take notice, it was the message that the transaction sent to the world: Africa is economically viable and preparing to take its place on the world stage. The twelve countries of the Southern African Development Community—Angola, Botswana, Lesotho, Namibia, Malawi, Mauritius, Mozambique, South Africa, Swaziland, Tanzania, Zambia and Zimbabwe—are defying generations of pessimism about the world's poorest countries…. The economies of SADS's members grew by an average 6.5 percent last year–well above the 2.4 percent of the United States–in all 12 countries inflation is coming down. Civil conflict is now changing into wars on poverty. While Africa may not be the most attractive foreign investment for the risk averse, anyone willing to invest now and stay the course could well reap the benefits of sustained economic growth over the long term." (The Year Ahead, 2000, pp. 101-103)

Religious Trends

As the center of world Christianity moves increasingly to the Dark Continent–now become the Continent of Light–more and more changes of mindset will have to be made. At a recent gathering of Anglican bishops in Britain, one question on the agenda was the ordination of homosexual men into the priesthood. The moral tone of England takes a very tolerant view of homosexuality, and following their culture the English Anglican bishops were in favor of the ordination. They were shocked, however, to find that their African brother-bishops took a very strong stand against ordaining gays. The English carried the vote, but they must have wondered, "How long will it be until the African Anglican bishops outnumber the British Anglican bishops?"

American theologians may be surprised at the appearance of a new star in the theological sky: ethnotheology. There have been numerous theologies in history: theologies of the Eastern church, theologies of the Western church, theologies of the Reformation churches and other theologies. It is predictable that African churches will produce their own theologies as well. It is embarrassing and awkward to the monocultural mind to have to confront the reality that our individual cultural systems are unavoidably blended into our perceptions of the Word of God. We fight ferociously for the impartiality of our perceptions, insisting that our cultural conditioning does not affect our perceptions of reality. Sometimes this works for our blessing, and sometimes for our curse. Africans, from cultures that place high value on tribal, clan, or family covenants, may feel a far deeper kinship with biblical history than democratic, individualized, industrialized, capitalistic Americans would ever feel. To the longstanding theological controversies of the last thousand years there well may come new viewpoints, alien to our own by reason of cultural roots, which by weight of African spiritual realities and numerical force will have to be seriously examined. And as the magnitude of African believers increases, we may be forced to recognize that the junior brother has slowly become the senior brother in this Kingdom of God. Ethnotheology can play some surprising games within this continuing family.

One such reversal is now well under way. By 1995 there had arisen 6,000 new indigenous African mission boards. At this point in time, these missionary boards are sending out 300,000 missionaries into the world (Christian Aid in Missions, 1999). The American cultural mind may object that this is no reality. When we think of mission boards, we think of a central agency through which 300,000 supporters organize themselves to send missionaries 12,000 miles to another continent. The reality is that the term "missionary "is best defined as one who leaves his mother language and culture to preach to people of another language and culture." Africans can, therefore, move out of their tribal boundaries into another language and culture only fifty miles away from "home." It may well be that in such a way Africans will claim Africa by becoming "missionaries" to some of the unreached peoples, tribes into which no believer in Jesus has ever come, where never has the word of God been read in their own mother tongue. In such a way, Africans are sending out legions of Word speakers, not only in their own continent, but to other continents as well. The little known reality is that African immigrants from Mozambique are now filling pews and roles of leadership in Lisbon, Portugal. Ads were run in an American church paper signed by three leaders of a London Church of Christ, two of which were Efik names from that Nigerian tribe. More African faces can be seen than Caucasian faces in a central Church of Christ in Paris, France. Ghanaian preacher-electricians have planted three congregations in a Muslim country where no American would ever be allowed to preach or teach. In 1985 a Nigerian went into the Ukraine for medical training. He taught himself Russian, translated from his Efik Bible, taught new friends the Word, and when the first American evangelist arrived in Kharkov he found a congregation of over fifty baptized believers worshipping together.

Africans have demonstrated that they plant new African churches better than Americans; they are starting more than three new churches every day somewhere on the African continent. Africans

40

have worked through some very tough moral and ethical problems for which it would take years for Americans to figure out valid, biblical answers. Uncountable men have been trained to preach in congregations and have gone out to nearby "ripe fields" to plant new churches. But this training has been outside our paradigm of academic structures. The teacher may not have had a degree, but whether in normal congregational sermons or through a mentoring, Paul-Timothy style relationship, a man learned to preach and for the joy of liberation from fearful ancestors, cruel charlatan sorcerers, or spooky demonic terrors, he cannot deny the fire in his bones or the divine impulse to share the joys of grace and love. African congregations answer the question, "How many men in your congregation can preach on Sundays or plant a new church?" by replying that two or three can in small congregations or twenty to thirty can in larger congregations, and do so often. This does not mean that all African preachers have arisen in this way. In Nigeria we have at least five accredited, academic kinds of preacher/leader-training schools. There are many advantages to this system, but we have twice that many small, unaccredited schools with only a dozen or so students, taught by one or two graduates of the older stronger schools. And from these variations come preachers of the Word, doing precisely what Paul told Timothy to do (2 Tim. 2:2).

Examples like these may make Westerners fearful of "losing our turf" and begin fighting to protect the spiritual dynasties that we have built. On the other extreme, it may make some American churches want to "pull up stakes and leave it with them," to terminate the troublesome battle of the budget that has been fought to keep our mission work going. There is, however, a third solution to this delightful multiplying of preachers and teachers. It is called "partnership."

Partnership

The idea of missions partnership is new enough to sound strange, perhaps too new to use until it can be tested by time and recommended to others. Recently an American church has made a covenant with a metropolitan African church to become partners in evangelizing and missions. They will select a place or country or tribe where there has never been a preaching of the New Testament gospel, or a Christian baptized believer, or any other kind of chance to know the grace and mercy of the cross of Christ or the power of his resurrection. From their team of Gospel preachers the African church will call a man (probably with his family) to go there and plant a church. Partners in the choice of the new plant location, the American church will share with the African church in the money necessary to send the man. The sending African church will supervise his going and work. The preacher (missionary) will be accountable to the nearby African church, and the American church will be kept informed. When the plant is completed, the work will be reviewed by the partner churches and the man brought home or sent on to the next door that the Lord may open.

As the "junior-become-senior" African brethren move ahead into their new roles and functions, Satan may be expected to throw up obstacles and hindrances galore. There will be moral problems (polygamy, unwed mothers, brothers taking into wifedom their dead brother's wife, etc.). There will be ethical problems (teachers paying application "fees" to get a new job, nepotism, estate settlement for a widow when her husband dies, surgeons on strike at hospitals refusing life-or-death surgery, school teachers teaching "Agricultural Science" by sending his pupils out to weed the teacher's vegetable garden, teachers showing up two weeks late because their salaries have not been paid for three months, etc.). Add to these troubles the problems of political life, technology, education, medicine, sci-

42

ence, longevity, the whole warp and woof of the cultural system. But don't forget "American" Christian problems—divorce, single parenthood, abortion, unwed teenage maternity, credit card debt, bankruptcy, student loan defaults, corporate campaign financing, philandering American presidents, etc. Satan plagues us as he does them, and the spiritual validity of the Kingdom still works among the children of God. Africans are not stepchildren, or grandchildren, or nephews of God. **They are sons and daughters of God by grace through faith, even as it has been from Pentecost.**

Concluding Thoughts

It may take awhile for us to become comfortable with God having genuine churches and preachers and elders in "Darkest Africa". The Anglican Church felt that way about "the colonies" in 1776, and strong ties had to be broken. New recognition of maturity and validity had to be accomplished. It will have to be again. And it will happen again. Western churches will learn to partner with African churches. There will be failures in some partnerships, but there will many fruitful successes. We can help with the ghastly AIDS problem (current African thinking is for an infected AIDS man to have sex with a young virgin in order to cure his infection) by teaching the church to speak boldly about culturally-forbidden "sex kinds of things," by dealing openly and honestly, by advocating sexual abstinence as the only prevention, by teaching how Aids can be contracted through moral but ignorant medicinal mistakes, and much more. We have help to be given in education, quality of life improvements, hygiene, status of women, industrial pioneering, farming improvements—partners are needed in dozens and hundreds of ways within the ability of partnering American churches to freely give as we have freely received.

In this process, many lessons will have to be learned by Africans and by Americans. What is the "10/40 zone" of resistance to the Gospel? What is the Joshua Project? Who are the Finishers or the New Horizon people? What should we be doing as China ripens for openness as its aged leaders (disciples of Mao) die off and younger, more approachable leaders move into the new roles of leadership at all levels of government? What can be done with the hundreds of thousands of orphans left by AIDS parents? What can be done to fill the employment needs of a society decimated by AIDS deaths? How can we "Adopt an Unreached People"? Where is the market where "Partnership African Churches" can be found? How do we get under the thin veneer of Christian membership and thoroughly remove the residual, core heritage of deadly fears of ancestors, sorcerers, evil spirits, devil covenants? How do we replace all of that with a solid core Christian worldview which puts total trust in atonement, integrity, life after death, resurrection, final and total judgment and accountability for both evil and good?

Just because Africa now has more congregations than the USA, the battle is not over. There are still the "unreached peoples." In the last two decades many of these "unreached peoples" have been evangelized; 90% of those evangelized have been reached by African evangelists from African churches, often from sending bases less than a hundred miles from strong established churches. The Word has yet to be translated into dozens of the minor languages and dialects of remote African tribes. Existing African churches must be persuaded that American churches are willing to and capable of "partnering" with them. We Americans need their insights into the folly of our American materialism and European secularism. Africa has enormous work to do to rebuild their failed infrastructures. They must be convinced of the unreality of their "Afro-pessimism," as Archbishop Desmond Tutu has called it (2000, p. 2). Had it not been for Chinua Achebe's heroic role in the literary life of his own country, he would have been assassinated for writing the scathing indictments of his own beloved people in *The Trouble with Nigeria* (1983). African attempts to "fix their society" have resulted in generational tragedies like the 40 years of war that Angola has been through after their "colonial masters" left in the 1970s (Michel, 2000).

The question arises then: "If Africa is the new Christian center of the planet, just what kind of churches are these?" There are 20,000 new, different denominations in Africa, yet we westerners feel like we have the real thing, and in the West we have but 300 denominations. Our belief is that despite all these realities the real saving truth of God in Jesus Christ can be found and can be valid for salvation. If Jesus could bring healing and life in the presence of 300 demons, can he not do it in the presence of 20,000? Did He not come out of the grave where more than that many legions of hell were trying to prevent His resurrection? And did not His truth prevail in a culture of Pharisees, Sadducees, Zealots, and Herodians in such a way that His truth could make men free. The power that is in Him (and therefore in us) is greater than the power that is within them. Churches of Christ have promoted a biblical approach that has led thousands out of imperfect knowledge of the Word and the Kingdom and into a New Covenant faith that goes far back beyond the hundreds of years of "Christian heritage" by holding to a "thus saith the Lord" and "speaking where the Bible speaks and being silent where the Bible is silent".

So, what a century that 20th was. And what a century this next one promises to be! Unknown demons lurk among the decades. Pitfalls lie hidden between the politics and the economics. Glorious progress rides on the new technologies not yet dreamed of. Ethical pitfalls open up where no one could have suspected them. Those who know not the times will be baffled at least, and terrified at most.

Those who know the God of history and the King who sits beside Him on His throne, those are the ones who can rejoice even in the days that seem dark, because they know the promises, the power, the glory and the victories of this supreme kingdom. And herein lies our hope, our courage, our assurance and our peace.

Maranatha, Lord Jesus!

WORKS CITED

Berryman, Mark, Broom Wendell, and Shewmaker Sam (2000). *Africans Claiming Africa Records.* Conference conducted at Johannesburg, South Africa.

Achebe, Chinua (1968). *The Trouble with Nigeria.* Enugu, Nigeria: Fourth Dimension.

Allen, Roland (1962). *Missionary Methods: St. Paul's or Ours.* Grand Rapids, MI: Eerdmans.

Allen, Roland (1962). *The Spontaneous Expansion of the Church.* Grand Rapids, MI: Eerdmans.

Allen, Roland (1962). *The Ministry of the Spirit.* Grand Rapids, MI: Eerdmans.

Barrett, David B. (1968). *Schism and Renewal in Africa.* Nairobi: Oxford University Press.

Barrett, David B. (1982). *World Christian Encyclopedia: A Comparative Survey of Churches and Religions in the Modern World, 1900-2000 AD.* New York: Oxford University Press.

Barrett, David B. (2000). Status of Global Mission. *International Bulletin of Missionary Research 24* (1).

Brockerhoff, Martin P. (2000). An Urbanizing World. In *Population Reference Bureau, 55* (3).

Broom, Wendell (2000). [Notes]. Unpublished records.

Christian Aid in Missions (1999). Christian Aid Mission agency. *Christianity Today.*

Haliburton, Gordon M. (1973). *The Prophet Harris: A Study of an African Prophet and his Mass-Movement in the Ivory Coast and the Gold Coast, 1913-1915.* New York: Oxford University Press.

Heijke, John (1966). *An Ecumenical Light on the Renewal of Religious Community Life: Taize.* Pittsburgh, Duquesne University Press.

Michel, Robert (2000). *Global Future.* Monrovia, CA: World Vision.

Mott, John R. (nd). *The Evangelization of the World in this Generation.*

Shewmaker, Stan (1969). *Tonga Christianity.* Pasadena, CA: William Carey Library.

The Year Ahead (2000). Author unknown, 300 pages on Internet.

Tutu, Desmond (2000). *Global Future.* Monrovia, CA: World Vision.

CHAPTER 3

Archery, Dentures, and Eagles: Missionary Metaphors of Wendell Broom

Gailyn Van Rheenen

Dr. Van Rheenen is professor of missions at Abilene Christian University. He and his wife Becky and family served as church planters among the Kipsigis people of Kenya for 14 years. Gailyn is the author of several books, including Communicating Christ in Animistic Contexts *and* Missions: Biblical Foundations and Contemporary Strategies. *He also conducts congregational seminars on missions.*

Wendell Broom is a master of metaphors. As he prays, adjectives describing the greatness and love of God roll from his lips. His sermons take abstract concepts and give them soul and life. Metaphors are his trademark—his way of helping us see beyond ourselves and our human dilemma to tangibly grasp allegiance to God, the priorities of the Christian faith, and distinctive ministries in God's kingdom. He has modeled the making of metaphors for three generations of missionaries by teaching and speaking in word pictures and graphic illustrations.

The following are some of his metaphors which have touched our lives.

Metaphors of Wendell Broom

On Theological Priorities: "Bowling or Archery?"

I remember how Wendell sought to clarify biblical priorities for those of us who live in North America by posing the question, "Is Christianity more like bowling or archery?" In bowling, each pin is of equal importance; special bonuses are given for perfection. In archery the focus is upon hitting the bull's eye. When Christianity is viewed as bowling, all Christian beliefs are held to be equally important. But when Christianity is understood as archery, Jesus Christ is the bull's eye, the center of the target, and all other Christian beliefs and values are understood in relation to this foundational doctrine.

In drawing his target, Broom argues that the Bible shows some aspects of the Judeo-Christian tradition to be more significant than other aspects and that the Bible must be allowed to set the theological agenda. Love is the foundation of the law—the greatest commandment of all (Matt. 22:34-40), the fundamental attribute of God and Christ. Jesus accused the scribes and Pharisees of emphasizing tithing while neglecting "the more important matters of the law—justice, mercy and faithfulness." He said that they "should have practiced the latter, without neglecting the former" (Matt. 23:23). In comparison to the spiritual gifts of miracle-working, healing, and tongue speaking, Paul considered love to be "a greater gift" and "the most excellent way" (1 Cor. 12:31). God desires heart-felt obedience rather than sacrifice (1 Sam. 15:22). Observing outward rituals in feasts, offerings, and prayer rites is meaningless if one is not showing compassion to the oppressed, fatherless, and widowed (Isa. 1:10-17).

Wendell taught us that we should not focus on the periphery of the target—on the least important items—and work inward toward the bull's eye. Rather, we should focus on God's distinctive work in Jesus Christ culminating in His death, burial, and resurrection. This is the gospel—the center of the theological target. I remember how these analogies helped me to clarify the message of the gospel and focus on its significant core in evangelistic outreach.

On Passing on Our Faith: "False Teeth Religion"

Rosalinda Walker, long-term missionary to Botswana and wife of Wimon Walker, remembers Wendell wrestling with how we pass our faith on to our children. He asked a very simple question, "What do your children want to inherit from us when you die?"

He asked, "Do our children want our false teeth? Our cane or walker? Do they want the medicines we need to survive? Do they want these things that you need to get by with?"

"Or," Wendell conjectured, "do they want the things that have brought us joy?"

"If our religion is something that we endure so that we will not burn in hell eternally, our children won't necessarily want that inheritance. On the other hand, if Christ is our greatest pleasure, if doing God's will is what makes us feel alive, if God's Spirit is something we just can't get enough of, then THAT is what our children will want for an inheritance."

"Ever afterwards," Rosalinda reflects, "I have checked myself to be sure I don't have a "false teeth religion" (personal communication, October 10, 2000).

51

On Church Reproduction: "Germinal or Terminal?"

I have heard Wendell preach in both North America and Africa on how churches become reproductive fellowships. In his lessons the metaphors change although the thought remains the same.

Many times unbelievers are converted and churches established without expecting them to teach others. They soon become like mules who cannot germinally reproduce but must return to the original sources, the horse and the donkey, in order to procreate. They are like seedless grapes, delightful to taste but with no reproductive power, or the fig tree that Jesus withered because it did not bear fruit (Matt. 21:18-19).

Wendell Broom graphically describes such churches as *terminal* (Broom 1976, 88-89). Terminal churches may have spiritual vitality but can reproduce only arithmetically (2, 4, 6, 8, 10, 12, 14, 16, 18, etc.). Missionaries are teaching others but not training their converts to become reproductive; they are initiating churches but not preparing leaders of these churches to plant other churches.

> Ten missionaries can each plant one church each year. If the churches they plant have terminal life, after ten years their field will have 100 churches. If the missionaries die or return home, the number of churches remains static, for they do not plant other churches. The same ten missionaries, by planting churches that have germinal life, will in ten years have 5,110 churches in their field. If the missionaries die or return home, the churches will continue to multiply, because they have germinal life (Broom 1976, 88).

These churches, according to Wendell, are described by the author of Hebrews when he wrote: "Though by this time you ought to be teachers, you need someone to teach you the elementary truths of God's word all over again. You need milk, not solid food!" (Heb. 5:12).

Germinal churches, according to Wendell, grow geometrically (2, 4, 8, 16, 32, 64, 128, 256, 512, etc.). They reproduce like rabbits in Australia, bananas in Bermuda, and papayas in fertile areas of tropical Africa. They are like starfish which multiply when cut into pieces. It is within the nature of each part to reproduce. Geometric church growth can be illustrated by strawberry plants or Bermuda grass, which send out runners in every direction; these runners develop their own root systems and send out still new runners until the field is covered. The roots each represent a new church or cell group planted in a new village or new area of the city. Once the Christian community develops sufficient roots, it is able to plant still other fellowships.

Wendell, then, tells how Paul urged Timothy to encourage his converts to become germinal: "The things you have heard me say in the presence of many witnesses (germination 1) entrust to reliable men (germination 2) who will also be qualified to teach others (germination 3)" (2 Tim. 2:2).

Wendell's illustrations of germinal and terminal churches and Christians have reverberated around the world.

On Being World Christians: "Mallards, Beavers, or Eagles"

Wendell Broom inspired many of us by describing three types of world Christians, all working together for world evangelization.

Some Christians are like *mallards*, wild ducks who travel great distances and consider two general areas of the world their home. In winter they fly south and in summer north. These are missionaries, like the apostle Paul, who traveled great distances to proclaim the message of Christ.

Beavers are the second type of world Christians. Because their bodies are plump, backs arched, necks thick, and hind feet webbed, the beavers do not have the gift of travel. But they are social animals

who can relate to other beavers around them. They also are characterized by hard work in the building of dams and cutting of trees in
the localities in which they live. Many Christians, like beavers, do
not travel to other environments or cultures. They belong at home
where they have perfected their ability to communicate the message
of God in all social areas of life and hard work, as is characteristic of
a beaver.

The great temptation of a beaver is to say, "Since the mallard is
not like me, what should I have to do with him?" or by practical
application, "Since foreign evangelists take finances away from what
we are doing at home, what should we have to do with them?" In
this way beavers are tempted to lose world perspective. Beavers, like
James, one of the pillars of the early church in Jerusalem (Gal. 2:9;
Acts 15:13-21), must not present the gospel only to those of their
home culture but also praise God for His work in distant places in
other cultures (Acts 21:19-21).

When making this presentation in Africa, where beavers are
non-existent, Wendell substitutes *rabbits*, who do the work that God
intended them to do but seldom migrate more than two miles away
from home (1992, 313).

Still other Christians are like *eagles*. The eagle's keen vision is
unsurpassed in the world of animals and birds. Eagles can spot their
prey at great heights and swoop down suddenly and seize them. An
additional characteristic is the tremendous height to which eagles
can fly. This height gives the eagle a vision that most other birds are
unable to obtain. However, the eagle is unable to travel great distances like the mallard.

Eagles symbolize special catalysts with a keen vision for the
world and the Word who are able to pass this vision on to others.
These catalysts see far but do not migrate. They motivate both individual Christians and churches to a higher, broader view of the

world. Jesus Christ, God's divine Son in human flesh, is the great example of an eagle.

This story helped many of my generation to understand that a world Christian perspective must be part of every church.

These metaphorical lessons have stirred at least three generations of Christians to reflect upon the nature of the gospel and the centrality of mission in the life of the church.

The Making of Metaphor

Metaphors, according to Wendell, "compare the known with the unknown." They are reflective responses amplifying understanding by asserting, "Oh yea, it's like..." (Broom 2000).

Developing metaphors takes special creativity similar to the forming and telling of jokes. While metaphors illuminate the unknown by comparing or contrasting it to the known, jokes pose a "discrepancy or contradiction between the expected and the stated." Thus those who make and tell jokes have an easier time developing metaphors (personal communication, July 24, 2000).

Wendell follows a three-step process in preparing lessons. First, he focuses on what his particular audience needs to hear. He then searches for biblical texts that will provide Christian understandings and solutions to meet the particular perceived need. Finally, with the truth in the abstract he searches for cultural metaphors that will explain the truth from the scripture.

For example, Wendell perceives that because Nigerian Christians have difficulty understanding total forgiveness in Christ. He reads Isaiah's metaphors about cleansing from sin, "Though your sins are like scarlet, they shall be as white as snow" (Isaiah 1:18), but realizes that Jewish understandings of sin, scarlet, and snow do not adequately communicate to contemporary Nigerians. He then asks, "How can I illustrate total forgiveness to Nigerians? What in the African environment can illustrate forgiveness?" He has learned that Nigerians love to wear white robes, which can be very expensive. When those robes become soiled or torn, they know to wash or repair them so that they are "good as new." With these understandings in mind Wendell develops a story.

> Once upon a time a man worked and worked to save enough money to buy a fine, very expensive white dachika (festival robe). He was so proud that he put it on at the tailors shop. But on the way home the dachika was soiled when splashed by mud and torn when caught in the bike's chain. Upon arriving home, the man was greatly distraught. "Look what has happened to my beautiful, new dachika," he mourned. His wife, hearing her husband's cry, lovingly took the dachika, mended the torn spots and with her favorite soap, cleaned the robe. When she had finished, the robe was as good as new.
>
> Likewise, we have sinned. We have become as soiled and torn as the husband's new dachika. But God takes away our sins, when we believe in the sacrifice of his Son and participate in His death, burial, and resurrection in baptism. Our clothes are washed; the torn spots of our lives are mended. Galatians 3:26 says, "All of you who were baptized into Christ have clothed yourselves with Christ." Thus coming to Christ in like putting on new clothes. The old tattered, dirty clothes are totally cleaned and repaired by a loving Father and by the cleansing blood of His Son.

When giving a speech or a sermon, Wendell determines its impact from audience response. If the people do not get the meaning or are not touched by its content, he would "dump it". He says, "I watch their eyes and their understanding smile, their laughs and giggles, or their moans and groans if it is a sad parable."

When teaching Missionary Anthropology, Wendell used to ask, "How many cultures must a missionary know in order to make his own parables?" The answer, he said, is four: The missionary must understand not only the culture(s) of the New and Old Testament but he must also understand his own culture and the new culture of his audience. Thus the new missionary cannot expect to be an effective metaphor-maker until he understands the recipient culture. He should, rather, look and listen and find biblical passages which have metaphors that are already clearly understood by the people (personal communication, July 24, 2000).

THE CURIOSITY AND CREATIVITY OF THE METAPHOR MAN

The words *curiosity* and *creativity* characterize Wendell Broom.

His Curiosity

Wendell's curiosity manifests itself in his desire to know the Word of God. I remember a time that Wendell focused on the book of Romans, and his devotional reflections and sermons came out of this book. More recently Wendell has been fascinated by the book of Revelation. This book, he says, is the "mother of all metaphors"—a picture book containing vivid pictures of cosmic reality (personal communication, July 24, 2000). His curiosity always results in the asking of probing theological questions. "What is the core of the Christian faith–the glue that sticks it all together?" "How can we diagram the Christian faith so that both believers and unbelievers can capture the big picture?" "Who is God?" "How can finite humans fathom His majesty?" "What is grace?" "Why does God save us?" "What is the significance of the virgin birth? The miracles? The resurrection?"

As a missions teacher his questions are also practical: "What do your children want to inherit from you when you die?" "How do Christians having various gifts and ministries work together within the body?" "How can we encourage all Christians to understand

their roles as world Christians?" "What theologies motivate terminal Christians to become germinal?" He is fascinated with beginnings: "What are the origins of human culture?" "Why would God
create humans?"

His Creativity

Wendell's creativity is an extension of his curiosity. The aim of
his curiosity is not mere intellectual understanding, but to communicate the gosepl creatively in order to develop faith.

Thus Wendell asks, "How do we bring the eternal message of
God into living cultures?" "How do we communicate the Christian
message in broad strokes so both believers and unbelievers are able
to understand it?" Although the Christian message may be perceived as difficult or intricate, Wendell creatively uses metaphors to
communicate with simplicity, clarity, and impact.

The curiosity to fathom God's purposes and creativity to incar-
nate God's message into living forms have been Wendell's trade-
marks. He has effectively modeled missionary communication to
three generations of missionaries.

WORKS CITED

Broom, Wendell (1992). How to be a World Christian. In Sam Shewmaker (Ed.), *Africans Claiming Africa Conference.* Unpublished manuscript, Harding University.

――― (personal communication, July 24, 2000).

――― (1976). Church Growth Principles. In George Gurganus (Ed.), *Guidelines for World Evangelism* (pp. 81-104). Abilene, TX: Biblical Research Press.

Walker, Rosalinda (personal communication, October 10, 2000).

God's Call to a Continent: People and Places

CHAPTER 4

A Survey of Work in Southern Africa

Robert Reese and Wimon Walker

Robert Reese is a third generation missionary to Africa. He and his wife Marietta have worked in Zimbabwe for the past twenty years. They have three children. Wimon Walker teaches Bible and missions at Abilene Christian University. He and his wife, Rosalinda, served as missionaries in Argentina from 1979 to 1981, and in Botswana from 1985 to 2000. They also have three children.

ZIMBABWE AND ZAMBIA
Robert Reese

They came to the Dark Continent by ship, and traveled inland by steam train, ox wagon, or Model T. The pioneer missionaries of the Churches of Christ were a very unlikely group by today's standards. They were poorly trained and equipped for the unknown obstacles of this vast continent. Armed only with the skills they had acquired from rural American life and their Bibles, they went ahead to face the dangers of travel, of carving homes out of the bush, of wild animals, disease, and spiritual opposition. They faced strange cultures and languages with a faith in God and in the absolute reliability of His Word. Essentially they came only to share the message from God that could save the African tribes from centuries of witchcraft and superstition, and to create and nurture groups of believers into functioning churches. As with any group, the missionaries too had their share of "bad apples" with ulterior motives, selfish pride, strange doctrines and plain old bad behavior, but the works that stand today are a testimony to the dedication of the pioneers and to the grace of God.

The Beginnings, 1896-1945

The person who opened up all of south and central Africa to the American-based Church of Christ was not an American at all. John Sheriff, a New Zealander who made his living as a stone mason, arrived in Africa in 1896 and settled in Bulawayo, Southern Rhodesia (now Zimbabwe) the following year. Stone masonry was his trade but his heart was in African evangelism. One evening while walking in an African suburb, he noticed a light shining through the wall of a tin shanty. Peering inside, he saw several African men trying to read an English book. He promptly started a night school for African workers to learn English and salvation. His first converts were baptized in 1902, and he established Forest Vale Mission on the outskirts of Bulawayo for the purpose of raising up and training national evangelists. Sheriff was joined in 1906 by another New Zealander, F.L. Hadfield, who shared his missionary goals. Ironically, the New Zealand Church of Christ would be considered the equivalent of the Christian Church or Disciples of Christ, but at that time there was no discussion of such differences, and missionaries from all strains of the Restoration Movement felt free to work together. The New Zealand group later contributed from among the ranks of its missionaries a Prime Minister of Southern Rhodesia, Sir Garfield Todd, who held office from 1954 to 1958.

Sheriff issued a call to American Churches of Christ to send missionaries and in 1921 Will and Delia Short began their career which was to last almost 60 years. Sheriff needed the Americans to follow up the work started by his African evangelists, in particular Peter Masiye who had gone to Northern Rhodesia (now Zambia) and Jack Mzila who had started preaching in the Mashonaland province of Southern Rhodesia. After a year with the Sheriffs at Forest Vale, the Shorts set off to Zambia where they built Sinde Mission in the bush, about 20 miles north of the great Victoria Falls. Peter Masiye, who had already made some converts, was the Shorts' right-hand man, preaching, teaching and helping them to understand the Tonga culture of southwest Zambia and to be understood. When Masiye died suddenly, one of his converts named Kamboli resigned a job that paid three times as much in order to assist the new missionaries. Without such sacrificial help on the part of the Africans, it is hard to see how the Americans could have progressed in their mission work.

With further appeals for help and a visit by Sheriff to the United States in 1924, the missionary body of the Church of Christ in Zambia grew quite rapidly. Ray and Zelma Lawyer were first to join the Shorts at Sinde, followed by Dow and Alice Merritt in 1926. Merritt was to have a career in Zambia spanning over 5 decades. George and Ottis Scott, Alva and Margaret Reese, and Leslie (W.L.) and Addie Brown were the other American missionary families who arrived in the 1920's.

Missionary Ways

The basic mission approach, practiced by all denominations of that time, was to locate in a rural area, where a mission station would be built. The mission would have a church building and a school, since the goal was to raise up an educated African leadership.

Students would come from all over the surrounding areas for education, and while attending school would be evangelized, and many would become members of the church which ran the mission. The missionaries would thus be occupied with building and maintaining the facilities, teaching academic subjects and Bible, and evangelizing both students and the surrounding villages. In this way, for example, the son of Chief Musokotwane in whose area Sinde was located, became a member of the Church of Christ, got a good education, and went on to become Prime Minister of Zambia when Dr. Kenneth Kaunda was President of the independent nation.

With a sizeable group of missionaries, the Zambia Church of Christ soon had two more mission stations, Kabanga and Namwianga, which were to have an impact on African leadership. The latter mission, located near Kalomo in southern Zambia, is still producing Christian high school graduates and teachers, and is still manned by Roy Merritt, Dow's son, and his wife Kathi, who are some of the small handful of missionaries of the Church of Christ that remain in Zambia.

Despite the influx of missionaries in the 1920's, progress was slow and difficult with much hard work and long hours. Setbacks abounded, the most serious of which was the untimely death of Ray Lawyer who died as a result of a freak accident, just as Kabanga Mission was in the early stages of being built by Lawyer and Merritt. Lawyer, heading out on a hunting trip, was merely trying to chase an unwanted dog home using the handle of a spear, when the blade pierced his abdomen, and he died of the injury during the long journey to the hospital in Livingstone. A further setback was the Great Depression, which deprived all missionaries of much-needed support. They turned towards forms of self-support such as farming, however, rather than capitulate. They had a heart to evangelize the vast area of central Africa and they knew they had barely started. The pioneers were in their work for the long haul, and adversity was part of the job. Many of them lost children to disease, and Dow lost his wife Alice to breast cancer. He later married Helen Pearl Scott, the daughter of fellow missionaries George and Ottis Scott.

In the early stages John Sheriff acted as the main co-ordinator and senior missionary, although he was a full-time stone mason. New missionaries arriving in Africa would be met by him or his assistants at Bulawayo train station, and be accommodated at Forest Vale Mission while they got their African bearings, purchased supplies, and made plans to move inland. More than likely they would be infected by his orderly and evangelistic spirit, and probably bemused by his eccentric ways. When the Merritts first arrived in 1926, for example, Sheriff wanted Dow to accompany him on a 3-day trip by Model T to see the work started by Jack Mzila at Wuyuwuyu, northeast of the capital, Salisbury (now called Harare). When they arrived, they found 300 people assembled for Sunday worship, and this caused Sheriff to make the decision to give Mzila the kind of missionary backup that he gave to Peter Masiye in Zambia.

This resulted in the Shorts leaving Zambia to follow up Mzila's work around 1930, and in the end Nhowe Mission was started not far from Wuyuwuyu by the Leslie Browns in 1940. Nhowe remains a major center for the Church of Christ in Zimbabwe.

The 1930's saw the beginning of a relationship between Harding College in Searcy, Arkansas and Zambian mission work that endures to this day. Dr. George Benson, a missionary to China before the Communist takeover, became the President of Harding at about the time Dow Merritt took his first furlough, 10 years after arriving in Zambia. Benson thereafter took a personal interest in helping Zambia with funds and personnel for many decades, even after he had retired as President. New missionaries in the 1930's were the Shewmakers, Brittells, Hobbys, and Mrs. Myrtle Rowe.

Alvin Hobby became adept enough in the Tonga language that he was involved from the early stages of the Tonga translation of the Bible until its completion in 1964. World War II prevented much movement of missionaries and most of the Zambian team remained on the field throughout the war, though some of their children were called for military duty to the U.S.A.

Further Advancements and New Divisions, 1945-1963

There was an upsurge of new missionaries after the war ended, and this marks the second phase of the mission work of the Church of Christ in the two Rhodesias. The war had opened up the eyes of many American servicemen to the needs of a wider world, and missionaries from all denominations began to pour out of North America into Europe and the developing nations. This was the case for the Churches of Christ too. Some of the "new" missionaries were the children of the pioneers such as Boyd Reese and Ken and Iris (Merritt) Elder, but most were brand new, and brought with them many of the controversies that had been rocking the Churches of Christ in America, introducing them into the Rhodesias. The three main issues that created sharp cleavages among Christian workers who had previously co-operated were premillenialism, instrumental music, and the issue of financial co-operation of autonomous churches. Even children of the pioneer missionaries lined up on both sides of these issues and thenceforth refused to work with those on the other side.

In Bulawayo, the heirs of John Sheriff became firmly divided over the use of instruments. The family of the pioneer F.L. Hadfield even split down the middle over this issue, with one grandson Phillip remaining with most of the New Zealanders on the instrumental side, and another grandson Alan going non-instrumental. Bulawayo, however, remained a stronghold for both sides during this stage and numerous churches were planted of both persuasions. Although Will Short continued his major influence on the non-instrumental church in Bulawayo, his son Foy came under the influence of Ray Votaw in South Africa and began to preach non-cooperation of local churches, basing himself in Gweru, Zimbabwe in 1957 and training young preachers in his point of view. He contributed heavily to the Church of Christ in Zimbabwe being extremely conservative on numerous issues such as head-covering for women, the ban of kitchens in church buildings, and the rejection of any organizations other than the local church, and only ended his long career in the 1990's when he retired to the United States. Two of the pioneer missionary families, Leslie Brown's and DeWitt Garrett's in Zimbabwe, were premillennialists. Because of the strong attacks by Foy E. Wallace on the premillennialists in the United States, the sponsoring church of Nhowe Mission sent Boyd Reese to free the mission from premillennialism in 1949. This effort was successful, but also created permanent divisions in the non-instrumental Church of Christ. Although the post-World War II period did produce some outstanding new missionaries in the Rhodesias, especially Eldred Echols in Zambia and Loy and Donna Mitchell who arrived at Nhowe Mission in 1958, the main legacy was the introduction of controversies which divided and weakened the Churches of Christ, particularly in Zimbabwe, but also to some degree in Zambia.

Rising Expectations, 1964-1979

The third phase of missionary activity coincided with the end of colonialism. Together with rising expectations of African nationals as they were ready to assume leadership in churches, schools and organizations previously run by American missionaries, there came a new breed of missionary eager to try new mission methods. Africans everywhere were clamoring to be heard and to be equal to the white man. Zambia attained independence in 1964 under its first black President, Kenneth Kaunda. The new missionaries who came after this set of changing circumstances were much better trained in terms of not only seminary training, but also cultural awareness. The new pioneers in Zambia were determined to chart a different path in missions, that of avoiding mission stations, schools, hospitals and institutions, in favor of locating in an African village and planting indigenous churches. The team ironically chose to locate in the village of Kamboli, Peter Masiye's first convert, not far from where the three mission stations were operating in southern Zambia. They thus built on the work of the original pioneers and made use of existing national leaders. One of the team was Stan Shewmaker, the son of veteran J.C. Shewmaker who was principal at Namwianga Secondary School. Stan and his co-workers, Phil Elkins, Frank Alexander, Allen Avery, and Mel Evans were all trained missiologists from Fuller Seminary School of World Missions. They were joined later by Stan's brother, Sam. With their wives, they took up village living and culture learning before embarking on church planting. This Tonga team stayed on the field from 1969 to 1979, but did not have a great impact on the Churches of Christ in Zambia. No similar team went to Zimbabwe because of the escalating guerrilla war there that would eventually lead to independence in 1980. Although the Tonga team planted about 20 churches in southern Zambia, the major influence they were to have was on the concept of how missions were to function in the post-colonial period. Therefore they became a model followed closely by later mission teams that went to Kenya and Botswana.

1980-Today

The fourth stage of American missionary activity has been characterized by withdrawal of the missionary force, partly because the Africans were ready and eager to take over leadership and partly because Churches of Christ are sending out fewer and fewer career missionaries. In Zimbabwe, indigenization of Nhowe Mission was forced on the missionaries when the guerrilla war forced Roy and Jaxie Palmer to leave the country in 1977. Allen and Janelle Avery located in the city of Bulawayo in 1980 after independence and were joined by Robert (grandson of Alva) and Marietta Reese in a new church-planting effort that has affected Matabeleland Province for the past 20 years. However, although both families were from the non-instrumental Churches of Christ, they soon began using instruments and their 60 churches are known as Zimbabwe Christian Fellowship and are of a general evangelical persuasion. Foy Short moved to Bulawayo also in 1980, and tried to fill the vacuum left by the departure of most white leadership of the Church of Christ, when a new Marxist government took over. Foy's tendency toward controversy further weakened the once-strong Bulawayo churches. He retired to the United States in the 1990's. Loy and Donna Mitchell, after a long and distinguished career connected particularly with the Preacher Training School that was moved from Nhowe Mission to the city of Mutare in the early 1970's, became the final non-instrumental missionaries in Zimbabwe. They returned to the United States in the late 1990s.

SOUTH AFRICA
Wimon Walker

News of war in Europe and in the Pacific filled the newspaper, but the heart of one young man was filled with the conviction that he should serve God as a missionary. When Eldred Echols found the path toward India blocked, he decided to go to Africa. In the fall of 1942, he proposed to a young woman, Crickett Zenor. They began making plans to marry, but soon doubts about mission work for the couple began to gather. She was the only child of poor parents who had sacrificed to give her a Christian education, and she felt an obligation to help them. How could she do this if she were in Africa? Perhaps, she thought, it would be better to break off the engagement. Although he did not share them with her, Eldred too doubts of his own. He had little money, and even less idea of how he would get to Africa and survive there. How could he care for a wife, even if he could convince her to accompany him? Both believed that God had plans for them, but that they could not carry out their God-given missions together.

So on November 6, 1943, alone, Eldred Echols boarded a coal-burning freighter bound not for Africa but for Argentina. Travel was difficult because of the war, and this was the only berth he could find. After more than a month at sea, he landed in South America, where he waited another five months for a ship heading for Africa. When he finally got off the ship in Cape Town, Echols began a love affair with Africa that is still going on almost sixty years later. After those intervening years, Eldred and Cricket reunited, and were married.

Echols was one of the pioneer missionaries of the Churches of Christ in South Africa, Nigeria, Tanzania, and Botswana. His first work was as a teacher at established mission schools in Zimbabwe and Zambia. Even then he spent school holidays on evangelistic trips, traveling by foot, bicycle or truck to remote villages where the gospel had not yet been preached.

In May 2000, men and women from around the world came to Johannesburg, South Africa to attend the Africans Claiming Africa conference. Brother Echols was also in attendance and was honored on the occasion of his 80th birthday, which fell during the conference. Afterwards, he expressed frustration with the accolades, "All that about my being a modern-day Paul is ridiculous," he said. "I never did anything on my own; I was sent by others. And the reason they sent me is because I was single, and if I were gone for months at a time, no one would miss me."

Maybe it is true that Eldred Echols is quite ordinary, as he himself insists. One thing that is far from ordinary was his willingness to go anywhere and try anything for the sake of the gospel. Even his singleness was the result of a decision to seek God's kingdom above his own happiness and fulfillment. I continue this chapter with Echol's story because no American missionary has had a greater influence than his on the growth of the Church of Christ in southern Africa.

In the early 1900's Cape Town, South Africa was already home to a Church of Christ made up primarily of brothers and sisters from England (and possibly New Zealand). In 1943, the Scott family had left Zambia because of ill health. Even though Scott was 70 years old, he worked to plant a new congregation in Cape Town. By mid-century there were several other churches associated with the Stone-Campbell Movement scattered across South Africa, but the Churches of Christ in America were not in communication with them.

In 1948 Echols recruited three families to join him in South Africa: Guy and Jessie Lee Caskey, Waymon and Naomi Miller, and John and Bessie Hardin. The group began working in Johannesburg, but after they had gathered a congregation of about 80 members they decided to split up and preach elsewhere. With the aid of new missionaries from the United States, evangelistic work was soon underway in several South African cities. Many of the converts of these and other early missionaries became preachers and church leaders in South Africa. Two young men converted in this period have had a great influence on the church in America: Abe Malherbe and Ian Fair.

In 1950 and 1951, Echols made trips to West Africa to investigate the reports of a fast-growing indigenous restoration movement in Nigeria. The ultimate results of these trips is part of the Nigerian story in chapters 1, 2, and 10 of this book.

After working in Tanzania (1956-1964) the Echols and Hornes returned to South Africa to establish Southern Africa Bible School (SABS). Their original intention had been to start a preacher training school for black Africans. But other missionaries working in South Africa prevailed on them to begin a school for whites (Echols 1989: p. 237). (Please note that I use the words "black" and "white" not because I consider them the best terms, but because these are the labels used in South Africa.) Several questions might be asked at this point: Why did so many missionaries choose to focus their effort on South African whites rather than on other population groups? Was this decision a reflection of racism on their part?

The Effects of Apartheid

The Nationalist Party came to power in South Africa in 1948. The party codified into law the principle of "separateness" (*apartheid*). Mixed race meetings were not illegal, but they were difficult. Probably most of the missionaries who went to South Africa went with the idea of being color-blind, intended to preach the good news about Jesus to every lost person regardless of race or language. In fact, several of them had run-ins with officials for carrying out their church work in defiance (or ignorance) of the race laws. But social as well as legal factors encouraged "separateness." Language and culture differences also separated people. For many reasons, congregations in South Africa have tended to consist of people of the same race or language group (see discussions in Echols

1989:103-104; Chenault 1986:149-157).

*& they could
Communicate
easier
with
them.*

One of the factors that led Echols and others to focus on South African whites was the belief that the whites knew their black neighbors better than Americans did, or could. Americans could communicate easily with white South Africans because their cultures were so similar. But to communicate with most black South Africans would require learning an African language such as Zulu or Xhosa, or working through interpreters. Many white South Africans, on the other hand, already knew how to speak one of these African languages.

The fact is that most of the South African whites who received biblical training have focused their ministry on congregations made up predominantly by whites. There are, of course, exceptions, but generally it has been difficult for white South Africans to minister effectively to black South Africans. Even if the minister can eliminate from his own mind all negative attitudes or stereotypes, he or she still faces suspicion and prejudice from their non-white audience.

Extending the Mission

The first missionaries to dedicate themselves to ministry among the non-white majority of South Africans were John and Bessie Hardin (Chenault 1986:380). The Hardins returned to South Africa in 1966 and decided to turn their attention to the black and colored congregations. By this time, black and colored congregations were spreading all over the country. For twelve years John traveled extensively encouraging these churches and training men to lead them. One area he visited often was Vendaland, and it is among the Venda people that the Church of Christ has grown the most.

A few other missionaries have worked among the African people of South Africa, but no one can replace John Hardin in their affections. Some who have followed Hardin's footsteps in recent years are John Reese, Patrick Kenee, and George Funk. All of these men have found World Bible School to be a useful tool for making contacts. From his base in Cape Town, Roger Dickson has developed a correspondence school for church leaders, and has thousands of students from all over the continent and even around the world.

According to the latest estimates, there are 500 congregations in South Africa with about 32,500 members (Berryman & Broom 2000).

Lectureships

In 1967, Southern African Bible School, located at Benoni near Johannesburg, began hosting annual lectureships. In the past, most of those who attended the SABS lectureship were white. The lectureship idea caught on so well that congregations (again, usually white) began organizing lectureships in other parts of the country. The black congregations, too, saw the value in this, and began organizing lectureships over the long Easter weekend. The location for these lectureships varies from year to year, at times being held as far away as Gaborone, Botswana or Harare, Zimbabwe, but the thousands who attend the Easter lectureship dwarf the hundreds who attend the various white lectureships.

Dependence

One of the weaknesses of many South African churches, both black and white, has been dependence on funds from the United States. South Africa is the wealthiest country on the African continent, and many South African Christians—both white and black—have good jobs and a high standard of living. Nevertheless, U. S. dollars have poured into the country to fund special projects, pay for church buildings, and support local preachers. This generosity has sometimes helped the church to move forward, but it has also had negative consequences. Foreign support has, at times, caused men to care more about the sensitivities of the overseas supporters than about the needs of the members of the congregation. Congregations that receive help from overseas may also feel controlled; they may not experience the blessings that come from sacrificial giving; and they may come to see themselves as incapable of doing anything on their own.

Botswana

Echols and Tex Williams were among the first missionaries to make evangelistic trips into Botswana. In 1974 several graduates of Sunset School of Preaching moved to Gaborone, the capital of this sparsely-populated country, most of which is covered by the Khalahari desert. The last missionary of this group, Bill Smith, left Botswana in 1985. At the Smith's departure the Gaborone congregation dwindled, but the core disciples have dedicated themselves to building up the church. In spite of setbacks the congregation has continued to grow in both number and vigor. One member of the church, Dennis Malepa, was receiving help from the U.S. at first. But the other members decided that it should be their responsibility to support their preacher, so they wrote the overseas supporters to ask that brother Malepa's funds be decreased and then stopped altogether. Brother Malepa is a powerful preacher who has had an influence in South Africa and other countries as well as in Botswana. He spent 1999 teaching at SABS, and spent most of the year 2000 studying at ACU, where he received the MAR degree.

Preachers in other towns and villages of Botswana have been supported from the U.S., but in most cases the churches have stagnated or died. In one place, the preacher baptized hundreds of people over the years. Yet he seemed to feel a need to assert his authority as the preacher, and sooner or later drove away every man with leadership ability or the desire to take initiative in the work of the church. The few members who remained had learned to be passive and let the preacher be the "big man." Admittedly, this is an extreme case, but it again illustrates the destructive potential of money.

From 1984 to 2000, a team of missionaries worked in far northwestern Botswana in the area around the village of Shakawe. The team's desire was to evangelize unreached people groups, and this was a remote place where little organized evangelism had been done by missionaries from any denomination. Unlike most previous missionaries to Botswana, all the men and women on this team learned to speak Setswana.

Malawi

Churches of Christ have flourished in the small, land-locked country of Malawi. According to the most recent statistics one out of every fifty Malawians is a member of the Church of Christ (Berryman and Broom 2000). As of the year 2000, there are about 4,100 congregations of the Churches of Christ in Malawi. This accounts for almost a third of the congregations in all of Africa. This gives Malawi the highest membership per capita in the world, and causes Mac Lynn to assign it the lowest priority for new church planting of any country except for Vatican City (Lynn, 1990: p. xxvi).

G. B. Shelburne III, missionary in Malawi from 1961 to 1980, has written a short history of the Churches of Christ in that country (Shelburne, 1997). Elaton Kundago became a member of the Church of Christ in 1906 in South Africa, where he had gone to get a job. Soon after, he returned to Malawi and began to preach. Brother Kundago eventually fell away, but he influenced three African men who held office in the Church of Scotland (Presbyterian Church) to be immersed. These three men, Brothers Masangano,

Khonde and Kaundo, were well-known preachers among the Churches of Christ in Malawi for decades.

It was also through the influence of Brother Kundago that the first missionaries of the Churches of Christ came to Malawi. In 1907, George Hubert Hollis was sent by the elders of a congregation in Cape Town, South Africa, and was later joined by other missionaries from England. The first missionaries from America did not arrive until 1952. During the 20th century over forty missionaries (mostly from America) served in Malawi.

One sad note is that many of the Malawian congregations do not fellowship with each other. Some of the missionaries from the British Churches of Christ were liberal, similar to the Disciples of Christ. Several African church leaders broke away for one reason or another and started their own branches or denominations. A large number of the American missionaries were from "One cup" or Non-Institutional backgrounds and planted large numbers of congregations who remain separate from other Churches of Christ. The missionaries who founded Namikango Mission in 1961 were from a Non-Sunday School background, but their work has been a focus of unity for the majority of the Malawian church members.

Many of the missionaries to Malawi have learned to speak African languages, especially Chichewa, the native language of the majority of those who live in the southern part of the country. Lendal and Peggy Wilks (missionaries in Malawi for 31 years) estimate that 60% to 70% of the members of the Church of Christ are in the southern part of the country. Some of the missionaries who work in the north have learned Chitumbuka.

Malawian Christians have become involved in missionary outreach to neighboring Mozambique. More than 10% of the population of Malawi in 1993 was refugees who fled the 20-year long civil war in Mozambique (Johnstone 1993:363). Some of the refugees were converted while in Malawi, and since the end of the Mozambican civil war in 1993, a number of Malawian Christians have gone into Mozambique to preach and encourage the churches there.

According to Wilks the missionaries at Namikango mission have begun asking themselves and their Malawian brethren the question: "If all the missionaries were to leave, which of the things that we are doing could the Malawian Christians carry on doing without us?" This reflection has caused them to modify several aspects of their work to make it more easily replicable by African Christians without outside resources.

Members of the Church of Christ have printed books, teaching materials and a monthly magazine in the Chichewa language. Jim and Kathy Albright (1980-1992) have had an impact on the nation as a whole since 1992 with the "Why Wait?" program for teaching abstinence-based sex education in the public schools. This is a critical issue for many African countries in the face of the AIDS epidemic.

God has done great things in Malawi, and our prayer should be that He continues to work in and through the church there.

Mozambique

Mozambique, on the eastern coast of southern Africa, was a Portuguese colony for almost 500 years. The story of the growth of the Church of Christ in that country is similar in many ways to the growth of the church in Nigeria. Feliciano, a Lomwe-speaking man, enrolled in a Bible correspondence course written by missionaries working in Sao Paulo, Brazil: "O que a Biblia diz" (What the Bible Says). Soon Feliciano was preaching the principles he learned in this course, and dozens of congregations were established. The movement spread rapidly without any outside assistance. A Brazilian

Christian came to Mozambique to help but left after only a short time because of civil war. Until the war diminished in 1992, few people outside of the country knew what God was doing in Mozambique. Brother Feliciano fled Mozambique during the war and took refuge in Malawi for a number of years. He may have had earlier ties to Malawi as well. According to Shelburne, the church in Blantyre "sent Bro. Daisi Banda Feliciano to Mozambique as a Missionary in 1968."

The Church of Christ has grown primarily among the Lomwe people in the Zambezia and Nampula provinces in northern Mozambique. This heavily populated rural area was among those hardest hit by the civil war. For years, people gave up planting crops or herding animals because whatever they produced was seized by one or the other of the armies. In spite of the isolation and suffering, an ever-growing "army" of Christians diligently spread the message of "What the Bible Says."

The Church of Christ in northern Mozambique is an indigenous movement, and as a result has developed unique ways of doing the Lord's work. While the church has grown well among Lomwe-speaking people, it has had little success among nearby language groups. In fact, congregations outside the boundaries of the traditional Lomwe areas are still made up mostly of Lomwe people who have migrated to these areas. For instance, few Makua-speaking people have become members of the church, even though their language is closely related to Lomwe. The Church of Christ in northern Mozambique is a good illustration of the missions principles that suggest that people become Christians most easily when they can do so without crossing cultural barriers. The church grows naturally among people who are "like us," but it takes special effort and sensitivity for the gospel to cross social or language barriers. It may be that in some cases, Makua people who want to become Christians are discouraged from reading or singing in their own language. Rather, they may be told, they should fit in with the Lomwe-speaking majority of the church.

In 1992, Mozambican Christians wrote the Church of Christ in Lisbon, Portugal, to ask for help. Attached to the letter was a map showing the locations of congregations, and page after page of addresses, contact names, and numbers of members. All told, the document reported about 300 congregations and 10,000 members.

Working in Lisbon at the time was Manuel de Oliveira. Manuel had been born in Portugal but spent his boyhood in Angola and finished high school in South Africa. It was in South Africa that he became a Christian, married a young South African woman who was also a Christian, and decided to study at SABS (Southern Africa Bible School). After he finished at SABS he taught at the Bible school at Manzini, Swaziland, and at the same time continued his own studies and earned a degree in theology from the University of South Africa. The Richland Hills congregation brought him to Fort Worth to translate the easy-to-read translation of the New Testament into Portuguese, and then sent him to Lisbon as a missionary (Watson 1989:335-336).

At the time the letter from Mozambique arrived, the de Oliveiras had been in Lisbon for eight years with no intention of leaving. But Manuel made a quick trip to Mozambique to confirm what was written in the letter, and concluded that he was more urgently needed in Africa than in Europe. Manuel settled his family in Johannesburg, South Africa. Then he began to look for ways to help the churches in Mozambique. Between 1994 and 1996, he arranged for about thirty Mozambican church leaders to come to Swaziland where he gave them a year of intensive Bible instruction. He encouraged the most gifted teachers to establish a school in Mozambique to pass on to others the training that they had received.

A group of missionaries from the conservative Christian Church/Church of Christ also took an interest in nurturing the Christian movement among the Lomwe. These missionaries were based near Maputo, the capital city. One of the families, Jacob and Nila Michael, made plans to move to northern Mozambique to be nearer to where the churches were. Sadly, while they were in the process of building their house, Nila discovered signs of cancer and they returned to the U.S. for treatment, which turned out to be unsuccessful. Jacob has recently re-married and returned to Mozambique.

In 1999, the de Oliveiras moved to Maputo where they live and work with the Michaels' former co-workers. In January 2000, one of the missionaries, Cecil Byrd, was shot and killed by robbers who forced their way into the Byrds' home. This traumatic event caused Manuel to question whether or not he should remain in Mozambique. In the end he felt convicted that his duty was to remain there and rededicate himself to being an evangelist. "Heaven," a friend of his wrote, "is just as close to Maputo as it is to Fort Worth."

In addition to the overseas missionaries, Christians from Malawi have been going into Mozambique since the end of the war. Also, African evangelists from Zimbabwe (many of whom received training at the Bible school at Mutare) have established a number of congregations in Manica province near the city of Beira, the second largest city in Mozambique. Travel within Mozambique is so difficult that the Christians from Manica province have had almost no opportunity for contact with the Christians who live further north.

The church in Mozambique has persevered and grown even in the midst of great suffering. Unfortunately, they are also in danger from divisions and other attacks from our spiritual enemy. Some of the tensions are not so much about doctrine as about church

83

practices, such as the order in which things are done in the Sunday assembly. But the more significant issues have to do with personalities and the desire for power. The church continues to grow, now numbering about 500 congregations with 20,000 members (Berryman and Broom 2000). Let us pray that our brothers and sisters in Mozambique will also grow in love and a missionary vision which will allow them to evangelize people of other tribes and tongues.

Madagascar

Barry and Stacie Rosie and Rodger and Sue Moon worked for more than ten years among the Luo people of Kenya. The Rosies and the Moons, along with the elders of their sending congregations, had concluded that the Luo churches had become mature enough to keep growing on their own. Rather than draw back from the battle front, these missionary families chose to look for a place where the need was great and their experience could be put to good use. In 1995, these two families moved to Madagascar, an island in the Indian Ocean just off the coast of Africa, along with a family from Madagascar who were converted while working in the United States. The Rosies have learned both French and Malagasy, and have begun an orphanage in addition to establishing a congregation in Antananarivo.

Namibia

Bessie Hardin Chenault wrote about a number of congregations that were begun in Namibia in the 60's and 70's (1986: pp. 615-618). So far as I know, none of these have survived. During the past ten years, brother D'Alton from South Africa has worked in Windhoek (the capital) and in Tsumeb, a small town in the north. Also, Christians from Capetown, both South African and American, have been reaching out in Namibia using World Bible School. They have begun a congregation in the far north, in Oshakati, the largest town of Ovamboland, which is the district where the greatest number of Namibians live. Several of the congregations from Capetown have been involved in campaigns in Namibia, and at one point talked about sending up one of their own as a missionary to live year-round in Ovamboland.

Conclusion

Missions is God's work, but he has chosen to do that work through people. As a result, the story of missions has both a divine and a human side. Missions is a story of heroism, selfless dedication, and the triumph of love and devotion over all obstacles. Missionaries in Africa have suffered hardships and dangers in order to serve their Master. They left family and comfort behind and instead faced wild animals, disease, deprivation, and war. In order to take the gospel where it had not yet been preached, they jolted along over rocks, slogged through sand and mud, and blazed trails where there were no roads. They often carried on in spite of Christians back home whose support, both emotional and financial, often proved inadequate.

At the same time, missions is a story of a spiritual battle in which not all are victorious. Satan destroys marriages and divides brother from brother. Some Christian workers fall victim to greed or sexual temptation. Others remain in service but possibly do as much harm as good due to harsh attitudes or the desire to set up their own personal kingdoms. Yes, the Gospel goes forward, sometimes in spite of the messengers rather than because of them.

Despite the obstacles and setbacks, the Church of Christ is well established and growing in southern Africa. African church leaders are rising up and taking the baton from the hands of overseas missionaries. The direction and destiny of African churches is being decided by Africans rather than by foreigners. So what will be the role of missionaries in the twenty-first century? There are still opportunities to serve, especially among people groups where the church has not yet been introduced. But American missionaries on their own cannot complete the task of evangelizing Africa. Possibly the greatest need is for missionaries who can work alongside and even under the guidance of African leaders to equip and empower African men and women to be evangelists not only to their own peoples but also across barriers of culture, tribe, and language.

God does not want the church in Africa to be a mission church, under the perpetual care and tutelage of missionaries. Rather, he wants the African church to be a missionary church, his servants through whom he can reach out and finish his work of reconciling the world to himself.

WORKS CITED

Berryman, Mark and Broom, Wendell (2000). Church Growth in Africa: Statistics 2000 [on-line], http://www.bible.acu.edu/missions/page.asp?ID=323.

Chenault, Bessie Hardin (1989). *Give Me This Mountain*. Winona, MS: J. C. Choate.

Echols, Eldred (1989). *Wings of the Morning*. Fort Worth, TX: Wings Press.

Johnstone, Patrick (1993). *Operation World*. Grand Rapids, MI: Zondervan.

Lynn, Mac (1990). *Churches of Christ Around the World*. Nashville: Gospel Advocate.

Shelburne, G. B. III (1997). History of the Church of Christ in Malawi [on-line], http://www.bible.acu.edu/missions/page.asp?ID=412.

Watson, Joe (1989). *Three African Drums*. Winona, MS: J. C. Choate.

CHAPTER 5

A Survey of Work in West Africa

Mark Berryman

Mark Berryman has served as a missions instructor and African missions research specialist at Harding University since 1992. He has done extensive field surveys in Africa and led future missionaries on numerous survey trips. Mark and his wife Sandy live in Searcy, Arkansas.

LIBERIA

Slave, died soon into his mission.

Alexander Cross, as far as is known, was the first missionary of the Churches of Christ to work in sub-Saharan Africa. The restoration preacher and strategist, D.S. Burnet, had wanted to begin a work in Africa to go with the work that had started in Jerusalem in 1850. Alexander Campbell also began promoting the idea. Cross, while still a slave, was overheard preaching to other slaves in Christian County, Kentucky. Burnet recommended that Cross's freedom be purchased and the Hopkinsville, Kentucky church quickly began helping him become more familiar with the scriptures. Two individuals gave 407 dollars and the Hopkinsville church gave 28 dollars towards Cross's mission support. Cross, his wife, and eight-year-old son set sail from Baltimore on November 5, 1853, landing in Monrovia, Liberia in January 1854. "In an effort to build himself a house at a certain point on the St. Paul's River, Cross poled a canoe fourteen miles up the river under the hot African sun. In a few days he fell down with a fever, and died. His little boy, James, who was along, also took the fever and he too, soon died" (West, 1974, pp. 219-220). Thus began and ended the work of God through that first missionary family of the Churches of Christ to Africa. While Cross's life ended quickly and his worked seemed to accomplish little, his faithfulness to the calling is an example to us all.

New Beginnings

Over one hundred years passed until other missionaries with the Churches of Christ entered Liberia.

> Those missionaries found a country well prepared by God to receive the message of the gospel. The One Party Legislative government was at peace, and there was no fighting among the 28 ethnic groups who occupy the country. Several denominational groups who had been in the country for a few decades had introduced them to the idea of God, the Creator. A number of Liberians were added to the Lord's church during those first few years. Many have remained to become a stable foundation for the church for over 25-30 years (Drinnen, 2000).

There are conflicting reports concerning the first converts in Liberia. One report written after a visit to Liberia in July 26, to August 5, 1966 by Dwayne Davenport of Kumasi, Ghana and Elvis Huffard of Freetown, Sierra Leone reports that as early as 1961 the Herald of Truth radio program over WLBC had been "softening up" this mission field. It was not until January of 1966 that Charles A. Johnson in Monrovia, Liberia actually began a Bible correspondence course given him after a visit by Eugene Peden, one of the pioneers in the Nigerian work. V.M. Whitesell, visiting from Nashville with Copeland Baker and Roger Church, baptized Johnson and his wife in the Atlantic Ocean on May 19, 1966 shortly before midnight. Another report of an early convert (also in 1966), a Brother Gibbson, was reported in the January 1970 issue of the World Radio News by Don Yelton.

Billy and Gerry Nicks (who had previously worked in Nigeria from 1955-1960) were the first full-time missionaries to Liberia, arriving in February of 1969 (Gospel Light, 1969). They were followed quickly by Jerry and Jean Langford and Dr. Tom and Anita Drinnen (1970-1973). Dr. Drinnen opened a clinic in Fellehla on April 29, 1970 with Sara Young, R.N. assisting. Later, John and Karen Littlejohn and David Cron were involved in full-time evangelism along with national workers at the clinic (Joe Glenn, nd). Other missionaries to work in Liberia include David and Myra Underwood, Dr. Adalia and Delitath Arnold (who worked for four and one-half years with U.S. AID), David and Ann Moses, Willard and Shelby Pyles, Willie and Kay Orange, Robert and Susan Waggoner (with World Radio), and Clyde Elder (administrator for the Christian Health Clinic) (Waggoner, 1975).

From the onset, the Medial Mission work was centered up-country about 80 miles from Monrovia, in Fellehla. After Tom Drinnen (a physician) and his family returned to the States in 1973, brother George Tokpa, a Liberian national trained as a medical assistant, ran the clinic in Fellehla until the civil war began in 1989. George was a teenager when he first became a Christian. He was an eager Bible student and had an exceptional ability to grasp the medical training. George continues to preach and teach in the Fellehla area, but the clinic was closed due to danger to the workers and lack of supplies. George has had to send most of his family to Sierra Leone for safety, but he has remained in Fellehla to preach, teach and give aid to those in need in the area. The Liberian Christians hope to reopen the clinic when conditions become favorable.

91

In those early years, with no idea that war was imminent, the goal of the missionaries was to bring the nationals as much as possible to the point of becoming self-sustaining. With this goal in mind, they began elementary and Bible schools, and trained a few of the most promising workers as medical assistants. The civil war slowed mission efforts considerably. The war has caused death to many Christians and heartache to countless others.

Liberia Today

Most of the activity of the church in Liberia is taking place in the area of the capital city of Monrovia. Liberian workers operate at least five Christian elementary schools (Liberia has no public schools). There is a Bible College and the WBS work is very strong in and around Monrovia. The Christian Relief Fund supports one of the larger schools. The Liberian Missions Fund supports 7 Liberian preachers, a deaf-ministry at one of the large congregations, some help for the Bible College, and also help for the elementary schools.

The best estimate in 2000 was about 70 congregations with 3200 members in Liberia. An *ACTION* (2001) report by Maxwell Shea, Liberian preacher for the Smythe Road church, reported 102 churches, 11 Christian schools and one college. There are no missionaries from the United States presently in Liberia. The Smythe Road Church of Christ in Monrovia is perhaps the strongest congregation in the country. Charles Paegar, one of the first converts by American missionaries, is a strong pillar in the Smythe Road church. He donates his talent as a construction worker; he is an outreach preacher, a fundraiser, and a godly example of faithfulness in Liberia. Brother Paegar's work has been supported for a number of years by the Cox Boulevard church in Sheffield, Alabama, and the Chisholm Hills church in Florence, Alabama. There are also two other large groups of 400-500 in the Monrovia area as well as a small number of house churches in other parts of Liberia.

With God's help, these Christians have endured the 10 year civil war out of which the country is now slowly emerging. There is no electricity, running water, or mail service. Communication, transportation, schools and medical services are operating on a minimum level. Also, many Liberians fled the country and became refugees in surrounding countries. We have heard of meetings of the church in these countries. We also know of several pockets of Liberian refugees in the States; one group in Rhode Island numbers 100 plus.

The Christians in Liberia are beginning to experience some relief from the struggles brought on by war, but continue to have many physical needs. Nevertheless, all reports tell us that they are strong in their belief that God will continue to provide for their physical and spiritual needs. They have zeal and want the gospel to continue to spread in Liberia (Drinnen, 2000).

SIERRA LEONE

Dr. Willis Orlando Price, a Methodist preacher from Freetown, Sierra Leone, was converted in South Carolina in 1963 while studying with V.E. Williamson (Beckloff, 2000; Christian Chronicle, 1966). Dr. Price returned to Freetown in 1964 and arranged for Chester Vaughn to preach there for six weeks, at which time they baptized forty-nine people. The two men received favorable comments from the local newspaper, radio and even the minister of education. Price operated a primary school with about 200 students prior to his conversion; he continued to use that work as a ministry tool after his return (Daniel, 1964). The first American missionaries began their work with Price's school as well. John Beckloff came over from Nigeria in July 1965 and also preached on a short-term trip.

Opening Moves

The first congregation in Sierra Leone was established in Freetown at Spafield, the Methodist church where Dr. Price had worked previously, and from which he converted many. However, soon after his return Dr. Price was diagnosed with terminal cancer and died only a few months later. Eugene Peden from Nigeria continued to encourage this new work, as did other Americans including the Houston Ezells and John Dedmons. The first full-time American missionaries were the Elvis Huffard family (1964-1966), from Freed-Hardeman, who worked in Freetown. The Huffards briefly overlapped with Paul and Cathy Dillingham who arrived in July 1966. From that point on, the work began to see more and more missionaries coming and going until the height of American missionary presence during the 1970's (Beckloff, 2000; Dillingham, 1967; Greetings, 1965 and 1967).

Although the missionary force had continued to grow with two missionaries in 1966, three in 1967, four in 1968, five in 1969, six in 1971, and nine in 1972, the Spafield congregation eventually died out as many members, it appeared, were looking more for material gain than spiritual life. But new growth was occurring elsewhere. New congregations were planted in a radius of 40 miles of Freetown. In 1967 the new growth resulted in 850 baptisms (Trousdale, 1972, p. 15-17). By June of 1969 there were 25 congregations around Freetown (Greetings, June 1969). "During the years 1964-1968 the number of baptisms increased by 212 percent annually. From 1968-1972 the increase was 66 percent annually" (Trousdale, pp. 15-17). In August 1969 there were over 5000 students enrolled in Bible correspondence work and about 850 conversions reported in 16 congregations (*Action*, 1968.) The total number of baptisms from 1964-1972 was 2,238, with 1,173 of those in the Freetown area and the remainder upcountry. However, practicing Christians, those actually assembling on Sunday, were only 600. Sixty-three churches were planted during the years 1964-1972, but only 27 congregations actually met on their own without missionary assistance. Another 20 congregations met as long as the people knew in advance of the missionaries' coming. By 1972, sixteen congregations were no longer meeting on Sunday or any time during the week.

The height of the work appears to have been the last quarter of 1970 when there were fifty-three congregations actually meeting. Of the "forty-one national preachers in the country, twenty-six of these were on some type of American support" (Trousdale, 1972, p. 15-29). Besides the capital city of Freetown, missionaries also located in Bo, about 150 miles from the capital and in Taiama, about 118 miles away. (Greetings, 1970). From 1972-1974 Ken and Pat Beckloff, Larry and Kay Little and Jim and Ruth Woodard worked in Bo. Baptisms in the Bo area from February 1977 to August 6, 1978 were 45 in the village areas and 19 in the Bo congregation (Missionaries located in Bo, Sierra Leone, 1978). Later, the Beckloffs and James and Lorene Howell moved to Taiama where they planted 18 congregations within a 20 mile radius and three more 40 miles away. In 1975 there were 51 congregations with 1,600 members (Beckloff, 1977). By 1980 there were still approximately 51 congregations listed with 13 of those no longer meeting (*Missionaries and Overseers of the Work in Sierra Leone*, 1980).

Evangelism and Training Methods

There were various methods used in Sierra Leone to evangelize, including preaching in the towns and villages, preacher training schools (with many of them being employed as preachers after graduation), correspondence courses, distribution of Bibles and tracts in the English and Mende languages, and primary schools. The wives of the missionaries also participated in Bible studies for the women and public Bible classes in various church settings for the ladies and for the local children (Trousdale, 1972, p.16). Jim Woodard, along with the other missionaries and elders, made the decision to discontinue the main office in downtown Sierra Leone which they used for the Bible correspondence program and to dismiss the two paid national workers of the program. The office at one time had been a busy hub of activity, but it was felt that the correspondence work should be directly under each local congregation rather than through a central headquarters (Greetings, 1978 and 1980).

The work in Sierra Leone of training preachers was carried out in part by the Freetown Bible Training School. The school began in September 1967 in the house of M. F. Norwood. The school originally had both male and female students who met for 3 hours, 3 nights per week. It grew through the years and relocated several times until Houston Ezell came from the United States and helped construct a new building in the Murraytown section of Freetown. Later the school was completed with a dormitory, kitchen, dining hall, and a workshop. By August 1976 there were between 25-30 students along with national teachers. Several missionaries served as director of the school including M. F. Norwood (1967-1969 and again 1971-1973), J. Garvin Smith (1969-1971), C. B. Laws (1973-1974) and James Woodard (1974-1975). Mike Norwood began directing the school in 1976. The school was always under the oversight of the Vultee Church of Christ in Nashville, Tenneessee. (Greetings, 1976). The Freetown Bible School compound was sold to another religious group in 1982 (Lawrence, 2000).

A second Bible school was started in Taiama in 1972 and held classes for 6-8 weeks during the dry season for the subsistence farmers in local congregations around Taiama. Over 20 congregations were being served by 1976. There were several primary schools begun in various locations including Bo and Freetown, with nationals working alongside missionaries to establish them. South End Day School, Overlook Christian School, Garber's and J. Davis' school were among them (Beckloff, et.al., unknown date). A series of Bible Lectureships also began in 1976. Ken Beckloff also operated a Leadership Training by Extension program in 1979, late in the missionary phase of the work (Greetings, March, 1979). The missionaries in Sierra Leone used either English or Krio (a trade language using English, Portuguese and African words built on African grammar).

National Plans

A *Ten-year Plan to Evangelize Sierra Leone by 1990* was developed under the vision of the Vultee Church of Christ in Nashville, Tenneessee. The plan called for missionaries to plant churches in all the headquarter towns of each political district by 1990, with the goal of establishing strong, evangelistic congregations in the town and the surrounding district. These churches were not to rely on American paid, national evangelists, but rather on voluntary, local Christians. The missionaries were no longer to work out of institutions, but directly with the evangelism and church development. (Beckloff, 1979; Greetings, 1980). However, after much prayer and discussion with the national Christians, the Sierra Leone church felt that they should try to continue to grow on their own. They encouraged the missionaries to continue to make visits to them from time to time, but located missionaries were not part of the final plan (Norwood, 2000). The last missionary families in Sierra Leone were the Littles and Laytons who left in 1980 and the Greens who left in 1981 (Little and Layton, 1985; Norwood, 2000). The Vultee Church of Christ in Nashville along with the Una Church of Christ,

97

also in Nashville, were the primary supporters of the work in Sierra Leone. The Vultee congregation still maintains an active interest in the work in Sierra Leone.

The 1980's brought economic crisis to Sierra Leone which affected the churches and their plans. Many church members with family ties to neighboring Liberia migrated there and became involved in the work of several congregations in that country. When civil war broke out in Liberia in 1989, several of those returned to Sierra Leone. A few years later Sierra Leone became embroiled in its own civil war, which became a long and devastating struggle with great brutality. The church is surviving, although it has suffered greatly (Beckloff, 2000).

The Church in Sierra Leone, Present and Past

Currently there is one man who is supported from the States, Prince C.T.O. Samuel John who works with the Priscilla Street congregation in Freetown. Another brother, A.J.S. Koroma is with the Overlook congregation, also in Freetown. At most there are six full-time workers in the country. The number of congregations has fallen to approximately 15 to 20. There are 6 congregations in the capital city of Freetown, 4 or 5 in and around the city of Bo, one in Kenema, 2 in the area of Tungea, and one in Makeni. Possibly there are more, but due to the war they cannot be contacted. One estimate of the number of members still assembling is about 300 while other estimates are a bit higher. However, there could easily be others who are meeting without our knowledge. Quite a few members were killed, others suffered great loss of property (Lawrence, 2000; Norwood, 2000).

While the church in Sierra Leone has faced and continues to struggle with hardship, there remain stories from the past to give us hope. In one of the earliest missionary bulletins from Sierra Leone in December 1965, Elvis Huffard wrote of S. O. B. Morgan,

> He is a contractor of small jobs, but when it comes
> to the church he is available with a great big smile and lots
> of enthusiasm. His favorite expression in promoting the
> work is 'make big noise.' Another expression he often
> uses in encouraging others is, 'Be not ashamed for
> Christ.' He never misses a Bible class or a lecture...
> (Greetings, 1965).

Former missionary Mike Norwood, years later, reported S. O.
B. Morgan's continued faithfulness and that of another Christian, E.
O. C. Corkson.

> He (Dr. Price) was a Krio, the group of people given
> special privileges by the British. I was very closely associ-
> ated with S.O.B. Morgan, a convert of Dr. Price, and
> E.O.C. Corkson. Both were Krios who spent the rest of
> their lives trying to teach others. I was given the oppor-
> tunity to give the eulogy for Bro. Morgan to about 200
> prominent Krios who attended his funeral. He was ostra-
> cized by them because he broke with tradition, but (he)
> never stopped. He edited and published a Krio language
> paper called "Kam Ot Pan Dem,' which is Krio for
> "Come Ye Out From Among Them." He was a pro-
> moter and visionary and believed that we must make a
> 'big noise' for Jesus. My fluency in Krio was largely due
> to his teaching.
> Bro. Corkson was 67 years old when my father, M.
> F. Norwood, taught him. Perhaps I should say, my father
> completed the job that John Koroma began. Pa Corkson
> was from a prominent Krio family who retired from the
> Nigerian Railway about 1962 and returned to Freetown.
> After John left his Muslim background and became a
> Christian, he began trying to teach Pa Corkson who lived
> in the same compound. To Pa Corkson, John, at age 25,
> was much too young to know anything. However, John
> had such a grasp of the Scripture that he could not entire-
> ly dismiss him. Pa Corkson opted for study with a 'white
> man' and that is how my father became involved. This

deference to an American came from his education when he had an American as well as several British teachers. His classical education included Greek and Latin, which he could still recite. His classmates included Siaka Stevens who became the President of Sierra Leone (Norwood, 2000).

But no doubt Corkson's most important contact was not the President of Sierra Leone, nor the American missionary Norwood, but rather John (A. J. S.) Koroma, the young Muslim convert of Dr. Orlando Price, who began teaching Corkson. John Koroma, the former Muslim continues in the year 2001 to preach faithfully with the Overlook congregation, Freetown, Sierra Leone. May the evidence of God's power continue.

BENIN

"Benin: Home of Voodoo" says the tourist poster! Benin, formerly known as Dahomey, is one of the most animistic, pagan countries in the world. In Fon, the language of the largest people group in Benin, the word *Voodoo* actually means "spirit language." Truly, Satan has deceived this small West African nation for many centuries. The animistic religion of the people pervades every aspect of their lives and only God, through the blood of Jesus, can rescue them. Idols, sorcerers, diviners, ritual ceremonies, ancestral shrines, animal sacrifices, and voodoo cults are all part of the daily lives of the majority of Benin's people. Following is an excerpt of a history written by veteran missionary Richard Chowning who works among the Aja people in the southeastern part of Benin.

WORK IN BENIN
Richard Chowning

The first congregation of the Churches of Christ in Benin was planted in 1985 by a Ghanaian Christian who was teaching in an elementary school in the village of Se. Another Ghanaian evangelist, George Akpabli, moved his family to Benin's capital, Cotonou, and planted the first congregation there in 1992. Three years later Akpabli opened the *Centre de Formation Biblique* (Bible Training Center) in Cotonou. Eighteen students have graduated from its 3-year program. They are now evangelizing in Benin, Burkina Faso, Cameroon, Chad, and Togo. Outreach from these African—initiated congregations and the *Centre de Formation Biblique* has resulted in the planting of seventeen congregations with a membership of nearly six hundred.

The first American missionaries arrived in 1993 to work among the Fon people, Benin's largest ethnic group. The Vogts, Parker, Gordon, and Boyd arrived in 1993 and the Wilsons and Treadway in 1995. There are now seven congregations with a total of around 120 members. The team is phasing out of the work and will leave the area by the end of 2001.

The third mission effort in Benin is among the Aja people, involves five families: the Baileys (1996), Chownings (1997), Crowsons, Hicks and Kennell (1998) and the Vaughns (1999). The first Aja congregation was planted in May of 1998; there are now 30 congregations, totaling over seven hundred fifty members (Chowning, 2000). The total number of churches in Benin in April of 2000 was 46 with 1,278 members (Berryman and Broom, 2000).

Perhaps the most heart wrenching story of God's work in Benin occurred in August 1995 when Tod and Nancy Vogt went to the neighboring country of Togo to pick up new teammates from the

101

airport in Lome'. A simple flat tire on a busy street in Lome led to Nancy's eventual death in a hospital in Abidjan, Ivory Coast on August 16, 1995. As the women were waiting for the tire to be changed, a thief snatched one of their purses and headed across the busy street. Nancy instinctively pursued and was struck by a vehicle. There was nothing that could be done to save her life. Nancy died, leaving behind her husband and baby daughter Hannah. Her life, though cut short, was as an example of dedication to God. Our spiritual warfare with Satan continues. We are once again reminded of the brevity of life and the urgency to share the good news of Jesus in dark places.

TOGO

As is typical with so many countries in Africa, the history of the work of the Churches of Christ in Togo begins with an African as the first to take the message to his own people. Togo, like Benin, is one of the most animistic, pagan countries in the world in terms of percentage of the people. Idols, animal sacrifices, charms, witchcraft, ritual ceremonies, etc. are commonly seen. Voodoo is the common word into which we fit all of these behaviors. Pray that those in darkness may come into the light. The following is an excerpt taken from e-mail correspondence from Jeff Holland, an American missionary in Tabligbo, Togo.

WORK IN TOGO
Jeff Holland

The Lord has been blessing the Churches of Christ in Togo with wonderful growth over the past few years, but for many years, this work of the Lord was very difficult and slow. The first member of the Churches of Christ in Togo is believed to be Paul Gbedemah. He had attended preacher training school in Ghana in the late 1960s. In 1970, he arrived in Togo and started preaching. Soon after his arrival, a small congregation was meeting in his home in the capital city of Lome.

Togolese Christian Evangelism

For many years Churches of Christ could not obtain official recognition because the government of Togo only authorized seven Christian groups to hold meetings, conduct evangelism, and invite missionaries. The members of the first congregation often had to meet secretly for worship and fellowship. Paul and others caught meeting to worship often faced imprisonment and beatings as they practiced their faith. In the midst of the persecution and lack of official recognition, God continued to raise up members and church leaders. Many of the early members were converted to Christ in Ghana and Nigeria or through World Bible School; others were converted through the congregation meeting at Brother Paul's.

A second congregation was established in another area of Lome in 1990. In the early 1990's, political tension was rising in the nation. Members of the two young churches continued to be harassed by soldiers, and members were imprisoned on various occasions. The Christians prayed that God would provide for official recognition. It was in the midst of these tensions that national religious freedom was granted and protected by a new constitution. On October 29, 1991, the Churches of Christ were finally allowed to apply for official recognition. God, through the government authorities, provided official status for the Churches of Christ on July 22, 1992.

When this official recognition was granted, Togolese nationals trained in Bible schools in Ghana and Nigeria were ready to advance the gospel.   The following year, a Ghanaian brother (Douglas Boateng, a businessman and elder in the church in Ghana who lived in Togo several years) purchased land in a central location in Lome. The two congregations already meeting joined together in one assembly with the hopes of reaching out to Lome and eventually the rest of Togo. From this one congregation in Lome, evangelists launched efforts into the cities of Kpalime, Tsevie, and Abodrafo. In Vogan, a brother raised in the Christian Church in Ghana agreed to cooperate with the Church of Christ evangelists and started a church planting in his family's home area. Thus, by the end of 1994, nationals had already started five congregations, all among the Eve people of southern Togo (over 2 million people). Since that time, the full-time national church leaders have continued to engage in church maturation and church planting. They have also increased their efforts through new full-time evangelists who have been trained in the preacher training school located in Cotonou, Benin.

American Missionary Teams

A team of five families from the United States also wanted to work in Togo. When the Church of Christ was recognized, this missionary team chose to begin a church-planting work among the Watchi people, a subgroup of the Eve' peoples. Because French is the national language of Togo, the team spent the first several months of 1994 in France to study the French language. Then in August 1994, the team began to settle in the city of Tabligbo in the southeastern corner of the country. God has combined the national and missionary efforts. He is working through full-time national evangelists, missionaries, and local leaders to mature the 29 congregations among the Eve' peoples of Togo. He is also using them in numerous church planting efforts. The Lord has allowed for relationships of trust to grow between the missionaries and the full-time nationals receiving

American support. The churches are now enjoying a high degree of mutual respect and desire for unity. One of the ways this unity has been strengthened has been Project Timothy, which meets one weekend a month for three years. Leaders from all of the Churches of Christ among the Eve' are invited to participate. They are trained by the missionaries and experienced national ministers.

In addition to the churches among the Eve' peoples of southern Togo, four churches are meeting in northern Togo. This is the result of evangelistic efforts of Ghanaian brothers who have crossed the border in an effort to reach people groups that are in both countries. That makes a total of 34 congregations meeting in Togo. Our prayer is that one day the whole country will be reached and that strong evangelistic congregations from Togo will reach out into other areas of West Africa. (Holland, 2000).

God raised up another team of five families who joined the work in Togo in September 2000. They moved to the northern city of Kara to work specifically among the Kabiye people. Churches continue to be planted and Togolese leaders continue to work side by side with national leaders. Several Togolese have taught in the school of preaching in Benin, and others have studied in the two-year program there. Full-time national workers include Luk Agbekenou, Akalo Komla, Adjayi Innoussa, Koffi Koudahe, Paul Gbedemah, Dey Adomekoe, Walter Akoubia, Toulassi, Mark Agossor, Pougla Bienvenue, Amou Kokoutse, and Kwami Hammer Afakule (Holland, 2000). There are many others at the time of this writing, but these are some of those spreading the gospel in Togo. Others also deserving mention include Walter Bryan, an American who made trips to Togo prior to full-time American missionaries arriving.

The Bible in Eve' and the New Testament in Kabiye are available for the missionaries and the local people. The missionaries

105

have done an excellent job in learning both French and the local language of Eve'. In the April 2000 report of Churches of Christ in Africa, 34 churches were reported with 910 faithful believers in Togo. At the time of this writing there are a total of 20 American missionaries in Togo. God continues to add to his kingdom (Berryman and Broom, 2000).

NORTHERN NIGERIA

The work in the southern part of Nigeria is well documented in other chapters of this book. But the advancement of the church into the Muslim north, primarily among the Hausa people, is an important demonstration that there is a harvest possible among the Islamic peoples of Africa.

Identifying the Need

The work in northern Nigeria, especially in the Plateau State, received help in 1982 when a team of vocational missionaries arrived. This vocational mission team, consisting of Rees and Patti Bryant, Tim and Belinda Curtis, Gary and Kim Luallen, David Little, Craig Trudgen, and Clarence Wilson, went as schoolteachers to teach in the Nigerian school system. This first wave of teachers was joined later by Wallace and Tammy Sutter, Irving and Rhonda Everson and Ken and Deborah Klein. When President Shagari's democratic government was overthrown by the military in a coup d'etat on December 31, 1983, government funding was suspended for about six months. When teacher's salaries were finally paid, all expatriate teachers were notified that they were being retrenched. Most of the vocational missionaries left Nigeria to return to lives of service elsewhere. The Kleins were spared retrenchment because they were stationed in Gindiri, which had a long history of being a

106

center of education in the north, a school where many of the nation's leaders had been trained. The Kleins were able to complete their 18-month term of contract. Later, the Ministry of Education of Plateau State in north-central Nigeria hired them to teach Christian religious knowledge in various schools scattered throughout the state. Clarence Wilson continued on, unsalaried, teaching CRK (Christian Religious Knowledge) in the government teacher's college and serving as the CRK department head while preaching in the villages every weekend for three additional years. Wilson's home congregation in Selfs, Texas picked up partial support of him after he had gone over six months with no salary whatsoever. Many Muslims took Christian religious education because it was taught in English.

Another major component for evangelism in the north was World Bible School. Ralph Perry was involved in World Bible School follow up in northern Nigeria, as early as 1980. (Ralph and Joyce Perry first went to Nigeria in 1971 with their family to teach at the Ukpom Bible College.) In the mid 1980's, Perry proposed the "10-10-10 Plan" where 10 leaders from the southeastern part of Nigeria, sponsored by 10 churches from the southeast would plant churches in 10 major centers in the north. However, the Hausa of the north do not really trust the Ibo, Ibibio, or Efik of the southeast, or the Yoruba of the southwest part of Nigeria. Culturally and linguistically they are different and there is a long history that is difficult to overcome. Neither was it effective to send students from the north into the Bible schools in the south. By 1987 it became apparent that because of the ethnic differences, a school for training preachers was needed in the north.

School of Biblical Studies, Jos

Steve Worley, along with Ralph Perry, had been working in Nigeria since 1985 conducting World Bible School follow up.

Worley was going back and forth to the United States promoting the work when he met the Central Church of Christ in Gadsden, Alabama, who agreed to oversee the work of building a training school in northern Nigeria. Several experienced people were brought together in early planning discussions, including Elvis Huffard, John Beckloff, Ralph Perry, and Steve Worley. It was hoped that by seeking guidance from experienced educators that some of the mistakes made in southern Nigeria would not be repeated in the north. They wrote a charter for a school of biblical studies in Jos, Nigeria.

Solomon Aguh, a Christian who had been converted at Ole Miss in the United States while a student working on his MBA, was teaching at the University of Jos. Solomon was a very active Christian and enthusiastically involved with the Jos congregation. Steve Worley asked Solomon to be the director of the School of Biblical Studies. Solomon refused, as he had no formal training in the Bible or religion. It was agreed that Solomon would go to Freed-Hardeman for two years and earn his B.A. in Bible. Another Nigerian, Naphtali Dagasamah, a straight "A" student at Nigerian Christian Bible College in Ukpom, was also sent to Freed-Hardeman to earn a B.A. in Bible. About the same time in 1987 Clarence Wilson, one of the original vocational teachers, went to Nigerian Christian Bible College at Ukpom in southeastern Nigeria to teach and gain one year of administrative experience to be better equipped to serve in the new school in the north.

Following two years of preparation, the School of Biblical Studies opened in Jos in the fall of 1989 with Solomon Aguh as Director and Bible teacher and with Clarence Wilson as the Dean of Students and Bible teacher. Naphtali Dagasamah taught Bible and related topics and a local northern Nigerian, Avaka Terwasi, taught English. Meanwhile Steve Worley secured a campus site and contracted the building. The plan was that twelve students per year would be accepted in a two-year program of study with scholarships provided. The qualifications for entrance to the school were that a local Nigerian congregation had to recommend a student for study, he had to have a secondary school diploma, and he must pass an English proficiency exam, which was written and administered by the School of Biblical Studies.

The plan also was that students come from all twelve states in the northern region of Nigeria. However, due to the fact that there were very few churches in the north at that time, during the first few years many students came from the same general locations. Most of the students were and still are young single men, though families in their early 30's have also studied at the school. Support tends to be a problem when the families bring large numbers of children to the school. Another key aspect of the school that was put in place was an apprenticeship program with trades in the city of Jos. The administration of the school sought out local craftsmen who were highly skilled at their professions to help train the Bible school students. Thus a student would be one half day as an apprentice learning a trade and the other half of the day learning the Bible and related subjects. This was done in order to avoid the problem experienced in southern Nigeria where graduates often expected support immediately upon graduation and often from American sources.

The School of Biblical Studies (SBS) registered with the government in Plateau State to receive accreditation. A library was built, with additional materials being added through the years, to improve the standard for a B.A. in religion. After teaching in the school for a number of years, Naphtali went back to Freed-Hardeman to get a masters degree and has been back in Jos since 1999. Solomon Aguh received an honorary doctorate from Freed-Hardeman as well.

In 1991 Clarence Wilson married Patty Woods, a nurse, who

had a long-term affiliation with Nigerian Christian Hospital in Aba, Nigeria in the southeastern part of the country. Patty began to teach health related subjects along with English and literature at the School of Biblical Studies. The Wilsons were with the school until 1993.

After the first class graduated in 1991, a decision was made to expand the program to a three-year program. Evangelism has always been a chief part of the training program with students partnered together for church planting on the weekends for the entire three years that they are present. Normally there are converts and a church is planted. Thus the students learn first-hand about problems related to church planting and development. They are debriefed in chapel every Monday following the experiences of the previous weekend. Also, summer campaigns for Christ are conducted in conjunction with local congregations, with staff members taking students to various states in the north for evangelism. Steve Worley currently helps organize seminars for World Bible School follow up by the students. The "Outreach for Africa" program continues to prepare and motivate students to go as missionaries to other African countries such as Chad, Uganda, etc. Ji Mathias Ofon, SBS student, recently made a preaching tour in Chad and reported 11 new Christians in this primarily Muslim country (*Action*, 2001, p. 3).

Emmanuel Adegoroye, a young leader in his mid-30's who has doctorate level training from Nigeria, was sent to International Bible College in Alabama for two years of Bible training. He is from western Nigeria and began working with the School of Biblical Studies in 1993, he now heads the missions department.

Ken and Deborah Klein were part of the first families who moved to northern Nigeria with Rees and Patti Bryant in 1982. After a few years in Nigeria, the Klines moved to New York where Deborah earned a doctorate in teaching English as a second language. The Klines returned to Jos in 1995, where Deborah teaches at the University of Jos and Ken teaches part-time at the School of Biblical Studies and regularly teaches and preaches in towns and rural areas throughout Nigeria.

At the time of this writing, Solomon Aguh continues to serve as the Director of the School of Biblical Studies. Steve Worley is the Director of Development, World Bible School follow-up coordinator for northern Nigeria, and also an associate minister with the Church of Christ in Savannah, Tennessee, traveling back and forth to Nigeria two times a year. Enrollment has grown as high as 44 students in 1998. The trades that are taught include carpentry, photography, tailoring, typing, shoe cobbling, graphic arts, poultry raising, and electronic repair. It is hoped that students will be able to be self-supporting as they graduate and plant and develop new churches. Several Nigerians have earned degrees in Bible and now teach at the School of Biblical Studies in Jos.

Another family, Greg and Cathy Hamlin also moved to Jos to help with teaching and other activities. Greg, with expertise in television and video recording, began religious broadcasting with the Plateau State television station. He also trained students in lesson preparation and delivery for TV and video ministry (Wilson, 2001). Sadly, Cathy Hamlin died in December 1998 of heart problems while in Jos, Nigeria. She was buried in Scotland, her native land. She is survived by her husband Greg, and an adult son and daughter. Greg Hamlin continues to work at the School of Biblical Studies in Jos at the time of this writing. Cathy's work at the school, especially with the library in preparation for the accreditation team inspection, and her work among students, as well as her contributions in church and in her home, were valuable to the Lord's kingdom in Nigeria. May God be praised for another life lived for Him (Worley, 1998).

111

Works Cited

Adair, Truitt (personal communication, January 20, 2001).

Akpabli, George (personal communication, May 3, 2000).

Beckloff, John, et. al. (nd). *Missionary Efforts: A Re-Evaluation.* Unpublished manuscript, Harding University.

Beckloff, Kenneth, et. al. (1971). *Missionary Work of Churches of Christ in Sierra Leone West Africa: Evaluations and Recommendations 1969-1971.* Unpublished manuscript.

Beckloff, Kenneth (1977). *Fund-raising report.* Unpublished manuscript, Harding University.

Beckloff, Kenneth (1979). *Sierra Leone Report, January-June.* Unpublished manuscript, Harding University.

Beckloff, Kenneth. (personal communication, April 14, 2000).

Berryman, Mark and Broom, Wendell (2000). Status of Churches of Christ in Sub-Saharan Africa: May 2000. In Sam Shewmaker (Ed.). *Africans Claiming Africa Conference.* Unpublished manuscript, Harding University.

Chad Church Growth (2001, February). *Action.*

Chowning, Richard (personal communication, October 16, 2000).

Crowson, Murphy (personal communication, May 4, 2000).

Daniel, Carlyle (personal communication, September 20, 1964).

Dillingham, Paul M. (1966, October 14). In Freetown: Dr. Price Establishes Church. *The Christian Chronicle*, p. 8.

Dillingham, Paul M. (personal communication, November, 1967).

Drinnen, Tom and Anita (personal communication, May 8, 2000).

112

Glenn, Joe (personal communication, nd).

Greetings—from Sierra Leone (1965, December). Newsletter, Harding University.

Greetings—from Sierra Leone (1967, July). Newsletter, Harding University.

Greetings—from Sierra Leone (1968, October). Newsletter, Harding University.

Greetings—from Sierra Leone (1969, June). Newsletter, Harding University.

Greetings—from Sierra Leone (1970, October). Newsletter, Harding University.

Greetings—from Sierra Leone (1971, September). Newsletter, Harding University.

Greetings—from Sierra Leone (1973, June). Newsletter, Harding University.

Greetings—from Sierra Leone (1976, August). Newsletter, Harding University.

Greetings—from Sierra Leone (1977, April). Newsletter, Harding University.

Greetings—from Sierra Leone (1978, October). Newsletter, Harding University.

Greetings—from Sierra Leone (1979, March). Newsletter, Harding University.

Greetings—from Sierra Leone (1979, October). Newsletter, Harding University.

Greetings—from Sierra Leone (1980, March). Newsletter, Harding University.

Holland, Jeff (personal communication, April 26, 2000).

Lawrence, Neil (personal communication, April 28, 2000).

Little, Larry & Layton, Jim (1985). *Mission Survey Trip 1984* (unpublished manuscript, Harding University).

Missionaries located in Bo, Sierra Leone (1978). *Summary of Work in Bo*, (unpublished manuscript, Harding University).

Norwood, Mike (personal communication, April 20, 2000).

Parker, Anthony (personal communication, April 14, 2000).

Phillips, Gary (nd). *Dateline: Bo.* Newsletter, Harding University

Plans Made to Establish Church in Liberia, Africa. (May 5, 1969). *Gospel Light.*

Pray for Liberia (2001, February). *Action.*

Sierra Leone. (1968, August). *Action.*

Sierra Leone Missionaries and Overseers (1980). *Evangelism of Sierra Leone by 1990* (Unpublished report, Harding University).

Treadway, Jana ().(personal communication, January 21, 2001).

Trousdale, Jerry (1972). *The Churches of Christ in Sierra Leone: A Study of the Members and Congregations After the First Eight Years.* Unpublished manuscript, Abilene Christian University.

Wade, Jack (personal communication, March 20, 1975).

Waggoner, Robert L. (personal communication, August 19, 1975).

West, Earl Irvin (1974). *The Search for the Ancient Order: A History of the Restoration Movement, Vol. I. 1849-1863.* Nashville, TN: Gospel Advocate.

Wilson, Clarence (personal communication, January 20, 2001).

Worley, Steve (1998, December). *The Jos Journal 6* (4), 31.

BENIN MISSIONARIES

Name	Place	Years
Bailey, Greg & Melanie	Aplahoue'	1996-2000
Chowning Richard & Cyndi	Aplahoue'	1997-
Crowson Murphy & Christine	Azove'	1998-
Davis, Brian & Sandra	Abomey-Bohicon	1997-1998
		1995-1998
Gordon. Andrew & Pulcherie	Abomey-Bohicon	1993-2001
Hicks, David & Heather	Azove'	1998-
Parker, Anthony & Maureen	Abomey-Bohicon	1993-2001
		1996-2001
Treadway, Jana	Abomey-Bohicon	1995-2001
Vaughn, Randy & Kelly	Aplahoue'	1999-
Vogt, Tod & Nancy	Abomey-Bohicon	1993-1995
Wilson, Andy & Rhonda	Abomey-Bohicon	1995 -1998

SIERRA LEONE MISSIONARIES

Name	Place	Years
Adair, Truitt & Kay		1973
Beckloff, Dean	Freetown	1978-1979
Beckloff, John & Dottie	Freetown	1968-1970
Beckloff, Ken & Pat	Freetown &	
	Taiama	1969-1971
	Bo	1972-1974
	Freetown	1977- 1979
Beckloff, Randy	Freetown	1978-1979
Deason, Bobby & Jo Ann		1973
Dillingham, Paul & Cathy	Freetown	1966-1968
Frankie,Golden	Freetown	1971-1973
Green, Bill & Carolyn	Bo	1977-1981
Huffard, Elvis & Emily	Freetown	1964-1966
Howell, James & Lorene	Taiama	1970- 1974
Jones, Joe & Sally		1973
Lawrence, Neil & Annabelle	Taiama	1974-1976
Laws, C. Barton & Vivian	Freetown	1969-1971
Layton, Tim & Pat	Bo	1979-1980

Name	Place	Years
Menefee, P.T. & Evelyn	Freetown	1966-1969
Musgrave, Don & Dona		1973
Newberry, Catherine (Cathy)	Freetown	1966-1969
Norman, Alton & Sharyn	Freetown	1971-1973
	Bo	1975-1978
Norwood, M.F. & Inez	Freetown	1968-1971
		1967-1969
		1971-1973
Norwood, Mike & Sonnie	Freetown	1968-1971
		1975-1977
		1978-1979
Phillips, Gary & Margaret	Bo & Freetown	1971- 1973
		1975- 1977
Richardson, Earl & Helen	Freetown	1977-1979
	Bo	6 months
Smith, J. Garvin & Nancy	Freetown	1969-1971
Trousdale, Jerry & Gayle	Taiama	1971-1973
Wade, Jack & Patty	Freetown	1973-1975
Walters, Gid & Ruth	Taiama	1971-1973
Woodard, Jim & Ruth	Freetown	1974-1976
		1976-1980

TOGO MISSIONARIES

Name	Place	Years
Bunner, Frank & Jenna	Tabligbo	1994-
Cloer, Teresa	Tabligbo	2001
Harris, Scott & Lisa	Tabligbo	1994-1996
Holland, Jeff & Brenda	Tabligbo	1994-
Kennell, Mark & Nicole	Kara	2000
Koonce, Marty & Louise	Tabligbo	1997-
Miller, Matt & Andrea	Kara	2000-
Neal, Don & Jane	Kara	2000-
Reeves, David & Becky	Kara	2000-
Ries, Brian & Traci	Kara	2000-
Slack, Edwin & Patty	Tabligbo	1994-2001
Tacker, Jeff & Sherrie	Tabligbo	1994-1996
Wright, Sandi	Tabligbo	2000-

CHAPTER 6

A Survey of Work in East Africa

Stanley E. Granberg

*Stanley Granberg served as a missionary in Meru,
Kenya from 1983-1993. He holds the Ph.D from the Open
University: Oxford Centre for Mission Studies. He taught
as missionary-in-residence at Lubbock Christian University
and is currently associate professor of Bible and Missions at
Cascade College, Portland, Oregon.*

The eastern portion of Africa, which includes Tanzania, Kenya,
Uganda, Somalia and Ethiopia, is the Africa with which westerners
are probably most familiar. Travelogues and documentaries have
recorded life among the countless migrating plains animals traveling
the Serengeti plains of Tanzania and the Masai Mara of Kenya as well
as the forest gorillas hid in the Ruwenzori mountains in western
Uganda. Many of the names most associated with Africa–the Maasai,
Jomo Kenyatta, Julius Nyerere, Diane Fossey, Richard Leakey and
Lucy (apparently the oldest hominid-like creature yet discovered)—
have their provenance in East Africa as well. The greater story, however, is the work of God which has not only rooted in East Africa,
but has blossomed with strength and dignity.

This chapter surveys the mission works of the Churches of

Christ in Tanzania, Ethiopia, Kenya, and Uganda. The reader will notice three distinct patterns in the work within these countries. The first pattern of work began in Tanzania in the 1950s and continued with the early works in Ethiopia and Kenya. This pattern was characterized by loosely organized missionaries who shared geographic areas, institutional development projects and centralized, country-wide leadership training.

The second pattern developed exclusively in Ethiopia when a socialist government expelled or limited the work of foreign missionaries. This pattern was similar to the first pattern in that it used institutional development work and centralized leadership training. It differed in that the work was nurtured and led by national Christians. The work in Ethiopia has been tremendously fruitful. Much credit is due to both the missionaries who pioneered the Churches of Christ in Ethiopia and the national Christians who built on those early beginnings.

The third pattern developed in Kenya in the 1970s and is predominant today in Uganda and Tanzania as well. This third pattern is characterized by close-knit mission teams who work in limited geographic areas of the country, use tribal vernaculars or national trade languages, promote non-institutional development works and emphasize local-based leadership training.

These patterns are important indicators of the dominant, missiological thinking of their times and/or the historical and geographical forces with which God's people have had to contend. No pattern is right or wrong, better or worse, in and of itself. Each pattern exhibits strengths and weaknesses which are instructive as the church continues to spread in Africa. I encourage you, the reader, to reflect on these different patterns and the forces influencing them as you read God's story in East Africa. The following East African country surveys are arranged in chronological order of their beginnings to provide an historical perspective as well as sketching the history of the work of the Churches of Christ in each country and, finally, looking into the needs and challenges of the future.

TANZANIA

Map of Tanzania

Country Profile

Tanzania, situated on the Indian Ocean just south of the equator, is about the size of Texas and Oklahoma. The British took control of the colony from Germany after WWI naming it Tanganyika. Tanganyika became an independent nation in December 1961. The name Tanzania was adopted in 1964 when the Islamic, island state of Zanzibar united with Tanganyika to form the United Republic of Tanzania (Tanzania Country Profile, 2000).

The population of Tanzania is almost 30 million people,14 million of whom are below the age of 15, with a birthrate of 3.0% per annum. The majority of Tanzania's population is still rural. However, there are six cities with populations of over one million (see Table 1). The official language of Tanzania is Kiswahili, with English as the second official language. There are some 120 distinct tribes in Tanzania with the Sukuma being the largest single tribal group. The religious make-up of the country is almost evenly divided with 30% practicing traditional African religion, 35% Islamic and 35% Christian (Tanzania Country Profile, 2000).

City	Population
Dar-es-Salaam	1.6 million
Dodoma	1 million
Mwanza	2.3 million
Tanga	1.6 million
Mbeya	1.8 million
Arusha	1.6 million

Table 1. Tanzanian cities of over 1 million (Tanzania Country Profile, 2000).

Early Beginnings, 1952-1964

J. M. McCaleb, traveling to the US for a furlough from his work in Japan, was the first Church of Christ missionary to visit East Africa. McCaleb (1930) visited both Mombasa (Kenya) and Dar-es-Salaam (Tanzania). Since these were short port calls, McCaleb spent little time in these towns. But his record is important because it does not indicate any missionary activity of the Churches of Christ in East Africa in 1929.

It was Eldred Echols who had the dream to open East Africa to the Churches of Christ. Echols reminisces in his autobiography, "The work in South Africa was pleasant and rewarding, but I felt drawn to the vast plains, primeval forests, and towering mountain ranges of the eastern side of the continent" (Echols, 1989, p. 155). At that time permanent residency status in Tanganyika required land ownership. In September 1952 Echols and Guy Caskey investigated the opportunity to establish a Bible training school for evangelism in Tanganyika (Echols, 1989). They made an option to purchase two farms sixty miles east of Mbeya, Tanzania, near the small town of Chimala. Echols, Caskey and Martelle Petty, all South African missionaries, joined together to raise the funds for the Chimala farms. A fund-raising campaign by letter among American churches netted no response, so the three men each agreed to finance one-third of the purchase cost. As is the case more often than we sometimes realize, the sacrifice of missionary lives is seldom far removed from their commitment to the Lord's work. Martelle Petty raised his third of the purchase price by selling his automobile. While Petty was without a car, he was killed riding a borrowed motorcycle to visit his wife in the hospital who had just given birth to their daughter (Echols, 1989; Horne, 1986). But the work went on and in 1956 the men purchased "Chosi" farm, a 500 acre spread on the Usangu Plains and the 300 acre "Ailsa" farm atop the Rift Valley Escarpment. The Chosi farm was used to support the developing Bible training school through agricultural production. The new school, dubbed Tanganyika Bible School, was established at the smaller Ailsa farm with its clean water supply and healthy "highland" climate.

Tanganyika Bible School (TBS) consisted of a two year program of study for men training to preach with other classes for their wives. The students came from Tanganyika, Nyasaland (Malawi) and Northern Rhodesia. Teachers were Eldred Echols (1956-1964),

Guy Caskey (1957-1960), Roy Echols (1956-1959), Ahaziah Apollo (1956-1960, from Nyasaland) and Al Horne (1959-1964) (Echols, 1989; Horne, 1986). Classes at TBS were taught on a three month cycle with a break in between of 4 to 6 weeks. Weekends and school breaks had students gathering into preaching teams and spreading out into near and distant villages to practice their lessons from God. In 1964 TBS had 44 students, their wives, and families.

Details on the growth of the church in southern Tanzania during this time are sketchy, but students attending TBS included Efron Mtonga and Rastoni from Northern Rhodesia, Grandwell Ngulube from Nyasaland, and Sam John Nyrenda from Tanganyika. Efron and Grandwell later became tutors in the school. An example of the growth of the church is the "Safari for Souls" preaching tour from June through December 1963. Twelve college men from the US worked with the missionaries on this project. The crew made three safaris (trips) of twenty or more days each into the African bush, preaching from village to village. They brought a "new thing" with them in the form of a slide projector and generator, with which they showed biblical filmstrips. Over 500 people were baptized in this preaching campaign. Through efforts like this and the regular preaching excursions of the TBS students, churches were established in numerous villages in southern Tanganyika and Northern Rhodesia (Horne, 1986).

Chimala Mission Hospital

A persistent demand African governments make on church missions is the demand for practical, physical help for their people in return for admitting missionaries into their countries. In 1962 Echols contacted Andrew and Claudene Connally, asking them to consider answering the Tanganyikan government's request for the church to begin some kind of social development, or the missionaries would be asked to leave. Glenn Boyd tells the story of Chimala Mission Hospital in chapter 9. You may also read about the Chimala Hospital in Connally (1995) or at the Chimala Mission website.

As well as building the hospital, the Connally's were preaching and teaching. A small congregation was started on the mission compound almost immediately upon their arrival. Regular teaching classes were held on the compound and in surrounding villages. Eventually eight congregations were begun with over 450 people baptized. The Connallys returned to the States in 1963 and the mission work was continued by Wayne and Florene Smalling.

The Connallys returned to Tanzania in 1971 to work in the twin towns of Arusha and Moshi in the north central portion of the country. The Connallys and the Joel Hestand family (1972-1975), followed by Ron Cotton (1975-1976), planted eight congregations around Moshi with about 300 members. Most encouraging was that three African evangelists were major contributors in this work: Mordicken Mkandawire (from Nyasaland), Edwin Tusekelege and Wiseman Mbukwa (Connally, 1995, p. 167, 245). At the same time the Dennises, who had served in Chimala, were working with the Philips family in Dar-es-Salaam where they had moved TBS. There were three congregations in Dar in 1971. Chimala mission continues to provide Bible teaching, evangelism and medical care under the direction of Bob Stapleton. There are approximately 80 congregations with 1,600 Christians in southwestern Tanzania (Stapleton, 2000). Chimala, Dar, Arusha and Moshi remained the outposts of the church in Tanzania until a new wave of missionaries began arriving in the 1990s.

NEW PIONEERS, 1991-2000

A new period of Tanzanian missions began in 1991 as new mission teams began their works.

Mwanza

The Newtons (1993-1999) and Bentleys (1993-1998) moved into the city of Mwanza in northwest Tanzania in 1991 to work among the 5 million strong Sukuma people. These families are part of the third pattern of East African mission work. As has been common among the missionaries working in East Africa this team was known as the Mwanza team. The Mwanza families used Kisukuma, the tribal heart language, for preaching and teaching. The express focus of their work was to plant new churches and to develop these new bodies of believers into a stable, brotherhood of churches.

The Mwanza team found the religiously traditional Sukuma people to be highly receptive to the message of the gospel. In eight years 95 churches were planted with approximately 5,500 baptized members (Bentley, 2000). Using the nomenclature of Donald McGavran, father of the church growth movement, this type of growth qualifies as a people movement (McGavran and Wagner, 1980). A follow-up team moved into the Sukuma area in 1999-2000, including the Thomases, Guilds and Chris Boyce. These families are working to extend the network of churches established by the first Mwanza team. Updated reports on this work are available through the team website.

Mbulu

The Palmers (1990-1994) opened another area when they planted several churches in Mbulu in the north central portion of Tanzania. The Mbulu work was continued by a team of three Kenyan graduates of the Nairobi Great Commission School

(NGCS): David Busine, Jacob Randiek, and Charles Owino (1995-1997). This was the first African mission team, trained at the NGCS, to cross a national border. It was also a *multicultural African team*—David Busine is Abaluyia, Jacob Randiek is Kalenjin and Charles Owino is Luo—which had to surmount significant cultural differences among themselves as well as national differences (Bolden, 2000). Today Elibariki Tluway, an Iraqw Christian, continues to work among the three congregations and 60 Christians in Mbulu (Palmer, 2000).

Moshi and Arusha

Between the mid 1970s and 1990s, the churches which had been planted around the towns of Moshi and Arusha had all but died out. Ken Bolden, a Kenyan missionary, began preaching as a non-residential missionary (a missionary who works in the target area but lives in another area) in Moshi in 1998. His goal was to organize a "zebra" team of missionaries for Moshi, a team with both US and African missionaries working together (Bolden, 2000). Bolden focused on an urban church plant in Moshi. He and two NGCS students, Charles Ngoje and Mark Sure of Kenya, planted the Moshi Church of Christ in March 1999. In 2000 the Hammitts arrived as full-time team members. By God's grace this exciting work may mark the beginning of a new, fourth pattern of missionary work in East Africa as American and African missionaries join together in zebra teams to take the gospel to the African continent. Such partnerships recognize the need for Africans to be cross-cultural missionaries on their own continent (see chapter 2). These partnerships also recognize the talent and abilities of African Christians to do far more than any of us from the West could ever do, or would ever dream possible. One of the team's goals for 2020 is for the Moshi church to prepare and send a team of Tanzanian missionaries to China (Bolden, 2000).

A second zebra team is working in Arusha. Bolden found two congregations still active in 1984, one in Arusha of about twenty members and another of similar size at Usa River. Boaz Auma moved to Arusha from Chimala in 1996 to strengthen these churches. Presently Auma and Francis Wechesa work with non-residential missionaries Cy Stafford and Howell Ferguson. Today the churches in Arusha and Usa River number around 40, with two more similar sized congregations in Moshi.

ETHIOPIA

Map of Ethiopia

(oval indicates greatest concentration of Churches of Christ).

Country Profile

Ethiopia has a history which reaches back more than 2,000 years, to a union between King Solomon of Israel and the Queen of Sheba. A coup in 1972 overthrew emperor Haile Selassie and a socialist government espousing Marxist-Leninist principles took over control of the government. The socialist regime was overthrown in 1991 and the Federal Democratic Republic of Ethiopia was formed.

The 1994 census estimated the population of Ethiopia at 54 million with an annual growth rate of 3%. There are over 80 ethnic groups in the country speaking about as many languages. Religiously 80% of the population are either Christian or Muslim, with Christians being slightly more numerous; the remaining 20% practice traditional African religions. Ethiopia's capital city, Addis Ababa, has a population of approximately 2.3 million.

The Imperial Period, 1960-1974

The Ethiopian work has had a two-prong focus almost since its inception: development efforts based around a school for the deaf and evangelism/church planting. The first missionaries of the Churches of Christ in Ethiopia were the Thompson (1960-1966) and Gowen (1960-1962) families (see Appendix 1 for a list of Ethiopian missionaries). These families moved into Addis Ababa and purchased church property in the area of the city called Makanisa. Thompson and Gowen spent the first two years applying for registration for the church with the Ethiopian government and making initial evangelistic contacts. It was soon apparent that the only way to gain registration was to begin some sort of humanitarian project. At that time there were no schools, or attention, given to deaf children in Ethiopia. Bob Gowen was a deaf instructor and a deaf school seemed to be a good fit for the situation. Construction on houses and school buildings began in 1961. In September 1962 the *Makanisa School for the Deaf* officially opened with three pupils. The leadership of the school was shared by American missionaries and Demere Cherenet (Granberg, 1993).

The evangelism/church planting side of the work was directed primarily toward the rural areas of the country surrounding Addis. Thompson worked mostly in evangelism during his years in Ethiopia. In 1963 the nascent fellowship included five or six Ethiopian Christians, including Demere Cherenet, and three American missionary families. In 1965 God brought another member into this group, a young man named Behailu Abebe, who would eventually direct the mission. Artie Reed (1966-1969) followed Thompson as the director of evangelism. In 1968 John Ed Clark (1968-1970) took over the evangelistic work along with Behailu. Clark accomplished two significant events during his period of residency. The first was the development of a four month training program for church leaders in the Makanisa mission compound. This program brought men into the mission compound in groups of 20 to 30 for four months of intense Bible training. The first class had fourteen students who studied ten hours a day for the four months. Graduates of the school were powerful evangelists in the Ethiopian countryside. Between 1968 and 1974 graduates began almost 400 congregations. Clark brought Behailu into the core of the work as assistant director of the mission. Clark's second major accomplishment was opening a second school for the deaf in Mazoria in 1969. The Mazoria school would play a critical role for the church in the coming dark years.

Revolution and Famine, 1974-1991

The communist government commenced their rule with a period of bloodshed and government terrorism. Travel was restricted. Churches were often closed; sometimes their doors were literally nailed shut. Many Christians were called upon to make life and death decisions about their faith. But many faithful men and women also learned they could live as Christians in a communist country. It was not easy, nor without sacrifice. For example, sixteen year old Teurowerk Lema was arrested on the way to a church meeting. She was beaten and jailed for two months, where she taught two other girls about Christ.

With the travel restrictions many of the Churches of Christ were cut off from the fellowship which fed and sustained them. However, the school at Mazoria provided an acceptable reason to obtain travel permits. Behailu, Demere (now principal of the Deaf School) and other Ethiopian Christians would travel to Mazoria for school business, but also used those opportunities to meet with church leaders to prepare them for life under communist rule. Church leaders slipped into the compound at night in groups of six to ten for encouragement, planning, and instruction. In this way a communication system was established which held over 400 churches together despite severe persecution.

The Ethiopian famine of 1984 was one of the worst in modern history, with lack of rainfall exacerbated by government-enforced socialist farming practices. Some of the worst hit areas were those where the Churches of Christ were most numerous. Members of the Makanisa Church of Christ literally saw many of their brothers and sisters starving to death on government television broadcasts. The members committed themselves to give a month's salary to purchase food. It was a small gift, but based on a great faith. After much prayer and fasting the church decided to send Behailu to the States to raise relief funds from US churches. Their goal was $100,000. The Stockton Central Church of Christ and the White's Ferry Road Church of Christ partnered in a nation-wide effort which eventually raised over $8 million for Ethiopian famine relief.

The Ethiopian church, under Behailu's direction as director of the mission, administered this and other aid donated by USAID, Christian Relief Development Agency, World Vision, Band Aid and other organizations. Local churches of the Churches of Christ were the initial distribution points. Eventually major feeding and medical care sites were opened in Kambata, Jido and Fursi. When the relief program closed in 1976 over 130,000 people had been fed and $15 million of relief aid had been distributed.

Beyond the Revolution, 1991-2000

The fall of the socialist government in 1991 brought more freedoms with it, but also more challenges. The poverty of many areas of Ethiopia has kept the church busy with development works such as well-drilling and alternative construction methods. The Bible training school at the Makanisa compound was reinstituted as well as several extension programs in the countryside. The two deaf schools continue to operate under Demere's leadership. Leadership in the mission is provided by a committee of national Christians who organize and coordinate the various mission programs in partnership with the Central Church of Christ in Stockton, California and other partnering congregations.

The Ethiopian work is somewhat unique among works in Africa because of its history and its patterns of work. Since 1974, when missionaries were forced out by the government, the church in Ethiopia has been led by national Christians. This historical situation produced a well-developed partnership between Ethiopian churches and US churches. This work, with 670 congregations and a membership of about 50,000, may well provide the best answers available to the partnership questions raised in chapter 13.

KENYA

Map of Kenya

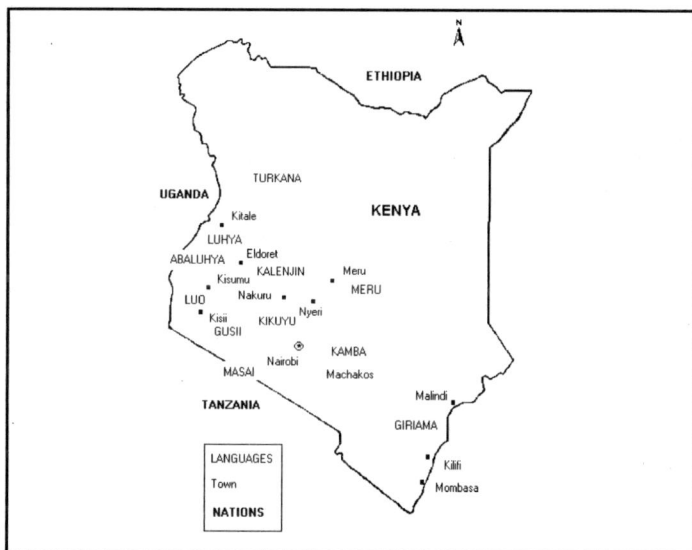

If there is a repeatable model for evangelizing an African country, Kenya may be as close to that model as one might find. In just forty years Kenya has moved from a beginning to a mature mission work. This does not at all mean there is no more need for mission work or partnership arrangements to strengthen and support national, Kenyan churches, but the time for ground-breaking work by foreign missionaries is essentially complete.

Country Profile

Kenya was a British colony from 1895 to 1963. The country is about the size of Texas with over 70 ethnic groups and a population of almost 29 million (Kenya), with about half of the population under 15 years of age. The population growth rate has slowed from

3.5% to 1.9 per annum, but population pressures are still a major concern. The official languages are English and Kiswahili.

Opening Doors and Establishing a Pattern, 1965-1979

The mission work of the Churches of Christ in Kenya began in 1965 when the White Station Church of Christ, Memphis, Tennessee sent the Tate (1965-1976) and Ogle (1965-1969, 1970-1971, 1989-present) families to Nairobi, Kenya's capital city (Kenya Mission Team, 1980). These families established a beachhead for the church in Kenya by gaining official registration for the church and planting three congregations in the Nairobi area. Since Kenya has had such a large number of missionaries, the reader is encouraged to use appendix 1 to identify the individual families involved in any work. The following survey focuses on the characteristics of the various works.

Nairobi

The work in Nairobi has had a wide variety of works reflecting the pluralism of the urban environment. The early work focused on planting the Ofafa Jericho and Makokgeni churches, both in working class areas of the city. The missionaries used printing, tent-meetings, street preaching and Bible correspondence courses as primary methods for evangelizing (Kenya Mission Team, 1980). In the 1980s and 1990s this work diversified with efforts into specific ethnic groups, middle-class works at Rainbow and Koma Rock, poverty work in the Mathare Valley slum, and ministry to "street" children. The largest ministry is the Kenya Christian Industrial Training Institute (KCITI) polytechnic school, a registered technical college with 2,050 students, a staff of 80 and a Bible training program. Nairobi-based missionaries also started churches in these other towns: Naivasha, Nakuru, Nyeri, Muranga, Meru and Machakos.

Another important work is the Nairobi Great Commission School, which provides advanced academic training for African church leaders (see chapter 10).

		1979	1986	2000
Nairobi				
	Churches	8	11	23
	Christians	83	232	2,000
Machakos				
	Churches	2	na	12
	Christians	na	na	600
Naivasha				
	Churches	2	na	4
	Christians	60	na	130
Muranga				
	Churches	2	na	2
	Christians	40	na	35

Table 2. Churches and Christians in Nairobi.

Rural mission teams with a focus on specific ethnic groups began to arrive in the 1970s. These teams worked among the Abaluyia people around Kisumu, the Luo in South Nyanza district, and the Kipsigis people around the town of Sotik.

Kisumu

The first rural team settled first in Kakamega and later moved to Kisumu. These missionaries preached and wrote in Kiswahili, the lingua franca of East Africa, and a widely used language among the different Abaluhya peoples. This work has been characterized primarily by village teaching, a printing ministry and Back to the Bible seminars for World Bible School correspondence students. There is also a strong urban church and a training center now associated with the Nairobi Great Commission School.

Kisumu	1979	1986	2000
Churches	39	94	200+
Christians	1,019	1,852	≈ 4000

Table 3. Churches and Christians in Kisumu

Kisii

Missionaries had moved into Kisii town in 1972, working with the Luo people of South Nyanza. The first missionaries who worked with the Gusii began their work in 1981. The Kisii missionaries worked primarily in English, using national Christians as translators. The work has thus had a strong, central core of Kisii leaders.

Kisii	1979	1986	2000
Churches	0	7	16
Christians	0	na	≈ 450

Table 4. Churches and Christians in Kisii

Sotik

The Sotik work began in 1972 when two families who had been unable to move to Uganda went to Sotik instead. These were the first missionaries in Kenya to use a tribal vernacular: Kalenjin. These missionaries influenced many later teams who would follow in using the tribal vernacular, a strong village-based, church planting

134

approach and employing church growth studies and strategies. A second team of missionaries followed up this first team in 1989, continuing the maturation of the Kipsigis churches and opening up new areas for evangelism. The arrival of a completely new mission team raised to the fore issues dealing with missionary/national partnerships, disengagement procedures and leadership/decision-making issues.

Kipsigis	1979	1986	2000
Churches	19	94	200+
Christians	582	3465	≈ 7500

Table 5. Churches and Christians in Kipsigis

Expanding Efforts, 1980-1991

A definite pattern to the mission work of the Churches of Christ in Kenya solidified in 1979 when missionaries to the area wrote *Church Planting, Watering, and Increasing in Kenya.* In the forward Bill Humble observed that the Kenya missionaries were never a mission team in the sense that they worked under a single church or mission plan (Kenya Mission Team, 1980, p. 2). However, the Kenyan missionaries, for the most part, have coordinated their individual works in a spirit of camaraderie and mutual support based on a unity of purpose which has overcome most individual differences and preferences, even through issues which created strong tensions.

The pattern developed in Kenya was characterized by close-knit mission teams working in specific, geographic areas of the country (usually a single ethnic group), the use of tribal vernaculars or Kiswahili (the national trade language), non-institutional development and local-based leadership training. This pattern was guided by the following five principles:

1. A body orientation – the goal of evangelism was not just baptisms, but the establishment of local churches (pp. 5-6).

2. A harvest orientation – in order to reach full maturity, churches must be involved in going and preaching themselves (p. 6).

3. Identification – the missionaries go to the people to learn their languages and ways of life so as to present the gospel message in ways which make sense to people in their life state (p. 7).

4. Autonomous churches – the goal was to produce churches which were self-governing, self-propagating, self-supporting and self-theologizing (Kenyan Mission Team, p. 8; Van Rheenen, 1983, p. 37).

5. Interdependency – the mutual support and encouragement of the church across multiple levels of structure.

This principle of interdependency developed slowly as the missionaries looked to strengthen the internal structure of the developing church. Interdependency was promoted at different levels. At the most basic level were "church clusters," several congregations geographically close enough to combine resources for teaching, evangelism, building, etc. The next level included area or district meetings and programs. These were nonformal events such as evangelists' seminars, women's meetings and Bible training by extension. At the national level, a Kenyan annual national meeting was instituted in 1989 in the form of a theme lectureship taught by national leaders. The annual meeting was intended to open communication between the widespread mission works across the country and to develop personal relationship networks among the Christians of different tribal groups. This concept was expanded to the entire continent in 1992 with the "Africans Claiming Africa" conference (see chapter 8). Finally, at its broadest level, the concept of interdependency is seeking ways to build partnership relationships between national, African churches and US missions-sponsoring churches which do not require on-field, missionary-based oversight (see chapter 13).

Kitale

Kitale, in northwest Kenya, is populated by people from the Luhya, Kalenjin, Turkana, Masai, Kikuyu, Teso and Luo tribes. The first two missionary families arrived in Kitale in 1981 and began learning Kiswahili, a logical language choice in this mixed tribal area. The Kitale work focused on church-planting and leadership training. Leadership courses were held in Kitale town for two and half weeks, six days a week. In 1987 the team decentralized the courses into cluster groups of churches. Another major development was the Mkristo ("the Christian") newspaper which was used to extend biblical instruction and to provide a medium for sharing news among churches. This paper soon was distributed throughout Kenya, primarily via missionaries in their individual works. In 1991, a 20-bed orphanage was opened under the oversight of an African/missionary board of directors and with national Christians as houseparents.

Kitale	1979	1986	2000
Churches	0	34	120
Christians	0	1,106	1800

Table 6. Churches and Christians in Kitale.

Eldoret

Four families arrived in the North Kalenjin town of Eldoret in 1982 and worked in the Kalenjin language. The first Christians in the north Kalenjin area were Jackson Rono and Zephania Kittony, both World Bible School students who were trying to start churches in their homes (Kenya Missionary Workshop, 1987, p. 41). A thriving group of churches soon blossomed among the Kalenjin peoples. The team emphasized relationship with God, evangelism and developing strong churches. Their primary teaching forums were local meetings for women, evangelists and large groups. An urban church was planted in Eldoret town 1990. The Eldoret team also has been inventive in developing small-scale development projects, such as improved cooking stoves, alternative building techniques, agricultural projects, and micro-business projects.

Eldoret	1979	1986	2000
Churches	0	34	110
Christians	0	576	2,500

Table 7. Churches and Christians in Eldoret

Meru

A team of five families entered Meru in central Kenya from December 1982 to February 1984. This team learned the Kimeru language and followed the dominant missions pattern of this time period, focusing on evangelism and church-planting. In 1985 the team began developing Leadership Training by Extension (LTE) courses using programmed instruction booklets and 4-6 week meetings among church clusters (Meru Mission Team, 1987). In 1989 a third major emphasis developed as the team began to implement development projects such as fiber-cement roofing tiles, soil building blocks, and various gardening and animal husbandry projects. The Kambakia Training Center was built in 1993-1994 to provide a central meeting point for advanced training of church leaders and to house large meetings for men, women and teens among the Meru churches. Kambakia was integrated into the NGCS extension program in 1995.

Meru	1979	1986	2000
Churches	0	10	40
Christians	0	266	2000

Table 8. Churches and Christians in Meru

Malindi and Kilifi

A two family Malindi team arrived in 1985 to work among the strongly traditional Giriama people on the coast of Kenya north of Mombasa. The Giriama people were highly unreached and very poor, even by Kenyan standards. The Malindi team constructed a training center in Malindi in 1991 which they used for week long training courses for men, women, and youth. This center is now a working part of the NGCS extension program. The newest mission team in Kenya arrived in 1998, expanding the work among the Giriama into the Kilifi and Kwale districts. This team is partnering with Manna International in well-drilling projects to provide clean, safe drinking water in remote Giriama villages. The team is also tapping into the strength of the Giriama women who will be great contributors to the church among the Giriama people.

Malindi, Kilifi and Kwale	1979	1986	2000
Churches	0	1	41
Christians	0	38	1500

Table 9. Churches and Christians in Malindi, Kilifi and Kwale districts.

Mombasa

The work in Mombasa was seeded by World Bible School students and Christians from other parts of the country who moved to Mombasa for work. Two families from Nairobi moved to Mombasa in 1989 and began ministering in this, the second largest city of Kenya.

Mombasa	1979	1986	2000
Churches	0	0	6
Christians	0	0	200

Table 10. Churches and Christians in Mombasa

Establishing Partnerships, 1992-2000

At one time in the 1980s there were more missionaries of the Churches of Christ in Kenya than in any country in the world. But in the 1990s many of these missionaries and mission teams began to phase out their work and return to the States or begin new works in other countries in Africa. Monte Cox in chapter 13 discusses a number of issues involved in the Kenyan transition. Just a few comments are made here.

First, the strength of the Kenyan work, which has allowed missionaries to phase out, is the existence of a strong communication and relationship network across the entire country. The Mkristo paper, the annual meetings, the NGCS were all tools which have helped Christians to develop important relationships with one another.

Second, the focus of missionaries typically has changed from a general, all-purpose mission effort to specifically-focused mission efforts such as the street kids ministry in Nairobi, the Nairobi Great Commission School (NGCS), the Eastleigh Polytechnic school and Good News Productions (GNPI). GNPI produces multimedia presentations for evangelism and teaching purposes. Their most successful project was the *Tough Choices* video, promoting sexual abstinence outside of marriage, which has been aired on the national television stations in both Kenya and Uganda. The sequel, *Promise of Love,* will be broadcast on primetime Kenyan television December 2000.

Finally, there is an important transition occurring as the Kenyan church moves into a new stage of development as a sending church. A number of Kenyan churches are beginning to send out their own missionaries. Some go to new areas within their own tribal boundaries, some go to neighboring tribal peoples, and others are being sent to surrounding countries in East Africa.

UGANDA

Map of Uganda

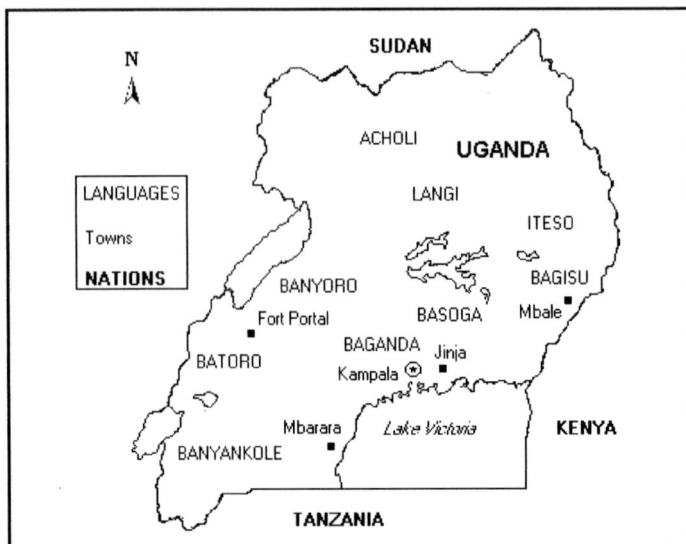

Country Profile

Uganda is the smallest of the East African countries with a land mass slightly larger than the state of Pennsylvania. Under British administration Uganda was nicknamed by Winston Churchill as "the Pearl of Africa." The country gained its independence from Britain October 9, 1962. Uganda's most infamous president, General Idi Amin Dada, terrorized Ugandans from 1971 to 1979. Uganda has since achieved a remarkable level of stability and economic growth under its current president, Yoweri Museveni.

The population of Uganda in 1990 was 16.9 million people, of whom nearly one-half are below fifteen, with an annual growth rate of more than 3.2 percent. The AIDS epidemic hit Uganda first, so its growth rate moderated in the 1990s as many of its child-bearing

142

adults succumbed to the HIV virus. Uganda's people are still largely rural farmers, with about ten percent living in urban centers, of which the capital, Kampala, is the largest. Uganda's people are divided into roughly forty tribal groups. The country's official language is English, but Luganda and Kiswahili are spoken as trade languages. Approximately 66% of Ugandans claim Christianity as their religion, 15% are adherents of Islam, and the remainder practice either traditional African religion or claim no religious affiliation (Uganda Country Study, 1990).

Initial Plantings, 1969-1972

The first definitive efforts of the Churches of Christ in Uganda are described by Joe Watson in *Three African Drums* (1989). Leonard Gray and Watson, from South Africa, and Jack Minter from the US arrived in Kampala on March 1, 1971. The visitors met for worship on March 7 with a small group of Christians: Belika Andika (from Kenya) Abulitsa, Sospater Akwenyu, Daniel Ssemakade, Johnson Arago, Jim James (a US visitor) and Tom Reynolds, a USAID agricultural worker living in Kampala (Watson, 1989, p. 108). This young church had received periodic encouragement since 1969 from Kenyan missionaries Van Tate, Hilton Merritt and Gaston Tarbet. The positive response from these Christians and a good look at Kampala convinced Watson that Uganda was ripe for full-time mission work.

The Watson family arrived in July 1971. They met with the Church of Christ in Kampala at the YMCA at No. 3 George Street. Their work was primarily following up contacts from English Bible correspondence courses. Watson also began to explore other parts of Uganda, making preaching trips to Fort Portal, Kasese, Mbale, Masaka, and Jinja as well as a survey trip to Kigali, Rwanda. A new church began in Mbale when Nathaniel Odokotum, his family and others became Christians. A church was planted in the Kasese/Fort Portal area with the conversion of Yona Muhindo (Watson, 1989, pp. 183-185). These and the other scattered churches were officially registered with the Ugandan government under the newly acquired registration of the Uganda Church of Christ. Like Joshua (Josh. 1:3), many of the places Watson went now have vibrant works as new teams of missionaries followed in his footsteps.

During 1972 other American families began to arrive in Uganda preparing for full-time mission work. The Van Rheenens and Moores arrived in February 1972, joined later by the Allisons and the Barrs. Meanwhile, the political climate soured under the increasingly dictatorial Idi Amin. Peace in Uganda began to unravel and finally collapsed in 1972 as Amin expelled most foreign personnel and deregistered all but a handful of church organizations. The Watsons left Uganda for South Africa; the Reynolds family moved back to the US; and the Moores, Van Rheenens, Allisons and Barrs went to Kenya. The registration of the Churches of Christ in Uganda was left in the care of Kampala Christian Sospater Akwenyu and the first chapter of our work in Uganda came to an end.

Interlude, 1972-1992

For the next decade Uganda underwent horrific suffering at the hands of the increasingly irrational Idi Amin. Meanwhile, the Ugandan Christians in the scattered Churches of Christ persisted in their faith. In 1983 a team of missionaries surveyed the western region of Uganda, around the towns of Fort Portal and Kasese, for a possible mission site. The continuing instability of the country made that move inadvisable. This team became the Meru, Kenya team. In 1984 another team from Lubbock, Texas made definite plans to move into Uganda. The week of their scheduled arrival, Uganda again erupted into civil war. The Uganda bound team shifted their landing point to Kenya and began the Giriama work. Uganda's time had not yet come.

New Beginnings, 1993-2000

Two decades of turmoil and healing—supported with prayer—opened the doors again for missionaries to enter Uganda. Kenyan missionaries had continued to maintain contact with Ugandan Christians. In 1985 and 1986 Shawn Tyler, Gailyn Van Rheenen, and Larry Stephens investigated the status of the Church of Christ registration in Uganda. Because of difficulties with the Ugandan Christians who were in charge of the original registration, it was decided that a new registration should be sought. Shawn Tyler applied for a new registration, New Testament Churches of Christ, which was accepted by the Ugandan government in November 1988. The following year the Hatch and Babcock families sought to enter Uganda under the original Uganda Church of Christ registration but were denied work visas. All the missionaries and churches since then have worked under the New Testament Churches of Christ registration. Up-to-date information on the Uganda work is available through the Uganda missions webpage.

Kampala

With the work in Kenya coming to maturity in the 1990s the focus of new missionaries for East Africa shifted to Uganda. The Carrs and Jenkins arrived in Kampala in 1993. The Jenkins family continues this work of establishing, "a church in Kampala, Uganda with its own elders and property who will plant other churches through dynamic worship, creative community service, and small groups" (Uganda Missions, Kampala, 2000). The Kampala church reaches into the urban community through the Better Living Resource Center which serves as the church meeting place, a weekday café, book and video library and community center. They also do campus work at Makerere University.

Jinja

In 1994 a team entered Jinja to work among the Busoga people (see appendix 1). This team's vision is "for the Churches of Christ to be a well-established, culturally-relevant, Christ-like presence in Busoga" (Jinja Team, 2000). The Busoga team typifies the third pattern of East African mission work as team members minister in the Busoga language, focus their efforts on the Busoga people, engage in small-scale development work and more local based leadership training. At present the churches number about 37 with over 600 Christians. The team's goal is to have at least two Churches of Christ in each of the 68 Busoga sub-counties by 2010. Their ministries include the Source of Life Resource Center located in Jinja, peace projects designed to promote economic progress among Busoga people, the Busoga Bible School in Jinja (affiliated with the NGCS), and mobile health care work.

Mbale

Two more works were opened up in 1995. The Mbale team is unique in that different team members focus on different tribal peoples or parts of the work according to their interests and ministry gifts. The Tylers (1995-present) and Shelburnes (1996-present) focus on church maturation and leadership training associated with the NGCS certificate course. The Vicks (1997-present) focus on the Sebei people, whose language is very similar to the Kalenjin people with whom the Vicks had worked in Kenya. The Sheros (1998-present) work with the Bagisu and the Palmers (1999-present) focus on the Teso people (Mbale Team, 2000). Sandi Piek (1996-present) designs and teaches courses to strengthen the faith among the women members. The Mbale (town) Church of Christ began in 1999 and already sets aside 20% of its contribution to support its own missionaries in another part of Uganda. The team has also made successful use of short-term workers in specific areas such as women's and primary health care courses.

Fort Portal

The Cashes (1995- present) moved into Fort Portal in 1995. This work was dominated early on by the physical needs of a guerrilla war as armed raiders hide in the Ruwenzori Mountains and raid farms and villages. Food, medical and public relief efforts in the name of Jesus have elicited the gratitude of even the President of Uganda. Jeff Cash has also been successful with a "Servants in training" program, preaching through the film media, drawing crowds of thousands to see the *Jesus* film and to be offered further teaching. Ellen Little, a pediatrician from Abilene, TX joined the Cashes in 2001 to extend medical services in the area (Cash, 2000). There are now 17 churches with approximately 250 Christians in the Fort Portal area.

Mbarara

The newest Uganda team settled in southwest Uganda in the town of Mbarara. This three-family team began their work among the 2 million strong Banyankore people in the Ankole region in 1997. The team's purpose statement reads,

> We believe that God will work through our team to plant clusters of churches among the Ankole of Uganda, whom we assess to be a highly receptive people group. Our goal is to establish bodies of new creations in Christ who develop spiritual maturity and resources to evangelize to the fringes of their group and beyond (Ankole Team, 2000).

147

These missionaries have started six congregations with 180 members through 2000.

Challenges for the Future

East Africa presents a series of challenges for the future. The following are the top four challenges.

Challenge #1: Develop Strong Relationship Networks

The first challenge for the future is to bridge this isolation through relationship networks so that these churches can grow towards greater maturity. East Africa is a large area with poor rail, road, and communication infrastructures. It is physically difficult to travel long distances. Christians have little ability to finance travel or even to use the limited communication facilities of mail or telephone. These factors limit the interactions between churches and isolate churches or groups of churches from churches in other parts of their own countries as well as from the church in neighboring countries. There is an important maturing influence and activities generation which occur when Christians from different areas come together and share with one another. The geographic isolation of many East African churches tends to limit their dynamism, resulting in more passive, inward looking churches. Activities such as national meetings and the ACA conferences provide models for meeting this challenge.

Challenge #2: Increase Vision

Part of the relationship network challenge is the need to increase the vision of the East African churches. The isolation of many churches means they have a very limited vision of the world around them and its need for the gospel. The "Africans Claiming Africa" conferences, the Kenyan national meetings, the Nairobi

Great Commission School extension program and the Mkristo paper have all contributed to expanding the vision of these churches for the world and their place in it as ambassadors for Christ.

Challenge #3: Reaching the Smaller Populations

The majority of the 300 ethnic groups in East Africa have small populations. There are too many of these small groups to send missionaries, even African missionaries, to each one. The third challenge is how to plant viable churches in this multitude of ethnic groups. One option with great potential is to develop multiple, strong centers of the church in East Africa which can cast a joining network between themselves and thus encompass many of the smaller ethnic groups. In a sense this option employs Broom's "Meet in the Middle" strategy (Chapter 17) on a country level. There are, or soon will be, such centers in Kenya, Ethiopia and Uganda. More centers of church activity are needed in Tanzania. All the countries need to emphasize "Meet in the Middle" efforts both within country and cross border.

Challenge #4: The Concept of Partnership

Through the decade of the 1980s the work in East Africa was in a foundational stage as missionaries worked to build a critical mass of Christians and churches who had both the maturity and the resources to sustain themselves in a vibrant brotherhood. In those earlier years American missionaries went into new places alone or with other Americans to open new territory to the Gospel. But as Bolden states, "Today, American missionaries are without excuse in going into new countries without taking their 'Timothy' and 'Titus' with them. Biblical example demands it" (Bolden, 2000).

This year marks the first time there are more congregations of the Churches of Christ in Africa than in the US (see chapter 2).

Soon, perhaps by 2010, there will be more members of the Churches of Christ in Africa than the US. The American church must recondition its self identity as the primary senders and enter into partnerships with Africans in multitudes of zebra mission teams. American churches have vast financial, educational, medical and developmental resources to share. African churches have the cultural expertise of Africans, a sense for the felt needs of the lost people of Africa and an unyielding faith in the efficacy of God's Holy Spirit (Shewmaker, 2000). Ethiopia provides an excellent model of how partnership arrangements between American and African churches can produce a strong, effective working union.

Priority Areas for Missionaries

Tanzania tops the priority list for missionaries in East Africa. Two people groups, the Ha and the Nyamwezi, stand out. The Ha live in the far west central border area of Tanzania on lake Tanganyika. The Ha number 800,000 (Ha, 2000) and are considered a highly receptive people group. The Nyamwezi are cousins to the Sukuma and number almost 1 million people (Nyamwezi, 2000). Missionaries to the Nyamwezi could work on a bridging strategy with the Sukuma work. Another set of priorities for urban missions are the major cities and towns of Tanzania: Tanga, Morogoro, Iringa (one congregation at present), Dodoma, and Tabora.

WORKS CITED

Ankole Team (2000). http://www.praisegod.org/ankole/team-purpose.html.

Bentley, Bob (2000). E-mail correspondence, December 5.

Berryman, Mark & Broom, Wendell (2000). Church Growth in Africa.http://www.bible.acu.edu/missions/page.asp?ID=323.

Bolden, Ken (2000). E-mail correspondence, December 9.

Cash, Jeff (2000). E-mail correspondence, November 14.

Chimala Mission (2000). http://www.dallasnw.quik.com/chimala/chimala.htm.

Echols, Eldred (1989). *Wings of the Morning: The Saga of an African Pilgrim.* Fort Worth, TX: Wings Press.

Ethiopia (2000). http://lcweb2.loc.gov/frd/cs/ettoc.html.

Granberg, Stanley E. (1993). *Behailu Abebe: Called to Served, Leadership Emergence in Ethiopia, 1943-1993.* Unpublished manuscript, Cascade College, Portland, Oregon.

Ha (2000).http://www.sil.org/ethnologue/countries/Tanz.html.

Horne, Donna (1986). *Meanwhile, Back in the Jungle . . . Tanganyika Tales.* Winona, MS: J. C. Choate.

Jenkins, Dave (2000). Personal communication, November 13.

Jinja Team (2000). http://www.ugandamissions.org/jinja/team.htm.

Kenya (2000). http://www. kenyaweb.com.

Kenya Mission Team (1980). *Church Planting, Watering, and*

Increasing in Kenya: The Study of Church Growth among Churches of Christ in Kenya, 1965-1979. Austin, TX: Firm Foundation.

Kenya Missionary Workshop (1987). *Advancing the Kingdom: Church Growth through Leadership Development.* Unpublished manuscript, Cascade College.

Mbale Team (2000). http://www.ugandamissions.org/mbale/mbale.htm

McCaleb, J. M. (1930). *On the Trail of the Missionaries.* Nashville, TN: Gospel Advocate.

McGavran, Donald & Wagner, C. Peter (1980). *Understanding Church Growth.* Grand Rapids, MI: Eerdmans.

Meru Mission Team (1987). *Church Growth among the Meru: Ministry of the Churches of Christ in Meru, Kenya–1987.* Unpublished manuscript, Cascade College.

Mwanza, Tanzania Mission Team. http://www.sukuma.net/main.htm.

Newton, Greg (2000). Telephone conversation, December 6.

Nyamwezi (2000). http://www.sil.org/ethnologue/countries/Tanz.html.

Palmer, Phil (2000). E-mail correspondence, December 24.

Shoemaker, Sam (2000). E-mail correspondence, October 25.

Stapleton, Bob (2000). E-mail correspondence, December 15.

Sukuma Home Page (2000). http://www.sukuma.net/main.htm.

Tanzania Country Profile (2000). http://www.tanzania-online.gov.uk/Business/ businessdirecto/ countryprofile/countryprofile.

Tyler, Shawn (2000). E-mail correspondence, November 23.

Uganda Country Study, (1990). Library of Congress Country Studies. http://lcweb2.loc. gov/frd/csquery.html.

Watson, Joe (1989). *Three African Drums.* Winona, MS: J. C. Choate.

APPENDIX
EAST AFRICAN MISSIONARIES

The following list is as accurate as the latest information allowed. This listing includes only those who worked "in-country." It does not attempt to list the many hundreds of short-term missionaries who have made important contributions. Corrections or additions may be sent to Stanley Granberg, Cascade College, 9101 E. Burnside, Portland, OR 97216.

Notations:
(A) apprentice
(T) teacher of missionary children

TANZANIAN MISSIONARIES

Name	Place	Years
Agutu, Boza	Arusha	2000
Bentley, Bob & Michelle	Mwanza	1993-1998
Bolden, Ken & Ann	Arusha	1984-2000
	Moshi	
Boyce, Chris	Mwanza	2000-
Busine, David	Mbulu	1995-1997
Caskey, Guy	Chimala	1957-1960
Caskey, Guy David & Lavern	Chimala	1962-?
Christopher	Mbeya	1999-2000
Connally, Andrew & Claudene	Chimala	1962-1972
	Arusha	1972-1975
	Chimala	1975-1995
Cotton, Ron	Arusha	1975-1976

Name	Place	Years
Dennis, Dale	Chimala	?-1998
	Dar	
Dockery, Tom & Patsy	Chimala	1962
Echols, Eldred	Chimala	1956-1964
Echols, Ray	Chimala	1956-1959
Ferguson, Howell	Arusha	2000
Guild, Eric & Susan	Mwanza	1999-
Hammitt, Ryan & Lynda	Moshi	2000-
Hestend, Joel	Moshi	1972-1975
Horne Al & Donna	Chimala	1959-1964
Huddleston, Ron & Maxine	Chimala	1963-?
Mays Jerry & Shirley	Chimala	1962-1963
Newton, Greg & Marsha	Mwanza	1993-1999
Ngoje, Charles	Moshi	1999-
Owino, Charles	Mbulu	1995-1997
Palmer, Phil & Elaine	Mbulu	1990-1994
Randiek, Jacob	Mbulu	1995-1997
Stafford, Cy	Arusha	?-1994
Stapleton, Bob	Chimala	2000-
Sure, Mark	Moshi	1999-
Thomas, Todd & Theresa	Mwanza	1999-
Tluway, Elibariki	Mbulu	1999-
Wechesa, Francis	Arusha	2000

ETHIOPIAN MISSIONARIES

Name	Place	Years
Blake, Gary	Deaf School	1962-1963
Clark, John Ed	Evangelist	1968-1970
Curl, Billy	Evangelist	1964-1969
Darden, Lennie	Deaf School	1963-1964
Davidson, Jimmy	Deaf School	1964-1965
Gowen, Bob	Deaf School	1960-1962
Leach, Lyle	Evangelist	1970-1974
Lee, Duward	Deaf School	1975
McDonald, Carl	Deaf School	1971-1975
Reed, Artie	Evangelist	1966-1969
Thompson, Carl	Evangelist	1960-1966

KENYAN MISSIONARIES

Name	Place	Years
Allen, Amos & Ann	Eldoret	1982-1992
Allison, Fielden & Janet	Sotik	1973-1988
	Mt. Elgon	1989-
Barnes, Jim & Lisa (A)	Kisumu	1984-1986
Barr, Lawrence & Faye	S. Nyanza	1973-1985
Bates, Daryl & Laurie	Sotik	1989
	Nairobi	
Beck, Jim & Phyllis	Malindi	1985-1995
Beckloff, Ken & Pat	Nairobi	1985-1989
	Mombasa	1989-1995
Beckloff, Randy	Nairobi	1984-1989
	Mombasa	1990-1995
Bell, Dan & Beverly	Kisumu	1984-present
Bolden, Ken & Ann	S. Nyanza	1978-1983
	Nairobi	1983-
Boyd, Dick & Sharon	Nairobi	1986-1991
Buchanan, Neville & Doween	Nairobi	1994-1995
Bush, David & Mary Helen	Kisumu	1981-1985
	Nairobi	1986-1990
Camp, Lee and Laura (A)	Nairobi	1992
Carr, Greg (A)	Nairobi	1985-1987
Chowning, Richard & Cyndi	Nairobi	1972-1974
	Kipsigis	1974-1988
Clodfelter, Greg	Nairobi	1992-94
	Nyeri	1994-
Conway, Larry & Holly	Eldoret	1986-
Coulston, Charles &	Nairobi	1992-
Cox, Monte & Mary	Eldoret	1982-1992
Deal, Lloyd (campaigns)	Nairobi	1990-1997
	Mombasa	
Earles, Lori	Soltik	1983-85
	Eldoret	1988-94
Ellis, Paul (A)	Kisumu	1977-1979
Evans, Shelly (T)	Meru	1992-1994
Fowler, James & Judy	Sotik	1977-1982
French, David & Lorie	Meru	1982-1984
Geer, Carter & Ruth	Kisumu	1984-1987
Granberg, Stanley & Gena	Meru	1983-1993
Greek, Stephen & Claudia	Eldoret	1984-

Name	Place	Years
Guild, Sonny & Eunice	Kisumu	1970-1979
Hackett, Berkeley & Charlotte	Nairobi	1970-
Hamilton, David (A)	Kisumu	1977-1979
Hamm, David & Lori	Kisumu	197?-198?
	S. Nyanza	?-?
Harrod, Dan & Traci	Kitale	1988-1990
Hayes, Kirk & Susan	Kitale	1984-1994
	Nairobi	1995-1999
Hemphill Preston & Janet	Kisumu	1979-1980
	Nairobi	1981-1985
High, David & Becky	Kisii	?-?
	S. Nyanza	
Hofschild, Dennis & Gaila	Sotik	1976-1977
Honey, Keith & Robin (A)	Kisumu	1979-1980
Joliff, Daniel & Allison	Nairobi	1988-1989
	Mombasa	1989-1995
Jones, Joe & Sally	Nairobi	1979-1983
Jones, Mike (A)	Nairobi	1985-1987
Kehl, Kevin & Susan	Sotik	1989
Kennamer, David & Betty	S. Nyanza	1978-1980
	Nairobi	1982-1984
Labnow, Keith (A)	Nairobi	1990-1992
Lane, Roy & Nora	Kisii	1981-1995
LeSeur, Michael (A)	Nairobi	1985-1987
Marcelain, Bob & Elaine	Nairobi	1981-1986
Mauldin, Tony & Janice	Nairobi	1996-1999
McKinney, Brittney	Kilifi	2000-
McLarty, Bruce & Ann	Meru	1984-1985
McLean, Dean &	Kitale	1981-1983
Meeks, Stephen & Donna Jo	Eldoret	1982-1987
		1991-1992
Merritt, Hilton & Avonelle	Kisumu	1969-1981
Moon, Rodger & Sue	Sotik	1980-1982
	S. Nyanza	1990-1996
Moore, James & Wanda	Uganda	
	S. Nyanza	1973-1977
Moore, Mike, (A)	Nairobi	1990-92
Morrow, John & Denise	Malindi	1986-1988
Moudy, Gabe & Jill	Kilifi	1998-
Nicholas, Mark & Debbie	Meru	1990-1999
	Nairobi	2000-

Name	Place	Years
Ogle, Ted & Martha	Nairobi	1965-1969
		1970-1971
	Nyeri	1987-1993
	Nairobi	1994-
Palmer, Phillip (A) & Elaine	Nairobi	1979-1981
Phares, Vic (A)	Nairobi	1979-1981
Pritchett, Roger & Karen	Meru	1987-1995
Ramsey, Roy & Margaret	Kisumu	1979-1986
Reppart, Jim & Laura	Nairobi	1983-1999
Rogers, Eddie & Kathy	Sotik	1989-
Rosie, Barry & Stacy	Kisii	1985-1997
	S. Nyanza	
Schrage, Mike & Karoyn	Kitale	1984-1994
	Nairobi	1995-
Scott, Sewell (A)	Nairobi	1990-92
Scudder, Jim & Faye, Jim & Grace	Sotik	1976-1977
	Molo	1979-1985
	Kisumu	1986-1989
	Nyeri	1990-
Searcy, Bill & Kathy	Meru	1992-1994
	Nairobi	1995-
Sharp, Becky	Nairobi	1984-1989
Shewmaker, Sam & Nancy	Nairobi	1986-
Smoothey, Craig & Jeane	Nairobi	1995-2000
Stephens, Larry & Diane	Kisumu	1977-1985
	Nairobi	1986-1999
Sullins, Jerry & Edith	Nairobi	1978-1981
Swift, Jamie & Ginger	Kilifi	1998-
Talley, Tim & Rebecca	Malindi	1985-1995
	Mombasa	1996-
Tankersley, Oneal & Betsy	Eldoret	1982-
Tarbet, Gaston & Jan	Kisumu	1969-1976
		1979-1980
Tate, Van & Jean	Nairobi	1965-1976
Taylor, Lavonne (T)	Meru	1992-1993
Thomas, Sam & Judy	Meru	1983-1984
Thompson, Carla Dean	Nairobi	1984-
Trull, Richard & Marinda	Meru	1984-1994
Tyler, Shawn & Linda	Kitale	1981-1994
Van Rheenen, Gailyn & Becky	Sotik	1973-1985

Name	Place	Years
Vesel, Louie (A)	Nairobi	1978-1980
Vick, David & Brenda	Sotik	1989-1997
Wells, Tara (T)	Meru	1992-1994
Williams, Keith & Lisa	Meru	1990-1995
Yoder, Paul & Naomi	Nairobi	1970-1973
Young, Stephen (A)	Kisumu	1977-1979

UGANDAN MISSIONARIES

Name	Place	Years
Abney, Brent & Heather	Jinja	1994-
Allison, Fielden	Kampala	1972
Baker, Jay & Andrea	Mbarara	1997-
Barr, Lawrence & Faye	Kampala	1972
Barton, John & Sara	Jinja	1994-
Carr, Greg & Debra	Kampala	1993-1998
Cash, Jeff & Cheryl	Fort Portal	1995-
Davis, Betty	Jinja	1998-
Davis, Clint & Briley	Jinja	1994-
Fouts, Nick & Renee	Mbarara	1997-
Gage, Shane & Carole	Mbarara	1997-
Hall, Mark	Jinja	1998-
Jenkins, Dave & Jana	Kampala	1993-
Moore, James & Wanda	Kampala	1972
Moore, Mark & Marnie	Jinja	1994-
Palmer, Phil & Elaine	Mbale	1999-
Piek, Sandi	Mbale	1996-
Raymond, Bret & Johnna	Jinja	1994-
Reynolds, Tom	Kampala	?-1972
Shelburne, Ian & Danetta	Mbale	1996-
Shero, Phillip & Laura	Mbale	1998-
Smith, Deron & Becca	Jinja	1994-
Tarbet, Gaston & Jan	Kampala	1994-1997
Taylor, Greg & Jill	Jinja	?-
Tyler, Shawn & Linda	Mbale	1995-
Van Rheenen, Gailyn	Kampala	1972
Vaughn, Ken & Nova	Kampala	1998-1999
Vick, David & Brenda	Mbale	1997-
Watson, Joe	Kampala	1971-1972

CHAPTER 7

World Bible School: A Timely Tool For African Evangelism

R.H. Tex Williams

> *R.H. Tex Williams spent 14 years as a missionary in southern Africa working in South Africa, Swaziland, Botswana and Lesotho. He taught at Sunset School of Preaching and Missions for 15 years training preachers and missionaries. He has directed World Bible School since 1986. He has served in churches as a pulpit minister and now serves as an elder. World Bible School, P.O. Box 2169, Cedar Park, Texas 78630-2169.*

For 27 years Ruth Orr of Lewisville, Tennessee and her husband had been World Bible School teachers. Most of their students were in Ghana, West Africa. Ruth continued the correspondence course teaching after her husband died. Her local church buys WBS lessons and Bibles for her and pays for the postage to send them. Ruth sent, received, and graded lessons for her students, convinced that "God gives the increase" though she never expected to personally meet any of those she taught. Unexpectedly, Ruth was invited to go to the city of Takoradi in Ghana with a campaign group to follow up on World Bible School students. Weeks before the group's departure, Ruth contacted all of her students in Ghana by letter, letting them know she was coming and where she would be staying. On the night of the group's arrival, four of her students were waiting for her. Three had come over 600 miles to see their WBS teacher. Other students had ridden buses and vans for 10 to 12 hours to meet their teacher and receive more teaching. In all, 43 of Ruth's students came to the special campaign and stayed for three or four days to continue their study. Thirty-eight were converted during the campaign and four had already been baptized before they arrived.

These were not the only conversions to Christ that Ruth had experienced in her career as a WBS teacher, but these were the first she had met face to face. It was the first time she had actually witnessed the baptisms of those whom she had taught. It was an encouragement and an assurance that her work over the years was real and productive.

The above story is special, but in one sense it could be repeated thousands of times. Not every World Bible School teacher will be able to travel to other countries and meet their students personally, but when one "plants" the gospel and "waters" receptive minds, the end result is the same...souls are saved.

WBS as a Method of Mass Evangelism

The tremendous population growth and high receptivity of the peoples who live in sub-Sahara Africa demands the attention of all who are interested in seeing that the Kingdom of God grows rapidly. Over the past 75 years, Christian missionaries have gone into various parts of Africa. Their work has made possible the establishment of the Lord's church, preachers have been trained, and churches have been established. Many of the churches and evangelists have matured and there is no need for missionaries in the areas where those folks live and work. Still, there are many cities, towns and villages where the truth of the gospel has not gone and where people are open to Bible teaching. Every method available must be implemented to reach those receptive hearts. *Mass evangelism* is one of the viable ways of teaching the gospel to African people and its many facets will assure that souls are saved and churches are established.

World Bible School is one method of mass evangelism or "evangelizing the masses." Its methodology is the use of correspondence courses sent through the mail systems of the world. It includes the one-on-one concept of evangelism, but is farther reaching because of its ability to contact large numbers of prospects for conversion in a nation or a particular geographical area. Advertisements are placed in newspapers, magazines, on radio and other popular media offering a free Bible correspondence course to those who write in requesting it. Many people of all ages write for the Bible studies. However, the largest number of students come from "referrals"—those names sent in by families and friends.

There has been some aversion to or dismissal of WBS as a practical mission method. These concerns have been in all good conscience. One concern is that WBS is a "shotgun" method of evangelism and that the students are too scattered and therefore cannot be formed into spiritual and productive churches. Another concern is that some missionaries have been overwhelmed with too many students to contact and proper follow-up cannot be made. To overcome such objections it would be good to look at the *concept* of mass evangelism as a New Testament command and practice. Then it is important to look at mass evangelism as a practical and efficient *method of evangelism* in modern times and the success of WBS in reaching the lost as an example of it.

Mass Evangelism: A Biblical Concept

Mass evangelism is a biblical concept. It characterized the preaching of Jesus, especially in Matthew's account of the Lord's life.

The Sermon on the Mount began because Jesus "saw the crowds" (Matt. 5:1). As Jesus went through the towns and villages during his ministry, he "saw the crowds" and "had compassion on them." Those experiences resulted in a challenge and command that were capsulated in his statement, "The harvest is plentiful but the laborers are few. Ask the Lord of the harvest, therefore, to send out workers into his harvest." That principle remains the same with the growing population of the world and the need for more committed Christians to have the desire and the opportunity to work in "the harvest."

In Matthew 13, Jesus sat by the lake and "such *large crowds* gathered around him that he got into the boat and sat in it, while all the people stood on the shore. Then he told them many things..." (italics mine, TW).

The concept of mass evangelism was implied in other teachings of Jesus. In Matthew 24:14 he said, "And this gospel of the kingdom will be preached throughout the whole world, as a testimony to all nations...." His eventual command to "go make disciples of *all nations*" and to "go into *all the world* and preach the gospel to the *whole creation*" certainly smacks of a notion of mass evangelism.

As the gospel was preached by the disciples of Christ, evidence of mass evangelism was certainly apparent. The preaching of the eleven and Peter on the day of Pentecost produced 3,000 souls. Later in Jerusalem, Luke wrote that ". . . more than ever believers were added to the Lord, *multitudes* both of men and women..." (Acts 5:14).

According to Luke's account, the preaching of Paul and the work of the new Ephesian church made it possible to say that "all the residents of Asia heard the word of the Lord, both Jews and Greeks" (Acts 19:10b). Paul and those who labored with him usually spent brief periods of time evangelizing in one place and then moved on to others very quickly.

The concept of mass evangelism today as a practical and useable method of reaching the lost certainly has a larger, more complex agenda than in New Testament times. Jesus, Paul, and others could only orate publicly. Their only "printed matter" was the Old Testament Scriptures usually found in the synagogues. Kenneth Latourette wrote:

> Of the methods of spread [of Christianity] we know something, although not as much as we could wish. In the first century we hear much of the public address, often given in the synagogue. We read, too, of private conversations and meetings with small groups. (A History of the Expansion of Christianity, Vol. 1).

But the important feature of their work was that they *maximized what they had to reach as many as possible.* They preached to both small and large crowds as opportunities presented themselves. They took advantage of and even sought chances to evangelize by preaching openly. Paul preached from the Areopagus in Athens where he knew the learned men would gather. But he also preached to an angry crowd in Ephesus after it was stirred up by Demetrius.

Mass Evangelism in the Modern Era

Historically, the spread of Christianity for the first twelve or thirteen centuries was by the same method; that is, by determined men and women who spoke whenever and wherever they could to as many as could be gathered. Later, the writings of the patristic church fathers were circulated but they were not readily available to the masses. Their content was usually passed on by those who preached publicly. The eventual printing of the Gutenberg Bible in 1456 probably brought the first major change in the method of spreading the gospel to the masses.

Now it is different! The challenges and potential of mass evangelism are greater than ever before. It can be better understood when we have specifics or some tangible expressions about the focus and size of our task. It is important that we understand what we mean when we speak of the need for mass evangelism methods.

Mass evangelism simply means preaching the gospel of Jesus Christ to the mass of people or the population of the entire world. The *American Heritage Dictionary* gives a definition of "mass" as "A large but unspecified amount or number." When applied to people, which is our interest, it is referred to as "the masses". But what does that mean? How many people are we talking about?

Statistics relative to the masses and to population change and growth are sometimes hard to digest because the numbers are so large. Changes are recognized more readily when we look back and see what has taken place; i.e. hindsight. However, statistics cannot be ignored, and they have a profound effect when presented in a unique way.

In an example of raw statistics, looking backward and ahead within an 18 years span, the *Population Reference Bureau* estimated in their "World Population Data Sheet" that in mid 1992 there were 5,410,000,000 people living in the world. The birth rate per 1000 population was 26 while the death rate was only 9 per 1000 population. With that kind of increase, the population of the world was projected to double in only 41 years. If those projections were correct, by the year 2010, the population is projected to be 7,114,000,000 and by 2025 the population is projected to be 8,545,000,000. In the year 2000 the population of the world reached 6,000,000,000, so population estimates are probably on track. It means that the church of our Lord is living in all generations in an emergency of catastrophic proportions. **We must**

develop adequate methods and skills to meet the challenges and potential of evangelizing the masses.

The impact that information has on the Lord's people is contained in the command to "go into all the world and preach the gospel." How is it to be done? Sending missionaries is important and should be increased, but there are not enough missionaries being trained and sent to meet the opportunities that are available and demanding our attention. Not only that, there are places where western missionaries are not permitted to live and evangelize. Other means of evangelizing must be used and that involves mass evangelism.

As the Lord commands, and as the need to fulfill his commands increases, so does he provide. With the growing population of the world has come printing presses, radio, television, computers, and internet to name a few media that can and should be used for the spread of the gospel. World wide travel has become so common that evangelists and teachers can travel to various parts of the world other than their homes in a reasonably short period of time. It would be foolish to neglect the use of any of these blessings from God and center attention on only one method of evangelism. Again, World Bible School is one method of mass evangelism that God has placed in our hands to be used until something better replaces it.

History and Development of World Bible School

World Bible School was the brainchild of Jimmie Lovell. Jimmie was born and grew up on a farm near Portland, Tennessee. Many things shaped his personal and spiritual life, but his innate driving character probably caused him to be a front-runner in everything that he did either in his work earning a living or in the work of the Lord. In the Foreword of Bill Young's book, *The Man of ACTION, the Story of Jimmie Lovell*, Dr. M. Norvel Young made this statement about the story of Jimmie:

165

> It is the story of a scrapper. As a boy and a young
> man Jimmie loved physical contact. In his mature years
> he has continued to fight verbally for the things in which
> he strongly believes. . . It is the story of a man of serv-
> ice—selfless service to God and his fellowmen.

After his discharge from the army during World War I, Lovell
began working for the DuPont Company, selling gun powder in the
western part of the United States. He was a crack marksman in both
rifle and pistol and gave shooting exhibitions all over the western
part of the United States. He settled in Denver, Colorado and produced a paper, *The Colorado Christian,* which helped to strengthen
and unify the churches in Colorado. He also sent copies of the paper
to Christians in the "Bible Belt" and encouraged them to move to
the western states and establish the church where it did not exist.
Evangelism was an important part of his thinking and his life. When
the use of gun powder diminished, Jimmie was transferred to Los
Angeles where he sold explosives to builders and miners.

His first push for correspondence teaching probably had more
of a concern for Americans teaching Americans. In the first issue
(December 1937) of *The West Coast Christian,* a paper published in
California by Jimmie, the idea appeared. He wrote,

> There is not a member who reads these lines who
> does not have some relative, neighbor or friend interest-
> ed in religion but still out of Christ. You have wished
> many times that you had the opportunity to sit down and
> tell this person about the church, and it is possible that
> you have talked to such a person off and on for years but
> never got to explain the Bible just as "we" understand it.
> I have been in this same position and finally decided that
> I would start at the very beginning and tell the story by
> making up mimeographed lessons so that I could send
> them to people I knew, one lesson at a time, over a peri-
> od of weeks, and if and when they read all of these they

would know the gospel story and if refused their blood would not be on my hands. I have made these lessons so that you can use them as though they were written by you, and you can hand or mail them to anyone just as I have done. Thousands of these have already been printed and distributed and I know from my own experience that souls have been brought to Christ through them, and one preacher advised me that he had not only started a new congregation in a new town, but converted 14 members by using these simple lessons of Christ. My idea has never been to sell the lessons but the demand has been so great I had to ask for the cost of paper, but it is not my purpose to ask for full costs which includes postage and other expenses. Those who have friends, relatives or neighbors and want to be a missionary for Him can do it with these lessons. Each set includes 15 lessons covering the following subjects: 1- Introduction (explaining the matter), 1a- The Bible, 2 - God, Son, Holy Spirit, 3 - Creation, 4 - Sin, 5 - Heaven and Hell, 6 - Jews and Gentiles, 7 - Ten Commandments, 8 - Prophesy, 9 - Christ, 10 - Teachings of Christ, (These are all I have ready for distribution just now, but the others will be ready soon) 11 - Death, Burial, Resurrection of Christ, 12 - Holy Spirit and Pentecost, 13 - Plan of Salvation, 14 - Church, 15 - Christian Living. Each lesson is written just like a conversation. No person seeking the truth could fail to find it, therefore, for $1.00 you will receive 10 sets, which means that you can carry the full gospel story to a lost soul for ten cents. Does someone's soul mean that much to you? I cannot afford to mail to any one address less than ten sets, but the wide awake church would make these lessons up for themselves, and if used, will double the membership of any church in one year. I am a preacher "pusher" and will work my heart out helping any of them, but the job is too big for preachers alone. They can never convert empty seats and those seats will remain empty until you and I are ready to help fill them up. You show me a Christian who WORKS and I will show you a person interested in SOULS. Help bring a soul to Jesus.

I have included the entire text of the quotation because many of the facets of methodology in the statement were already being done when the name, World Bible School, was added to the program and are still used in today's WBS. Some of those are: 1) contacting people who could not be contacted personally; 2) teaching by correspondence courses; 3) using the mail systems; 4) using Christians to do the teaching; 5) providing correspondence courses to teachers as cheaply as possible; 6) recognizing the value of a soul and the necessity of doing something to see that they are taught about Jesus.

Jimmie continued to use the above correspondence courses whenever and wherever he could find someone who was like-minded or when he could persuade someone else to use them. However, its full development came sometime after he moved to California. He settled in Los Angeles proper at first, but later moved to Redondo Beach to be closer to his daughter and son-in-law, Doug and Patsie Trowbridge and their family. He worshiped with the church in Redondo Beach, but eventually moved his membership to the church in Torrance.

In January 1962 Jimmie began publishing the newspaper ACTION which was dedicated to world evangelism. He recruited several to assist him in the publication and mailing of ACTION, among whom were Howard and Margaret Cox. Howard worked for what was then North American Aviation, but he and Margaret committed one day a week to assist Jimmie with ACTION. In the course of their work together, Jimmie's interest in correspondence course evangelism was discussed, and Jimmie persuaded the Coxes to start a correspondence course teaching program in the Torrance church. They procured 100 names from Doris Pennick who was working with Richard Kruse and International Bible Correspondence School which had already started in Canada. All the names were from Africa. Another 100 names were obtained from Brother Jolly Meyers who was active in mission work in the Caribbean. Eventually, there were 54 teachers in the program in Torrance and the number of their students quickly grew to over 2500. That number exploded to 200,000 and Jimmie talked the Coxes into working with him in getting other churches involved and using ACTION as the means of spreading the challenge. Howard Cox took an early retirement from his job, and he and Margaret have made WBS their lives since that time. The name World Bible School was first assigned to the program in 1973.

When Jimmie Lovell died, he had already made arrangements with Reuel Lemmons to transfer the international headquarters of the ACTION and World Bible School to Austin, Texas where Reuel was to direct and promote the program. When Jimmie died April 29, 1984, the transition was already complete. However, shortly after Reuel took over the direction of WBS he discovered that he had a congestive heart condition that would end his life in a matter of a year or so. He contacted me at Sunset School of Preaching and Missions where I had been teaching for 15 years. At first my wife, Mary Jane, and I refused the offer since we had plans to return to South Africa to continue our work there as missionaries. Reuel persuaded me to come to Austin and visit with him and look at the possibilities. We made three visits and also I made trips overseas to see what results the WBS program was producing. We were persuaded that the work was important and potentially it was just beginning to grow and develop into a spectacular outreach.

We moved to Austin, Texas in February 1986 bringing most of our support from congregations with us. The Westover Hills Church of Christ committed office space for WBS and volunteers from the congregation had already set up the mailing of ACTION paper. Reuel Lemmons' debilitating health caused him to pass the direction of WBS to me very shortly after my arrival in Austin. He lived until January 25, 1989.

Over the years, by God's grace, WBS has grown so much that we have had to add new staff. The Westover Hills church continued to give us more office and operational space, but with the growth of both WBS and the Westover Hills church, we bought our own building and moved in August, 2000. One of our major continuing projects is to develop new correspondence courses. John Reese, long time missionary in Africa has been responsible for course development.

Why World Bible School is an Important Tool in Africa

The above bits of historical information all contribute to some extent as to why World Bibles School is an effective tool for evangelism in Africa which is the focus of this book.

First of all, WBS gives American Christians an opportunity to participate in world evangelism in an active, one-on-one method of teaching the gospel; or, as one teacher said, "pen-on-pen" method of teaching. When responses come in from our advertising, the names and addresses of the respondents are sent to volunteer WBS teachers who live all over the U.S.A. who have committed to do the teaching. Giving American Christians an opportunity to participate in world evangelism on an individual basis not only strengthens them and the churches they represent, but enhances their interest in Africa because of their students. Many teachers regularly respond to the needs of African evangelism by sending Bibles, printed materials, correspondence courses, and even go on campaigns as mentioned in the beginning of this chapter.

A good example of this was my first introduction to WBS, its teachers, and its impact in Kenya, East Africa. We at the Sunset School of Preaching and Missions had recruited and placed a team in Nairobi. My wife and I periodically visited with teams we had helped to train and put on the field and consequently, we visited with the Nairobi team. One of the team members asked me to go with him to meet with a group of new Christians among the Kikuyu tribe. The work had been started through the conversion of one man who had made contact with the missionary team. On our visit to the Kikuyu area, we found that two congregations had been started and a church building had been built. The man's name was Gabriel Muchiru and he related that he was a WBS student of Sister Perry McComb of Conroe, Texas. I took pictures of the Muchirus and the churches and sent them to Sister McComb. She wrote a very encouraging letter back about some of her activities, but the closing paragraph illustrates the value of WBS, its teachers, and the spread of the gospel in Africa. She wrote, "I am teaching over 600 students in Kenya, Uganda, Zimbabwe, Nigeria, Liberia and Ghana. I love the work. To think that I can sit at my desk in Conroe and teach the gospel to those in Africa who will continue teaching, is something I never dreamed of before. I am delighted but sobered to have such a gift in my hands." She was 90 years old when she wrote the letter. There are probably dozens - perhaps hundreds - of such illustrations that might be used to illustrate the value of WBS and its teachers in African evangelism.

Secondly, WBS makes it possible for churches to become involved in African evangelism. World Bible School initially was the work of individual Christians who bought their own materials and paid for their own postage. However, church leaders began to see the value of the program as a project of the church for mission outreach. They committed to buying lessons for their teachers and also paid the postage for mailing costs. They set up WBS offices and rooms and contributed computers to keep track of all the African students who were being taught. They help to send Bibles, tracts, religious books, and other things that assisted new converts, preachers and churches in their growth and outreach. Others focus on particular areas of a nation in Africa and follow up on their students by taking campaigns into the country using their own members and other recruits. For example, the Oldham Lane Church of Christ in Abilene, Texas sends campaigns to western Ghana and they convert hundreds each trip and establish and strengthen the churches that result from their work. All such efforts also create an evangelistic spirit in the churches where WBS is used though not everyone participates in WBS teaching.

WBS also contributes to the work of missionaries. Many African missionaries have made contacts in their particular area of work from the names and addresses they receive from American WBS teachers. John Reese, who now works with the WBS office here in the States wrote of his experience in South Africa using WBS:

> During the years of intense local work we contributed to teaching hundreds. Then we teamed up with WBS, pioneered its use in the same region. Through amazing American teachers our search after several years extended to perhaps 100,000 students. We know the number of advanced WBS students passed on to us, because we entered their information into our computers. After five or six years, 5,000 had already been referred to us. Some 500 were baptized after the follow-up studies.

WBS contacts also assist missionaries in opening up new areas of work. Some missionaries and mission teams now contact WBS before going into a new area asking for names of WBS students whom they can use in the beginning of their work. They usually find people who are already well taught in the scriptures and ready to obey their Lord in baptism.

WBS is effective in Africa also because most Africans are very spiritual. Culturally, and probably innately, they feel it necessary to search for answers to some of the things in and about life that they do not understand. They have the time and the environment that makes them "seekers." African WBS students are generally searching for answers to questions like, "Who am I and why am I here?" "What will happen to me when I die?" "Does God really know who I am and is He interested in me as a person?" "Is there something better for me than the poverty I have to live in all of my life?" "What is the Bible about...what does it teach and how can it help me?"

WBS is effective in Africa also because of the desire that many Africans have to get an education. Educational opportunities are many times limited to a few years in grammar school. Some areas have private schools and sometimes public schools are available but in many places getting an education is beyond the financial reach of many whom would like to study. Most students are very pleased to finish their WBS courses and get a certificate for completing the studies.

WBS has been an effective tool in such West African nations as Nigeria and Ghana where some churches are very strong and are sending their own missionaries to neighboring countries. WBS is helping to sustain the preaching of the gospel by churches in Liberia even though no mail can be sent between the U.S.A. and Liberia. Some Christians here in the U.S. have found a way to ship WBS materials into the country and the brethren there are doing the grading and follow-up on interested students.

Though most of the influence of WBS is in sub-Sahara Africa, it has also begun to have an influence in some parts of northern Africa which is mostly Muslim. Using WBS in the Arabic language converts are being made in Egypt, Eritrea, Ethiopia and Morocco.

Conclusion

Like all methods of evangelism, WBS has difficulties and problems. It is time consuming and takes patience and perseverance on the part of the teacher and the student. Mail systems in some countries lack a lot in being effective and fast. Some take the courses in hopes of benefiting financially from their studies and they ask for funds, trips to America and a number of other such requests. However, in spite of all its short-comings, World Bible School has contributed greatly to the spread of the kingdom in Africa and its influence continues to grow.

CHAPTER 8

"Africans Claiming Africa" and the ACA Conferences

Sam Shewmaker

Sam and Nancy Shewmaker have been missionaries their entire careers. Sam was born to missionary parents in Northern Rhodesia, now Zambia. They have worked in Zambia and Kenya as well as criss-crossed the continent to promote the ACA conferences and develop communication networks among the African churches. They currently reside in Searcy, Arkansas. sshewmaker@earthlink.com.

The expression "Africans Claiming Africa" is the name of an African missionary thrust. It is also a slogan denoting the need for Africans to be about the business of claiming their continent for kingdom of God. For four centuries and more, explorers and adventurers, colonists and companies, merchants and missionaries from far and near have been about the business of claiming Africa for one interest or another. Now it is time for African churches and African Christians to claim their own continent for Christ. So "Africans Claiming Africa" is a vision to mobilize God's churches in Africa to join the great missionary enterprise of finding the lost of Africa and leading them to saving faith in Jesus Christ.

In fact, this has been happening in a few isolated cases for nearly a century and a half. To name a few examples, Alexander Cross, a freed slave from North America became the first Church of Christ missionary to Africa in the modern era (about 1856). John Sherriff, a missionary from New Zealand, trained and sent African missionaries throughout the African subcontinent in the early decades of the 20th century (see Dow Merritt, *The Dew Breakers* and George Benson, *Missionary Experiences*). Wendell Broom mobilized Nigerian evangelists to take the gospel to Cameroon in the late 1950s. But by and large the African church is a sleeping giant in terms of its potential for missionary endeavor.

A Rationale for an African Missionary Movement

In the mid-1980s some missionaries in Africa began to feel the burden of their own inadequacy to complete the task of spreading the gospel throughout the continent. The dreams born in the heyday of Church of Christ missions in the 1960s of 'winning the world to Christ in our generation' were not being realized. With only about 200 of our missionaries in Africa and fewer than 40% of the countries of Africa with a Church of Christ presence, not to speak of the hundreds of unreached tribes, it was evident that completing the task of evangelizing Africa in our generation was simply not going to happen.

While Africa was becoming increasingly receptive to the gospel, missionary recruitment and training was not meeting the demand. Money for missions was difficult to find among churches in North America. Many would-be missionaries were discouraged by the daunting task of raising funds among churches preoccupied with their own local programs. In addition, new missionaries from the West generally were limiting their commitment to five to ten years of service on the field. Much of their time in the first two to three years was focused on learning the vernacular language of the people among whom they had come to work, so that their window of effective ministry was quite limited in many cases. In short, it was apparent that we needed a broader missionary base and that we needed an alternative approach to developing that base.

At the same time, churches in a number of countries were maturing and developing leaders with a vision for evangelism beyond their local communities. While many of these national African leaders lacked adequate training, they were gaining experience in crossing cultural barriers to take the gospel in to enemy territory, crossing both tribal and national boundaries in their preaching. These men and women also typically lacked the financial resources to do more than make occasional short-term preaching trips. But the ranks of these short-term soldiers of the gospel were growing. It was becoming clear that the western missionary was not going to be the lone pioneer of missions of the Africa of the future.

In 1987 several missionaries met in Nairobi, Kenya to consider how we might devise a plan to reach the rest of the continent. Some of the questions that arose in those discussions were: Can western missionaries alone ever accomplish the task of missions in the continent of Africa? How can we multiply and mobilize adequate human resources for the task of mission? Is there a way to leverage out the sum total of mission resources to achieve greater effectiveness in our missionary endeavors? The strategists resolved to form an organization that was dubbed SPEAR - Strategic Planning to Effect Africa's Redemption, to begin devising ways and means of entering unreached peoples and areas of the continent. Some missionaries in Kenya were adamantly opposed to forming such an entity and the idea was temporarily shelved.

But the urgency to do something continued to lie on the hearts of some missionaries. It was clear that we did not know enough to begin realistic planning. Research was necessary to find out the state of the church across the continent, to get to know the major players, and to forge a unity of purpose before we could even clarify the problems and define the goals. We needed to understand what had been accomplished in order to define the unfinished task.

Toward this end, in July, 1989, a meeting of several Kenyans and missionaries was convened in Nakuru, Kenya to make preliminary plans for a continental conference in 1991. (Because of the Gulf War and resulting oil shortages and higher airline fares, the conference was delayed until 1992). Don Yelton agreed to enlist the support of the White's Ferry Road Church of Christ to provide matching funds of up to $10,000 of the estimated $20,000 needed to underwrite the cost of the conference. Much of that money was used to subsidize the costs of airfares for African Christians who attended the conference from all over the continent.

The Thuchi River, Kenya ACA Conference - 1992

In April 1992, nearly 200 Christian leaders, evangelists, elders, teachers and missionaries met for ten days at Thuchi River Lodge near Embu, Kenya. They represented 16 nations of Africa and the United States and 39 different languages. The purpose of the conference was "to inform, to inspire and to equip" each other for the spread of the gospel and the expansion of the kingdom of God.

The conference was far more than a lectureship. Its program included devotional messages, major morning and evening addresses, classes, workshops, country and project reports and on the last day a tremendous parade of the nations that culminated in a marvelous period of prayer and worship. Numerous informal meetings occurred during meals and unscheduled time that fostered connections and networks of different interest groups that would form the basis of a movement later.

Strategy Formulation

A key feature of the Thuchi River conference was the development of national strategies for evangelizing unreached groups. The
groups representing each nation were given several sessions to identify a people group they knew who had not been reached with the
gospel. They then developed an initial strategy and a timeline for
reaching this people group and planting a church among them. The
purpose of these strategy sessions was both to train the participants
in thinking and planning for evangelism as well as to go home with
something to share with others to inspire them for evangelistic outreach. Each group representing a nation then designated a
spokesman to present their national strategy in a plenary session of
the whole conference.

Some of these strategies showed the initiative and creativity of
the participants. The Nigerian strategy was to focus on training
evangelists and missionaries at the School of Biblical Studies in Jos,
with a view to reaching the predominately Muslim countries north
and east of Nigeria where the *lingua franca* is the Hausa language.
These Islamic governments typically do not allow professional
Christian missionaries entry into their countries, so the Nigerians
planned that evangelists would also be trained as 'tentmakers' who
could support themselves as teachers or businessmen while sharing
the good news privately.

The Malawians resolved to increase their evangelistic efforts
among the Mozambican refugees along their common borders and
to train the Mozambicans to evangelize and plant churches in their
own country.

The Zambians presented a three-prong approach. They wanted to reach the deaf of Zambia and to evangelize among the refugees
in Angola to the west and Mozambique to the east. As we will see

later, each of these strategies was activated in the years that followed the conference, with varying degrees of success.

Mission Practicums

All participants in the conference were urged to take part in one of the mission practicums planned to follow the conference. The visiting national Christians were sent to five or six mission locations throughout Kenya where churches and missionaries hosted them for 5 to 7 days. These men had the opportunity to experience a new culture, to meet other church leaders, to preach and teach in situations very foreign to them and generally to get a feel for what it is like to be a missionary. These short missionary journeys had a profound effect on many of the visiting brethren as well as their host churches.

Overall the conference and the practicums deeply impacted the ACA participants. Wendell Broom's lecture on becoming a 'world Christian' broadened the world view of many. Jim Reppart's classes on culture helped Africans and missionaries alike unravel long-standing confusions over each others' motives, assumptions and presuppositions. The daily worship and prayer periods led us all to new heights of fellowship and nearness to God in a 'mountain top experience' the like of which few had ever witnessed. It was referred to by different ones as a 'second Pentecost' and the 'mother of all conferences.'

Outcomes of the Thuchi River ACA Conference

In the closing days of the conference two questions were voiced by the African brethren: 1) how will we communicate with each other? and 2) when and how will we meet again?

In answer to the first question, a newsletter was suggested. Norm Rhodes, editor of World Radio News, volunteered to publish

180

an African newsletter as a section of World Radio News until such time as another arrangement could be made. This writer volunteered to serve as editor of the newsletter. The newsletter was named 'DRUMBEAT' and was published quarterly in World Radio News for two years. The first issue of DRUMBEAT as a separate entity appeared in Kenya in April 1994.

The second question resulted in the forming of a continuation committee made up of one representative of each country present. The committee decided that another conference should be convened in 1996 and accepted an invitation from Nigeria to host the next conference. Zimbabwe was listed as a backup in case Nigeria could not host the meeting.

How the Thuchi River ACA Conference Affected the Church and Missions

No conference with the purpose of the Thuchi River ACA conference is successful in and of itself. Its success can only be measured in how it changes the status quo of the church and its mission.

Some of the countries that developed strategies at the conference were serious about implementing them. In the next two years the Zambians activated two prongs of their strategy. Jim and Linda Hawkins learned sign language and established a fellowship of deaf Christians in Lusaka. While there was still a civil war in progress in Angola, Leonard Mujala moved to the largest refugee camp in Central Africa to work among the Angolans in exile there. He planted three churches with a total of nearly 1,000 converts among these refugees and laid plans to return with them to Angola when they were resettled at the end of the war.

The Malawian evangelists increased their work among the Mozambican refugee camps along their borders and began regular preaching trips across Lake Malawi and into Mozambique itself.

In a parallel development in Nigeria, Steve Worley at the School of Biblical Studies at Jos, introduced a concept called 'C-TEAM' for 'Christians Training and Equipping African Missionaries.' The plan was to recruit Nigerian preachers as missionaries, give them one year of training in missions at the Jos Bible school then send them to out to neighboring countries. These missionaries would be overseen by Nigerian churches and sponsored by partnerships between Nigerian and American churches.

The Nairobi Great Commission school was founded in 1990, with its purpose of 'equipping God's people for ministry and missions.' It was the first Church of Christ Bible school in Africa with a serious intention to train not only local church leaders and evangelists but also cross-cultural missionaries. In September 1996, the Rainbow Church of Christ in Nairobi recruited three graduates of the Nairobi Great Commission school and sent them and their families as missionaries to Mbulu, Tanzania. The missionaries were supported by a consortium consisting of the Rainbow church, an American church and two or three individuals all under the oversight of the Rainbow church and its elders who provided accountability for the Mbulu mission team. In the years that followed, the leadership and missions committee of the Rainbow church made several trips to Tanzania to encourage and assist the mission efforts there.

The churches in Ghana focused much of their mission efforts in the Islamic north of their country. From 1992 to 1997 some 250 new churches were planted in this region. Additionally, Ghanaian missionaries moved to such countries as Benin, Burkina Faso and the Gambia during this period.

These are only a few examples of the beginnings of the serious attempts at missionary endeavor in Africa following the Thuchi River ACA conference. Some of these efforts were direct products of the conference while others received encouragement there.

The Chinhoyi, Zimbabwe ACA Conference - 1997

Nigeria was to host the next ACA conference in 1996, but because of the political uncertainties at the time, the conference was moved and postponed. The brethren in Zimbabwe were asked to host the conference and they agreed to do so in May, 1997.

There was no funding from the American churches at this second conference so fewer participants could afford to come from distant countries. The church in South Africa, Zimbabwe, Zambia and Malawi was well represented. Thirty participants came by bus and plane from Kenya. All total nearly 170 church leaders, teachers, evangelists, missionaries and mission supporters attended from 16 countries, representing 47 vernacular language groups and nearly 9,400 churches.

The theme of the seven-day conference at Chinhoyi, Zimbabwe was 'Becoming a Sending Church.' Each day began with a biblical lesson from Galatians by Dennis Malepa of Botswana. Plenary addresses were given each morning and evening on an important topic facing the church in Africa. Again the primary focus of the conference was on evangelism and missions, but other tracks were also featured that reflected broader ministry concerns in Africa. These additional tracks included theological education, World Bible School, medical work, women's ministries, tent-making ministries, urban ministry and communications ministries. Each of the classes and tracks met several times during the week. One day was devoted to fasting and prayer. Special events such as prayers for the nations, a foot-washing ceremony and a 'passing of the map' ceremony took place in the evening sessions. The passing of the map symbolically represented passing on the responsibility for the future to the African church and its leaders. The participants again selected a continuation committee whose purpose was to plan where and when there would be another conference. In the spirit of the Thuchi

River conference, the whole week was bathed in great periods of worship and prayer culminating in the Parade of Nations that was becoming a tradition of the conferences.

Outcomes of the Chinhoyi ACA Conference

The move towards self-reliance and 'God-reliance' in terms of supporting evangelism was evident at Chinhoyi. One example of this was the "Tree of Life" project in Swaziland where Africans are using 200 acres of Bible School land to grow thousands of macadamia nut trees, the proceeds from which will be used to support evangelism and missions. Douglas Boateng of Ghana pledged support and housing for an African missionary to move to Dakar, Senegal. A Zimbabwean brother who has a rental house pledged the income from the house to support evangelism. In South Africa a construction company was formed whose profits would be used to support missions in Namibia. Farm land was bought in Kenya to develop and support a college of agriculture and other trades training. While some of these projects required U. S. funding for seed money, they primarily involved African commitment, financial support and hard work.

One of the major outcomes of the conference was the targeting of six important African cities that needed to be reached with the gospel: Niamey (Niger), Khartoum (Sudan), Luanda (Angola), Kigali (Rwanda), Windhoek (Namibia) and Maputo (Mozambique), each capital cities of their respective countries. In the urban missions track, individual participants took responsibility to see that a church was planted in each of these cities before the next ACA conference. While the conference experienced some undercurrents of dissent about certain aspects of the program and activities, overall it ended on a high note of determination to extend the kingdom of God throughout the continent.

The final session of the conference was open to all who had comments or thoughts to offer. In the spirit of Isaiah's statement, "Here am I, send me," several people, including school administrators, teachers, evangelists and missionaries expressed a willingness to do whatever was necessary to follow God's call in taking the gospel to the lost.

How the Chinhoyi ACA Conference Affected the Church and Missions

In August, 1997, Wendell Broom challenged an assembly of national preachers and church leaders in southeastern Nigeria to join with Christians in East Africa in a great evangelistic church planting effort. He presented the meeting with a pledge 'to meet in the middle' of the continent by reaching out eastward from Nigeria and westward from Kenya and Ethiopia. The pledge stated that the signers would pray, study, send, and go to towns and villages planting churches to form a chain joining the two areas of the continent. The pledge was signed by 178 preachers.

Fledgling evangelistic efforts began in two of the cities targeted at Chinhoyi. Manuel d'Oliveira who had planned to open a work for the gospel in Angola was prevented by the civil war in that country. Instead he and his wife Pam moved to Maputo, Mozambique in 1998 where Manuel trains church leaders and evangelists.

Justin Rudasingwa moved to Kigali, Rwanda in 1999. Though Justin is not a full-time evangelist, it is his hope to lay the groundwork for a church plant in that city. He is hoping for others to assist him in this effort.

...And beyond

Only God knows what is in the future for the ACA conferences. For the first time at Chinhoyi the phrase 'to Africa and beyond' was used.   With news that Africans are revitalizing the churches of southern Europe in such countries as Italy, France, England and Portugal, 'our eyes were lifted up.' How God will use his African people to reach out with the gospel beyond Africa's shores, we wait with anticipation to see.

CHAPTER 9

A Historical Overview of Medical Evangelism among Churches of Christ in Africa

H. Glenn Boyd

Glenn Boyd is president emeritus of International Health Care Foundation, formerly African Christian Hospitals, an organization for which he served as president for nineteen years. Glenn and his wife, Shirley, were missionaries in Germany for sixteen years and directed the Year-in-Europe program for Pepperdine University for nine years. Glenn is an elder at the College church in Searcy, Arkansas. International Health Care Foundation, 102 N. Locust, Searcy, Arkansas 72143.

The terms "medical missions" or "medical evangelism" were, as far as I can determine, not used by missionaries of Churches of Christ in Africa until in relatively recent years. Mission work included whatever methods were appropriate at the time, whether it was the feeding of the hungry or providing pure water, clothing, or medicine. It was understood that the missionary was there to communicate the gospel of Christ. This included both physical and spiritual help.

In a study of the history of medical mission work in general, it is interesting to note that for 87 years after its establishment, the American Board of Commissioners for foreign missions did not recognize medical workers as missionaries. In 1897 the Prudential Committee, the executive body of the American Board, decided that henceforth medical personnel in the service of the Board should have the status of "missionary," not assistant missionary (Dodd, 1964, p. 25).

In the 20th century, little emphasis was given to foreign mission work among Churches of Christ until near the end of World War II. There were a few scattered missionaries in Africa, Japan, China, the Philippines, the Caribbean and a few other places, but sending missionaries was not a high priority. The missionaries who did go were not usually asked to go by a sending church but rather had to search for a church to send them. Some of these were indeed qualified as medical professionals but were not recognized as "medical missionaries."

In the following pages we will give an account of the medical works that have been established in Africa over the past 75 years. There will be some, whose names we will mention who were medically qualified and did do some medical work, but who went primarily in an evangelistic or teaching role. We will also endeavor to trace the development of the more recent efforts to establish what is now termed "medical mission work." Most of those who went to Africa as missionaries, although not trained in medicine, were constantly called upon to treat the sick. Gerry Nicks, who, with her husband, Billy, were in Nigeria from 1955 to 1960 and again in 1971-1974, wrote:

> My husband is not a doctor and I am not a nurse, so we didn't hang out a shingle in front of our house. We didn't have to, because it wasn't long until the people

were coming day and night for us to help them with their physical problems. The most common complaints were headaches, malaria, tropical ulcers, and their 'belly trouble,' which could mean a lot of things. The serious ones were accident injuries, women with delivery problems, babies with tetanus, dysentery and other life-threatening situations (Nicks, 1997, p. 77).

This is the story of almost every missionary family who has lived in Africa.

J. D. Merritt, at age 19, joined the navy as a corpsman in 1913. He was given the opportunity to train as a nurse and to serve as the "doc" on various ships until after World War I, receiving his discharge in June 1919. In the same year he married Alice Drusilla Cook, whom he had met in 1912 at Odessa Bible School.

In 1926, having had the seed for missions planted in his heart while in Bible School and having had much experience in the navy as a nurse, Merritt and his family decided to go to Africa as missionaries, sponsored by the church in Morrilton, Arkansas. They had been invited by Will Short to come to Northern Rhodesia (Zambia). Merritt was confident that his medical skills would be very useful on the mission field, and indeed they were. Although he went as an evangelist and teacher, he expected to care for the sick while in Africa. Dow told me in the latter years of his life that his medical skills had opened many doors for preaching the gospel and had been invaluable to his mission work.

SOUTHERN RHODESIA (ZIMBABWE)

The first mission work of the churches of Christ in Africa with a medical component began in Southern Rhodesia.

Forest Vale Mission

When they first arrived in Africa, Dow and Alice Merritt went to the home of missionary John Sherriff at the Forest Vale Mission near Bulawayo, Southern Rhodesia (now Zimbabwe), to spend the first month. In his book, *The Dew Breakers*, Merritt says:

> Sheriff's elder daughter, Molly...was putting in full time working on the mission. She acted as her father's secretary, taught in the school, and also had the responsibility for caring for the sick on the place. She spoke Sindebele, the local language, like a native. Molly knew that I expected to make care for the sick my work in Northern Rhodesia, so she asked me to go along with her when she made her visits to the homes of the Africans who lived on the farm, or to the school and workers' hostels. I saw sore eyes, "seven-year" itch, tropical ulcers, boils, carbuncles and malaria, ulcerated gums, abscessed ears, burns, stubbed toes and other things and began to see that the "mission doctor's" practice would be a broad one (Merritt, 1980, p. 21).

Nhowe Mission

In 1940 Mr. and Mrs. W. L. Brown acquired land from the government in Southern Rhodesia (now Zimbabwe) and moved there to establish the Nhowe Mission. Since Brown had had some training as a nurse and had also had some hospital training, he was called "Dr. Brown" and was granted a license to practice medicine and dentistry on the Mission. The Central Church of Christ in Nashville, Tennessee, contributed to their support.

The W. L. Browns' son, Dr. A. R. Brown and his wife, Ruth, of Searcy, Arkansas, went to Nhowe Mission in 1947 to establish a hospital. Since the funds did not become available for a hospital, he built a clinic and practiced medicine on the mission until 1949.

In the late 1940s, Marjorie Sewell, MD, and Ann Burns, R.N., graduates of ACC, went to the Nhowe mission to work in the clinic established by Dr. Brown. They were successful in firmly establishing the clinic, and for many years the clinic served not only as an outpatient facility but also served as a maternity clinic. They left the mission sometime in 1957.

Andrew and Claudene Connally left the United States in 1957 to go to Nyasaland (now called Malawi). They landed in Cape Town, South Africa, and then began their journey "up country." On July 27, 1957, they arrived at their first destination – Nhowe Mission. Claudene Connally, in her book, *I Walked By His Side,* relates this story:

> When we arrived at Nhowe Mission, Dr. Margie (Dr. Marjorie Sewell) took us to her clinic and showed me how to recognize the most common ailments and how to doctor them. Among them were malaria, burns, dysentery, infected eyes, scabies, tropical ulcers, snakebites and pootsies (little worms that got under the skin). She gave me a list of medicines I should get and so helped me to pack my medicine kit. I felt confident and ready." (Connally, 1995, pp. 20, 21).

In 1998 the East Point Church of Christ in Wichita, Kansas, began the oversight of a program to build and operate a new hospital at the Nhowe Mission. In April of 2000, the new hospital was dedicated, consisting of 12 buildings, including a 50-bed unit with an outpatient clinic, maternity and pediatric wards, x-ray facilities, laboratory, pharmacy, kitchen, laundry, and other facilities. Housing for the medical personnel is also planned. The hospital was named after Brian Lemons, the son of Dr. and Mrs. Steve Lemons, of Wichita, Kansas, who had planned to go there to work as a missionary doctor at some time in the future. Brian was tragically killed in an automobile accident in 1997 at the young age of 18 years. Dr. Lemons has been largely responsible for the fund-raising for the new hospital. Two Christian physicians, Drs. Gwini, a husband and wife from Bulawayo, Zimbabwe, resigned their jobs to work full-time at the hospital with several Zimbabwean nurses. Short-term rotations of American personnel are also planned for the hospital.

191

NORTHERN RHODESIA (ZAMBIA)

The initial mission efforts in Southern Rhodesia soon spread to its sister country, Northern Rhodesia.

Sinde Mission

After staying a month at Forest Vale Mission, the Dow Merritts proceeded on to Sinde Mission, established by Will and Delia Short in 1922. (The Shorts had been contacted by John Sherriff, and in 1922 they went to Northern Rhodesia and established the Sinde Mission, working with Peter Masiya, an African converted by John Sherriff.) In 1924 Ray and Zelma Lawyer joined them, and in 1926 Dow and Alice Drusilla Merritt joined them.

Kabanga Mission

Dow Merritt stayed nearly 50 years in Africa, teaching, preaching, and healing. The earlier years were spent at the Kabanga Mission, which the Merritts helped to establish, along with the Ray Lawyers, after leaving Sinde Mission in 1928. They established a school and started building a hospital at Kabanga and lived in the "hospital" building while waiting to complete their own house. Actually, the hospital was never opened, but Merritt did treat people daily in his yard. They stayed at Kabanga until 1937, and then were invited by the Scotts and Browns to move to Namwianga to work with the school, which had been established in 1932.

Alice Drusilla Merritt died of cancer in the early months of 1941. Dow stayed at Namwianga and on May 14, 1942, married Helen Pearl Scott, the daughter of Mr. and Mrs. George Scott, at Sinde Mission, with J. C. Shewmaker officiating. They left Namwianga in 1945 and went back to Kabanga mission.

Namwianga Mission

A Magistrate, the head of the government in the large Kalomo District, wanted people to come to his area to purchase farms that were for sale. He approached the W. L. Browns, who at that time were working at Kabanga mission. In 1932 the W. L. Browns purchased a 1,300-acre farm called "Shamrock," and the George Scotts purchased an adjoining farm of 3,200 acres called "Eureka." The Scotts moved to Eureka in March 1932, and the Browns moved to Shamrock in July of that same year. This was the beginning of a mission called Namwianga, which was the name of the nearest river. Namwianga was established in order to centralize the efforts of the missionaries. They agreed that this area, about three miles from Kalomo, would be the ideal place for the mission. After Dow Merritt married Helen Pearl Scott, they purchased 950 acres of land; this is the land upon which the present Namwianga mission is built. Helen Pearl's father, George Scott, told the Merritts that if they would deed their 950 acres to the mission, he would also deed his 3,200-acre farm.

> Mrs. Scott, a long time teacher in Christian schools, had had a school for missionary children, which was attended by some farm children too, at Sinde Mission. So when she got to the new place at Kalomo she had no rest in her spirit until she planned and opened a boarding school for white children on her farm. Before the year was out a ten-roomed dwelling and a neat little schoolhouse were on the farm. The new school was called Eureka School after the name of the farm (Merritt, 1980, p. 152).

In 1937 the Merritts went to the United States on furlough, and while visiting Harding College, recruited Alvin and Georgia Hobby to join them and teach at the Namwianga Mission. The Merritts returned to Northern Rhodesia in 1937 and began making bricks to build a new school. In 1938 Alvin and Georgia Hobby joined the Namwianga Mission and began teaching in the new school. After teaching 24 years there, the Hobbys returned to the United States in 1962 to enter nurses training. Alvin completed a two-year degree; and Georgia, a B.S.N. and an M.S.N. Returning to Zambia at the end of 1968, they established a clinic at the Namwianga Mission, which is still in operation today. Before they established the clinic, they went to Kabanga Mission to observe how the government clinic there was run. At that time the school at Namwianga was also expanded into a secondary school, and Alvin Hobby ran the school. The Zambian government registered both Alvin and Georgia as nurses. Today there are clinics at all three missions – Sinde, Kabanga, and Namwianga. The Sinde and Kabanga clinics are government clinics, but Namwianga clinic is a part of the mission.

The Hobbys were in Zambia for a total of about 40 years. Not only did they do medical work and teaching, but Alvin also assisted with the translation of the Bible into the Tonga language.

At the time of this writing, plans are underway to build a hospital at Namwianga on school property. Each year since 1995, a large group of medical professionals, organized by Dr. Kelly Hamby of Abilene, Texas, has traveled to Zambia to hold village clinics. This has been a great source of encouragement to local churches as well as to the people in general. Many have been converted to Christ as a direct result of this effort.

Tanzania: Chimala Mission Hospital

In 1962, after a furlough in the United States, Andrew and Claudene Connally were making their plans to return to Nyasaland (Malawi) to start a preacher training school. They received word from Eldred Echols, who was working in Tanganyika (Tanzania), that unless someone came to Tanganyika to start some kind of social work, the missionaries were going to be expelled from the country. The Church of Christ was not a recognized religion in Tanganyika, and the missionaries were there as farmers. The government officials knew that they were not really there to farm, but were church workers (Connally, 1995, p. 110). So Andrew started raising funds to build either a clinic or a school or an orphanage, or something to gain official recognition for the Church.

> Echols had told us that the old hotel at Chimala was for sale and would be the ideal place for this work. We got a price on the property and Andrew, in three days, raised enough money to secure the property, and also enough to get whatever we were going to do started. Little did we know at that time that a hospital was what was needed. We realized that soon after arriving on the field. So, that is how Chimala Mission and Hospital came to be (Connally, 1995, p. 111).

The Connallys arrived in June of 1962 with the money in hand to buy the property from the Cormacks, who were returning to their home in Scotland. It soon became apparent that a hospital was what was needed. There were no other medical facilities in the area. Connally hired an Englishman, Ken Postlethwaite, to come from Nyasaland and help with the building. He and his wife, Sheila, both became Christians and were an asset to the establishment of the work at Chimala.

Connally and Postlethwaite traveled around the country looking at hospitals, gathering ideas as to how to build the buildings. They decided to build the buildings in the form of a square with porches around the inside so that the doctors and nurses and patients could go from one section to another during the rains without getting wet. After considerable travel and gathering of materials, the buildings were built.

In June of 1962 Chimala's first physician, Dr. Jerry Mays and Shirley, along with their two children, arrived at Chimala from Lake Jackson, Texas. The buildings were not yet completed when they arrived, so they purchased a metal building in which Dr. Mays treated thousands of patients while waiting for the hospital to be completed.

The Mays stayed nine months and were followed by Dr. Ron Huddleston and Maxine, along with their children. When the Huddlestons left, Dr. Raymond Wheeler and Leona and their children went to Chimala and spent several years at the hospital. Several other physicians have served at Chimala for short periods of time, but there was a time when no American doctors were there. Wayne and Florene Smalling and their children arrived in about 1963. Wayne acted as administrator and Florene was a nurse. She often had the responsibility of the hospital with only one African doctor in attendance. They went over to work in Kenya for a time but returned to Chimala and spent many additional years.

In 1992 Dr. Frank Black and his wife, Lou Ann, of Indianapolis, Indiana, took early retirement in order to give their time to medical missions. They went to Chimala, and after spending a few months in language school learning Swahili, spent the remainder of five years working at the hospital. More than 30,000 patients are treated each year at Chimala Mission Hospital, and at the time of this writing, the hospital is 38 years old. It is a 90-bed facility and was the first hospital ever to be built by Churches of Christ of the Restoration Movement, as far as we know.

NIGERIA

The first missionaries of the Churches of Christ arrived in Nigeria in 1952. They found a fast growing church already in place, and overwhelming medical needs among all the people.

Nigerian Christian Hospital

In March of 1958, Rees and Patti Bryant joined the work at Onicha Ngwa, Nigeria, to teach in the Bible Training College. Later the Jimmy Masseys, the Doug Lawyers and others joined them. Although no medical facility had been established, the missionary wives worked tirelessly, dressing wounds, giving aspirin, doctoring all kinds of ailments. It was not unusual for the men to interrupt a class at the Bible Training College in order to take some sick person in their car to the nearest hospital, about 15 miles away. It was often too late, since the patient was not brought until all else had failed. Rees Bryant tells of his first day at Onicha Ngwa:

> March 14, 1958, was my first full day of missionary service in Nigeria. Early that morning, as I walked toward the Onicha Ngwa Bible Training College, I met two Nigerians riding a bicycle. One of them, obviously very sick, was seated on the luggage carrier. The healthy man spoke to me through an interpreter and said, "This man is my brother. He is very sick. I am afraid he will die before we reach the hospital. Will you put him in your motor and take him to the hospital? Please help this my brother!" (Bryant, 1979, p. 1).

Of course Rees took the man to the hospital, about 15 miles away, but he also began to ask himself why Christians could not provide medical help to the thousands in that area who were desperately in need of a medical facility. He began to discuss this with Billy Nicks and with others who were teaching there. In the meantime their wives set up tables at their back doors and saw up to fifty or more people almost every day.

Bill and Jerry Nicks, in their book *Short Stories of West Africa Long Remembered* (1997), relate that when they returned to the United States in 1960, the first person they visited was Dr. Henry Farrar, whom Bill had known from his youth in Nashville,

Tennessee. They got a commitment from Dr. Farrar at that time, but Dr. Farrar's uncle encouraged him to finish his surgical training before going to work in Nigeria (Nicks, 1997, p. 144).

In 1962, when Rees Bryant and his family were visiting Dr. Billy Mattox, Bryant was telling Dr. Mattox of the great medical needs of Nigeria, whereupon Dr. Mattox asked Bryant if he had ever heard of Dr. Henry Farrar. Bryant called Dr. Farrar on the phone and asked him if he would consider going to Nigeria to help establish a hospital. According to Bryant, Dr. Farrar thought for a moment and replied on the telephone, "Well, yes! I'll do it." (Bryant, taped discussion, October, 1982.) Those who know Dr. Farrar recognize this as typical of his willingness to do the Lord's work. Consequently, in 1963 the West End Church of Christ of Nashville, Tennessee, Farrar's home church, sent him to Nigeria to explore the possibilities of establishing a medical work. As a result of this encouragement, the missionaries at Onicha Ngwa began to negotiate with the village chiefs and landowners to secure property as well as their cooperation in this new venture.

After tedious negotiations between church leaders, missionaries and landowners from the three donor villages for 119 acres of land, the signing of the lease took place on Monday, October 18, 1965. The *Nashville Tennessean* reported:

> Upon hearing of the signing of the deed, the Green Lawn Church of Christ in Lubbock, Texas, immediately accepted the challenge to provide Dr. Farrar with a simple, though adequate, concrete block, tin-roofed facility in which to use his marvelous and sorely needed talents (Jim Massey , 1965).

On July 25, 1964, Dr. Henry Farrar, his wife, Grace (a nurse), and their five children arrived in Nigeria to begin a first tour of service. The West End church in Nashville, Tennessee, agreed to sponsor and support them. Two nurses, Nancy Petty and Iris Hayes, followed in 1965. Nancy was sent by the Vanleer, Tennessee, Church of Christ; and Iris, by the College Church of Christ in Lubbock, Texas.

An outpatient clinic, the first stage of the Nigerian Christian Hospital, was opened August 20, 1965, in a government rest house remodeled for this purpose. The clinic included a waiting room for 50, a small lab, a dispensary, three examination rooms, modern toilet facilities, offices, running water, and electricity. Dr. Farrar and his staff began by treating about 100 outpatients daily.

From this point onward most of the medical people who were recruited were reached through brotherhood (Churches of Christ) papers and through personal contacts made by former missionaries. Articles such as this one appeared in various papers:

> Dr. Farrar urges Christian doctors to come to Nigeria for even a stay of two months as this will provide great stability to the work. All missionaries and others agree that unimaginable good toward the spread of the gospel in West Africa will result from this effort to practice what Christians preach. Nigeria's human misery and suffering, together with its sordid superstitions and sin, provide the blackest possible backdrop against which the brilliance of the gospel shines forth in its marvelous light (Jim Massey, June, 1966).

One of the many physicians who answered this plea was Dr. R. Maurice Hood, a good friend of Dr. Farrar, who along with his wife, Jonnie, went to Nigerian Christian Hospital for the first time in 1971. He made 15 subsequent trips of about one month each over a period of 23 years, at one time staying for six months. He has served on the board of International Health Care Foundation (African Christian Hospitals) since its inception in 1972.

The first buildings at Nigerian Christian Hospital were built with the contributions of many churches in the United States. Brother F. F. Carson, a highly respected preacher, began his fund-raising campaign throughout the United States. Others joined him in soliciting contributions. In November of 1965, Houston Ezell, a Nashville contractor and dedicated Christian, went to Nigeria to supervise the building of the new buildings. Construction plans for the first two years included the following facilities: laboratory-x-ray-operating room building; maternity unit, five beds; isolation unit, five beds; male ward, 30 beds; female ward, 30 beds; kitchen-laundry building; and a mortuary.

The Biafran war, which began in May of 1967 in the eastern section of southern Nigeria, forced the missionaries of Churches of Christ, including the medical personnel at Nigerian Christian Hospital, to be evacuated in July.

Dr. Henry Farrar related that the hospital was occupied by military forces and used for the care of the wounded and as a distribution center for food during most of the Biafran war. Toward the end of the conflict everyone fled the area, leaving the hospital buildings empty for just a short while. During this time, looters took nearly everything from the hospital. The buildings were stripped of wiring and everything removable. The walls were full of bullet holes and were left in such a condition that everything would have to be rebuilt (Henry Farrar, 1980).

About six months after the war, Dr. Farrar was able to return to Nigeria by working with the Kaiser Foundation, a humanitarian organization sending doctors and nurses to Port Harcourt to help in the aftermath of the war. On weekends Dr. Farrar was able to take a taxi out to the hospital to begin to re-establish it. In October 1971, his family joined him, and in December they moved back to Onicha Ngwa, where they stayed until May 1973. The Christian Council of Nigeria assisted with the rebuilding of the hospital by donating $40,000. Dr. Farrar wrote the following to the Gospel Advocate:

> The civil war in Nigeria has been over for a year now, and rebuilding is going along. Some five hundred Churches of Christ here are in many ways stronger than ever. The poverty in some areas is worse than before the war, but the brethren continue to spread the gospel though we have few missionaries. Nigerian Christian Hospital was damaged and completely looted in the war, but through the generosity of many brethren, rebuilding is proceeding nicely. The patients have to be on the floor now, but we have beds on order from a local maker (Henry Farrar, January 14, 1971, p.30).

The beds soon came and the hospital was constantly full with patients needing treatment for malnutrition and other diseases that resulted from the war. From the time the Farrars left in 1973 until Dr. Robert Whittaker of England came in 1975, there was no full-time doctor at Nigerian Christian Hospital. Nurse Nancy Petty, who was one of the founding nurses of the hospital, had evacuated to Cameroon during the war. She returned to Nigerian Christian Hospital after the war and was the medical officer in charge for the two years after Dr. Farrar left in 1973. There were some visiting doctors from time to time, but the burden of the responsibility was upon her.

In 1975 Dr. Robert Whittaker arrived and remained at the hospital for nearly three years on his first tour. He returned in 1985 and has continually served the hospital as chief medical officer since that time. Numerous other physicians and nurses have served over the years, some for as long as two or three years. Several missionary administrators have also served throughout the years. It is worthy of note, however, that Dr. Farrar and his wife continue to go each year to work in the hospital for one month, usually taking a number of medical professionals with them. They have been making these annual trips since the early 1970s. Drs. Farrar and Whittaker and other medical missionaries at Nigerian Christian Hospital have established many congregations in the surrounding area of the hospital by accepting invitations from patients to come to their villages to preach. One of the larger congregations of the entire area, the church at Etungua, was established by Dr. Farrar.

The hospital has 100 beds, approximately 165 employees, and serves at least 30,000 patients each year. Two evangelists serve in the hospital all day each day, visiting and praying with patients, counseling, visiting family, and teaching.

In 1972, after a futile attempt to find a church to oversee the program of the Nigerian Christian Hospital, Rees Bryant, Dr. F. W. Mattox and Dr. Jesse Paul formed a non-profit corporation called African Christian Hospitals Foundation. This organization has been responsible for facilitating the work of the Nigerian Christian Hospital and other medical facilities in Nigeria, in Ghana and other places. In 1998 the name was changed to International Health Care Foundation (African Christian Hospitals).

Palmer Memorial Hospital

Lucien and Ida Palmer and children, Patsy and Eddie, were in Nigeria from 1954 to the end of 1957 when they returned home due to the illness of their son, Eddie. Lucien continued to make regular trips back to Nigeria for many years, serving at times up to six months. In 1984 the African Christian Schools Foundation, at the bidding of the churches among the Efik people, agreed to establish a clinic/hospital in the village of Ikot Usen, the village of C. A. O. Essien, who had already established numerous congregations in Nigeria even before 1950.

When the clinic was to be opened in 1986, the people of Ikot Usen area insisted that it be named in honor of Lucien Palmer, who had lived in Ikot Usen on his first tour to Nigeria, and who has remained close to the people through the years. He also was the primary fund-raiser for the construction of the buildings. The clinic/hospital was therefore named the "Palmer Memorial Clinic/Hospital."

The African Christian Schools Foundation made a special appeal to African Christian Hospitals Foundation on May 2, 1991, to take over the ownership of the property and the complete operation of the clinic/hospital. The official transfer of authority and all properties was made on December 7, 1991.

Plans for the hospital were drawn up, and the buildings were built, including an out-patient area, a surgical room, an in-patient area, a large storage area, a lab, an office block, a generator building, a duplex for hospital staff, and a doctor's house. Much credit goes to John Beckloff, who oversaw the entire project, making the dedication possible on June 22, 1996. The Palmer Memorial Hospital serves in an area where there are more than 200 villages without a medical facility.

Akwabia Hospital

Akwabia Hospital was established in 1996 by Moses Akpanudo, Ph.D., under the oversight of the Church of Christ at Mt. Morris, Michigan. In 1995, in an effort to establish a private Christian university, Dr. Akpanudo established the African College of Management. One of the requirements of the Nigerian government for a private university is that a hospital be built. The hospital is located on the new campus.

At the present time there are 13 beds, and plans are underway to add a children's ward, a laboratory, and a maternity ward. The hospital, though small, is already having an impact on the community, and souls are being won to Christ through this ministry.

Cameroon

Phillip Eichman, in his book *Medical Missions Among the Churches of Christ* tells of the medical missions program that was begun in Cameroon, West Africa, in October 1968 when Drs. Ken Yearwood and David Willbanks and nurses Charlie Bridges and Iris Hayes moved to the city of Kumba. They had intended to work at the Nigerian Christian Hospital but were unable to do so because of the Biafran war. There were two permanent facilities in Cameroon, a clinic building at Ekombe Bonji and a building used for storage of supplies for the mobile clinics, located in Kumba. Regular mobile clinics were conducted in surrounding villages. Among the physicians who worked at the clinic were Dr. Dan Blazer, Dr. Mark Carnes, and Dr. Mike Kelly, along with a number of nurses, including Nancy Petty (Eichman, 1999, p.26).

The Averill Avenue Church of Christ in Flint, Michigan, assumed the sponsorship of the work in the early 1980s. In the late 1980s, due to pressures from the government to expand the clinic work into a hospital, they were forced to discontinue the work in Cameroon altogether.

Liberia

In April 1970 Dr. Tom Drinnen and family and nurse, Sarah Young, opened a medical clinic at Felleh Lar, Liberia. The clinic was supported by the Church of Christ in Decatur, Georgia, and the Arlington Church of Christ in Knoxville, Tennessee. Not only did Dr. Drinnen and Miss Young operate the clinic but they also trained primary health care workers, who were able to continue the work after Drinnen and his family left in 1973. An American nurse remained for about one year after the Drinnens' departure.

One of the works of the clinic was to conduct mobile clinics in surrounding villages. Dr. Drinnen spent much of his time in evangelism, along with missionary Bill Nicks, who had intended to return to Nigeria to work but came with his family to Liberia in 1969 because of the civil war in Nigeria. The Nicks family left Liberia in 1971 and returned to Nigeria to assist in the rebuilding of the work at Onicha Ngwa, where they had formerly worked.

Ghana

During and following the great drought in Ghana in 1982-83, the Churches of Christ in the United States under the leadership of the White's Ferry Road Church of Christ in West Monroe, Louisiana, gathered funds and sent many containers of food, clothing and medicine to Ghana. The Ghanaian churches distributed these supplies without discrimination throughout the country. This made a positive impression on the people of Ghana, especially on the government officials, who were also recipients. In 1984 Jerry Reynolds, former missionary to Ghana, asked me to go with him to Ghana to explore the possibilities of starting a medical work there. We visited the Ministry of Health, the World Health Organization, the Christian Hospital Association of Ghana (CHAG), and the headquarters of UNICEF. In each case we were encouraged to come to Ghana to assist with medical care. Although a government plan had been developed for providing medical care for all, the five-year-old program had scarcely begun. They had no funds to provide medicines, no funds for transportation, and too few medical workers in the entire country.

Kumasi Clinic

The board of African Christian Hospitals gave approval to proceed, and we began planning for the work. The White's Ferry Road Church of Christ agreed to commit the remaining funds from the food relief program to this work, so plans were made to open a clinic in Kumasi, the second largest city in Ghana. A large building, which had been used as a residence for staff members of the Ghana Bible College, needed only to be renovated to serve as a clinic. A center for training primary health care workers was built, and three apartments were prepared on Samuel Obeng's property to house the medical team. Application was submitted to the immigration office for a visa quota for the work, and the recruiting of a medical team in the United States was begun.

By September of 1987 a team of 10 workers had moved to Kumasi to begin the work. These were Royce and Cindy Reynolds, former missionaries to Ghana, Bob and Beth Williams, Jerry and Fran Thornton, John and Linda Glover, Jackie Willits and Mary Ann Brock. All of the women were nurses with years of experience, and the men were all capable in various areas.

Since its beginning, many missionary nurses and administrators have worked at the Kumasi clinic, along with about 20 Ghanaian employees, including an evangelist/chaplain, who works full-time in the clinic.

Yendi Clinic

Beginning in 1987 a water-drilling project in Ghana was started, sponsored by the Church of Christ in Traverse City, Michigan. With the encouragement of the water-drilling crew, it was decided that African Christian Hospitals Foundation should have a clinic in Yendi to assist with the tremendous health-care needs of that area. A clinic building was built on a four-acre piece of property, and the launching of the clinic took place in June of 1996. Today there are four missionary families living there, running the clinic and holding regular mobile clinics in the many villages surrounding Yendi, along with doing extensive evangelistic work. There are six Ghanaian evangelists living in Yendi who work with the water project and with the clinic project. The American families there are Royce and Cindy Reynolds, Richard and Linda Benskin and two children, Jerry and Fran Thornton, and Dan and Brenda McVey and their two children, who have worked in Ghana since 1982. More than 200 churches have been established in the north of Ghana as a result of the medical and the water-drilling work. In January 2000 the well-drilling operation became a part of International Health Care Foundation.

Nairobi, Kenya

In 1998 a clinic was established at the Rainbow Church of Christ in Nairobi, Kenya, as an outreach of that church. Nurse Jan Linck, of Tulsa, Oklahoma, spent about one year in Nairobi to help get the clinic established and running. It is now operated entirely by Kenyan personnel.

Conclusions

Medical missions is now recognized as an important avenue for evangelism. In recent years universities, Bible schools, and seminaries have begun to offer medical missions as a discipline. Harding University School of Nursing is currently considering offering medical missions as a minor. Mission teams are being encouraged to include a "medical component" to their teams. A team of eight families in Jinga, Uganda , has a physician as one of its team members, which has proven to be a great blessing to their work. Additionally, Dr. Ellen Little joined the mission team in Fort Portal, Uganda in April 2001.

Appeal

Opportunities for serving as medical missionaries are abundant today. It is my prayer that increasing numbers of medical professionals will step forward and serve for some period of time in Africa.

Many countries in Africa are still in the developing stages and are in dire need of assistance in delivering medical care to the masses. Some statistics tell us that 60% of all medical professionals in most developing countries stay in the large cities, while 80% of the people live in small villages and live on subsistence wages. The governments of most of the African countries do not have funds for proper distribution of medical care to the people and are therefore favorable toward any kind of humanitarian assistance. They also allow the missionaries to evangelize freely.

There are at least three avenues of missionary service for medical professionals: giving long-term service at one of the mission hospitals, going for one month each year to serve in one of the hospitals, or going on short-term campaigns. Unfortunately, we have had very few long-term physicians in the history of our work. Dr. Whittaker is the exception, having spent about 18 years to date at the Nigerian Christian Hospital. We need more men and women who will commit their lives to such work. Dr. Whittaker takes advantage of many opportunities to preach the gospel in villages on weekends. Many congregations have been established through the years as a direct result of the hospital work.

Nurses, laboratory technicians and pharmacists are also needed for long-term work in most of the clinics and hospitals mentioned in this chapter. For those who cannot go for a longer period, there is always the need for people to go for one or two months. It would be a blessing if we had physicians, nurses, and other medical practitioners going every month of the year to work in one of the hospitals or clinics.

Other needs include administrative personnel, accountants, bookkeepers, repairmen, carpenters, and electricians. Administrative personnel, accountants and bookkeepers are needed immediately for long-term work. Repairmen, carpenters, and electricians are always useful, especially on short-term trips. For those who plan to go for long-term work, a degree or diploma of some kind is usually required. The governments want to know that the individual is capable of teaching a national citizen to do the job. Those who go for short terms simply enter the country with a visitor's visa. For for further information and contacts, please see the bibliography.

It has been 19 years since I first became involved in the promotion of medical evangelism. In our works in Africa we have seen thousands of people helped through medical aid and the drilling of fresh-water wells. We have seen doors of opportunity for spreading the gospel of Christ open because of the compassionate care given to hurting people. Many people have been led to Christ and many new congregations of the Lord's church have been planted as a result of this work. When we consider all of the works of medical evangelism throughout the world, it is obvious that the Lord is using this avenue to reach many.

The medical evangelism seminars held in Dallas, Texas, each January have grown from a small gathering 18 years ago to more than 400 people, assembling to discuss what is being done and what needs to be done in medical evangelism. Many are attending the seminars to tell of their experiences, while others are looking for opportunities to serve. Organizations such as Partners in Progress, Health Talents International, Central American Missions and International Health Care Foundation are constantly recruiting medical professionals to work with them. Medical works are being carried on in numerous countries today. Many of our missionaries would not be allowed to live and work in their selected fields were it not for the medical or humanitarian aid that they are providing. Organizations such as Healing Hands International, in Nashville, Tennessee, and in Abilene, Texas; RAPHA, in Fort Worth, Texas; and CURE, in Fort Smith, Arkansas, are working together with missionaries to provide needed medical and relief supplies to their various governments.

It is my conviction that increasing numbers of Christians will decide to use their talents and their professional training to serve in this way. May the Lord be exalted and glorified in all that is done in His name.

WORKS CITED

Boyd, H. Glenn (1983). *A History of Nigerian Christian Hospital and the Spiritual, Medical and Economic Impact it Has Had on the Three Villages who Contributed the Property.* Unpublished manuscript, Trinity Evangelical Divinity School.

Boyd, H. Glenn (1988). *A Model Program For Primary Health Care Delivery in GhanaWest Africa For The African Christian Hospitals Foundation (Churches of Christ).* Unpublished doctoral thesis, Trinity Evangelical Divinity School.

Bryant, Rees (July 1979). *Medical Missions: A Justification.* Unpublished manuscript, Fuller School of World Missions.

—.(personal communication, October, 1982).

Connally, Claudene (1995). *I Walked By His Side.* Seagoville, TX: Connally Publications.

Dodd, Edward M. (1964). *The Gift of the Healer.* New York: Friendship Press.

Echols, Eldred (1989). *Wings of the Morning, The Saga of an African Pilgram.* Fort Worth, TX: Eldred Echols.

Eichman, Phillip (1999). *Medical Missions among the Churches of Christ,* Gallipolis, OH.

Farrar, Henry (1971, January 14). Nigerian Christian Hospital Needs Physicians. *Gospel Advocate,* 30.
Farrar, Henry (personal communication, 1980).

Hood, R. Maurice (1989). *Please Doctor: A Christian Surgeon in Iboland.* Dallas, TX: Gospel Teachers Publications.

Massey, Jim (1965, November 12). Nigerian Evangelism to be Broadened Through Medical Benevolence. *The Nashville Tennessean.*

— (1966, June). Farrar Urges Doctors to Serve. *The Christian Chronicle.*

Merritt, Dow (1980). *The Dew Breakers.* Winona, MS: J. C. Choate Publications.

Mitchell, Donna (1995). *Among the People of the Sun – Our Years in Africa.* Winona, MS: J. C. Choate Publications.

Nicks, Bill & Nicks, Gerry (1997). *Short Stories of West Africa Long Remembered.* Winona, MS: J.C. Choate Publications.

Rowe, Myrtle (1968). *Silhouettes of Life.* Searcy, AR.

ADDITIONAL SOURCES OF INFORMATION USED

Brown, A. R., M.D. (September 2000). Personal telephone conversations. Dr. Brown spent his teenage years with his parents, the W. L. Browns in Africa, and was there as a medical doctor from 1947-1949.

Merritt, Roy (September 2000). E-mail exchange. Merritt is the son of Dow Merritt and his wife, Helen Pearl, born and raised in Zambia and currently working there.

Hobby, Georgia (September 2000). Personal telephone conversations. The Hobbys spent 40 years in Zambia at Namwianga Mission. Mrs. Hobby lives in Searcy, Arkansas.

SOME ORGANIZATIONS DOING MEDICAL WORK AFFILIATED WITH CHURCHES OF CHRIST

C.U.R.E., c/o Bob Fisher, MD, in Fort Smith, Arkansas, (Tel) 501-452-2852.

Healing Hands International, 208 Space Park Drive, Nashville, Tennessee 37211,   (Tel) 615-832-2000.

Healing Hands International in Texas, at 949 South Judge Ely Blvd, Abilene, Texas 79601.

Health Talents International, 2624 Buttewoods Drive, P.O. Box 59871, Birmingham, Alabama 35259-9871, (Tel) 205-991-9939.

International Health Care Foundation, 102 North Locust, Searcy, Arkansas 72143   (Tel) 501-268-9511.

Latin American Missions, 1601 E. Park Avenue, P.O. Box 3799, Valdosta, Georgia 31604-3799, (Tel) 229-242-1069.

Manna International, PO Box 3507, Redwood City, California, (Tel) 415- 365-3663.

Partners in Progress, P.O. Box 150, Little Rock, Arkansas 72203, (Tel) 501-374-5761.

RAPHA International, 2313 Ludelle Street, Fort Worth, Texas 76105,   (Tel) 817-536-3383.

CHAPTER 10

Christian Education in Africa

"TEACH US": THE LINEAGE AND DEVELOPMENT OF
AFRICAN CHRISTIAN SCHOOLS FOUNDATION

Henry Huffard

*Henry Huffard was taken to Nigeria by his mission-
ary parents, Elvis and Emily Huffard, in 1953. He served
in Nigeria as a teacher and administrator at Nigerian
Christian Bible College (1983 to 1991) under the oversight
of Palisades Church of Christ in Birmingham, Alabama.
He was then appointed President of African Christian
Schools Foundation (1991 to the present). Henry also serves
as an elder at the Hillsboro Church of Christ in Nashville.
Contact: acsf@juno.com.*

Over fifty years have passed since C. A. O. Essien sent his
request to the United States for teachers to come to Nigeria and
ground a fledgling church in the Word of God. So much has been
accomplished, more than he or anyone else in those days could have
imagined. And yet, as glowing as the past has been, the future of
Christian education in Africa may be even brighter!

Providence Redirects Focus

In 1944, when Lawrence Avenue Church of Christ in Nashville,
Tennessee prayerfully embarked on a ministry through the mail, it

was not their intention to target Africa (Goff, 1964, pp. 2-5). Their correspondence program grew out of a desire to encourage faithfulness among men and women in the military while serving in Europe. Anna-Maria Braun, German founder of the Internationales Korrespondenz-Buro in Munich, obtained a copy of Lawrence Avenue's course and liked it. It's author, Gordon Turner, who was both preacher and elder at Lawrence Avenue, capitalized on Braun's interest. He sent stickers to Braun advertising the Bible course, which she placed on envelopes of all the various pen pals in her organization. One of these envelopes may have gone to Nigeria and changed the destiny of that nation.

C. A. O. Essien was intensely interested in studying the Bible. He learned of the Lawrence Avenue course through Braun, enrolled in it and completed it with top marks. He and a friend baptized one another. In a short period, he reported an unbelievable number of congregations. In 1950, Boyd Reese and Eldred Echols, missionaries to Southern Rhodesia and South Africa, respectively, made a special trip to Nigeria to investigate Essien's report. They arrived with skepticism but left convinced (Goff, 1964, pp. 6-9).

In the extensive Reese-Echols Report, they write, "Several thousand native Africans have, without the presence of a white man, fought their way out of denominationalism and have found the church of God. This is without precedent in Africa . . . In Nigeria, the initiative was taken by the people themselves when they requested the Bible Correspondence Course from Lawrence Avenue. Their fervor is evidenced by the fact that in three and a half short years they have established more congregations than we have in the whole of Southern Africa after thirty years of labor by white evangelists" (Goff, 1964, p. 10).

Essien Challenges Lawrence Avenue

Essien was aware that his fellow church leaders were not adequately prepared to meet the needs of young congregations. He didn't ask for foreigners to come and take over leadership. His request had a prophetic tone. "We can teach our people, but we need teaching ourselves. Send men to TEACH US, and we shall take Nigeria for the truth" (Goff, 1964, p. 8).

What follows in the history of Churches of Christ in Nigeria is the fulfillment of Essien's dream. Year after year, Nigerian men and women are trained for lives of Christian service in the classroom, during activities with local churches and on evangelistic campaigns. According to statistics compiled at the Africans Claiming Africa for Christ conference 2000, Nigeria has 2,850 Churches of Christ with 265,000 members (Berryman, 2000). This is one-third of the church membership of the entire African continent. God has richly blessed the restoration movement in Nigeria using Christian education as a tool.

Americans Respond to Nigeria's Requests for Schools

The first missionaries from American churches of Christ agreed with Essien regarding the need to train evangelists. The first four American resident missionary families arrived in Nigeria from December 1952 to December 1953. They were the Jimmy Johnsons, the Howard Hortons, the Eugene Pedens and the Elvis Huffards. Horton made a quick trip back to his overseers after six months on the field. From the four issues he urgently brought to their attention, one was a training school, one had to do with opportunities to manage village primary schools and another was the need for more missionaries, especially someone qualified to manage schools. He returned to the field encouraged and ready to go forward (Goff, 1964, pp. 22-26).

217

The Bible Training School

The missionaries' first attempt to train preachers was a three-month course of study. It was soon considered inadequate. In February 1954, the Ukpom Bible College was founded. When Ukpom village chiefs saw how aggressively the school was being developed, they increased the size of the land made available to the mission from fifteen to twenty acres. All four American missionaries taught at the school, two at a time on alternating days. This left half of the men free at any time to go on appointments and to see to the necessities of life.

Approximately thirty men were admitted annually to the two-year program. Classes were taught in English, the official (adopted) language of Nigeria. Before long, some Ukpom graduates started three-month Bible training programs in the Efik (regional) language. At one time, as many as fifty-seven such programs had 493 students. These smaller centers made up a "feeder system" for the more extensive program at Ukpom (Broom, 1970, p. 216). As one would imagine, at this time of amazing opportunity, more emphasis was placed on evangelism and church planting than on nurturing young congregations to maturity (Broom, 1970, p. 213).

Howard Horton was the school's first director (1954). From him, the mantle was passed to Lucien Palmer (1954-56), Sewell Hall (1956-58), Eugene Peden (1958-59), Glenn Martin (1959-61), Dan Gibson (1961-63), Phil Dunn (1964-65), John Beckloff (1965-66) and Robert Dixon (1967) (Broom, 1970, p. 130, Appendix A). No one blindly endorses everything that took place during these formative years of Bible training. But it should be noted here that in reports, to a man, every Nigerian and American who had first-hand experience stresses that the Ukpom Bible College was urgently needed and was responsible for much of the soundness and phenomenal growth in Churches of Christ prior to Nigeria's civil war.

Village Schools

In addition to C. A. O. Essien's appeal for adult education, Eldred Echols gives a practical reason for missionary involvement in the education of children. After a full explanation of the usual way mission agencies cooperate with village schools, he says, "This is such an established pattern that the people generally have no confidence in a religious body which will not assist them in getting schools. Theoretically, the church has full choice in whether or not its missionaries concern themselves with education. In actual fact, it is impossible to make any great headway without having schools" (Echols 1951 (d):3).

In a report, Howard Horton describes Elvis Huffard, who was selected to establish and to manage village schools, "Brother Huffard's ability, training and experience have combined to enable him to accomplish amazing results for the time he has been here. . . We all feel that the schools offer one of the richest opportunities of the work. Several hundred school children, even thousands later, can be handed to Brother Huffard for complete religious guidance, and that in schools supported by public funds" (Goff, 1964, pp.24-25).

Management passed in succession from Huffard (1954) to Lucien Palmer (1955-56), Leonard Johnson (1956-57), Eugene Peden (1957-58), Joe Cross (1959), John Featherstone (1960-61) and John Beckloff (1961-1967). By the end of the Huffard and Palmer years, eleven schools with an enrollment of approximately 2,500 were being taught Bible daily, primarily by graduates of the Ukpom Bible College. John Beckloff was forced to leave when civil war broke out. He was able to look back over six years during which he managed ten Christian schools with a consistent enrollment of

3,000. During his years he also arranged for Ukpom graduates to teach Bible to 3,000 more students who were in public schools that were not managed by him.

Another observation from Horton gives the reason for expanding from primary schools to a secondary school. "It has been saddening to see our students finish standard six (8th grade), and then enter high school under sectarian domination. I am convinced that we are already so late in this field that we may need to leap ahead very quickly into the next level of education" (Goff, 1964, p. 57). In 1962, the village of Ukpom gave the mission another eighty-five acres to build Nigerian Christian Secondary School (NCSS). The school was opened in 1964. From its meager opening enrollment of sixty, the school grew to over 500 by 1968, when its first class graduated.

African Christian Schools Foundation is born

When Lucien Palmer returned from his second tour of duty in 1958, it was decided that the needs of the village schools could best be met by an American school board. Former missionaries Horton, Huffard and Palmer and two successful Christian businessmen, Roger Church and Miles Ezell, Sr., were the charter members of Nigeria Christian Schools Foundation (Goff, 1964, p. 56). The foundation was incorporated in the state of Tennessee in 1959. Its name was changed to African Christian Schools Foundation (ACSF) in 1967, and its charter was broadened to include activities such as medical and benevolent aid.

The number of men on the board soon increased to nineteen. In its first five years, ACSF primarily served as proprietor of the eleven primary schools. The Nigerian government paid the bulk of the operating costs. The foundation's first financial challenge was raising funds to construct the first seven buildings of NCSS in 1963 (Goff, 1964, p. 57-58).

War Disrupts Schools, Validates Strength of the Church

In 1967 the southeastern portion of Nigeria, where the churches of Christ were strongest, seceded from Nigeria. Biafra, the newly formed state, suffered terrible losses of life and property. During the conflict, the Church of Christ lost one hundred thirty church buildings and about four thousand members, including twelve former students of Ukpom Bible College (Church, 2000). Resources in the schools were plundered. Houses on the Ukpom campus were seriously abused while being used as living quarters by troops.

During these difficult times, David Anako and others did their best to hold onto mission assets and keep programs going as long as possible. Critics thought the church would stop growing during this time because American funds were totally cut off. Nothing could be farther from the truth. Remarkably strong church leaders, in place after twenty years of solid groundwork, kept the movement going and growing.

Postwar Era Forces Change

Soon after the war ended, the Nigerian government confiscated the primary and secondary schools of all mission agencies. Since ACSF no longer had control of village schools or Nigerian Christian Secondary School, it redirected its efforts toward building the Christian Trade Technical School in Oyubia (1972). Three years later, when the Nigerian government took that school as well, printing presses were moved from Oyubia to Ukpom, and later, to Nung Udo Itak to start the Christian Printing and Distribution Center.

The Ukpom Bible College was not taken over by the government, but it could not return to business as usual. Immediately after the war, when U. S. citizens could not obtain visas to enter Nigeria, a Canadian, Ralph Perry, was asked to serve at Ukpom. Based on the fact that Canada and Nigeria were British Commonwealth countries, they had more open immigration policies. When Perry arrived, David Anako was principal, and Andrew Isiip and S. P. Ekanem were teachers. Anako (1970-72) was followed by Perry (1972-73), Isiip (1973), Okon Mkpong (1973-74) and Monday Akpakpan (1974-1978). These men worked hard to restore the Bible college to its former status. Ekanem and Isiip earned college degrees in the United States during the Mkpong and Akpakpan years and later came back to serve again in the administration of the school.

Sponsorship of the Ukpom Bible College moved with Lawrence Avenue members as they started the Concord Road Church of Christ. Later, Waverly-Belmont Church of Christ became the sponsor. In 1977 full responsibility for the operation of the Bible college was transferred to the African Christian Schools Foundation. After losing the school in Oyubia, never again did ACSF become involved in village schools. For the next ten years, all its attention was focused on the Ukpom Bible College and the Christian Printing and Distribution Center.

When Isiip returned with his graduate degree in 1978, he met with church leaders to determine the future direction of the Bible college. At their suggestion, more secular and commercial classes were added to the curriculum. Younger applicants were admitted. The school became similar in many ways to Nigerian Christian Secondary School across the road, which was the school the government took from ACSF. Unlike NCSS, the Bible college was controlled and staffed by members of the Church of Christ, generally had higher standards and offered extra Bible courses. For several years, the brotherhood in Nigeria used the Bible college to circumvent the government's actions to prevent them from having a Christian junior and senior high school for their children.

Focus Turns to Higher Education and Expansion

In the 1980s, the Nigerian government began to realize how much the mission organizations provided for village school development. The government offered to return schools to their former owners, but by then, the campuses were in a bad state of repair. Having been burned by government actions in the past, few agencies responded to the offer. But one good result of the government's more conciliatory attitude was their permission for mission agencies to have a greater influence over their former schools. Even if an agency refused to take back its schools, it was allowed to choose principals, Bible teachers, and chaplains.

In 1983, John Beckloff and Andrew Isiip revived the preacher training track of the Ukpom Bible College. It started with only twelve students. Nigerian Christian Bible College (NCBC) became the new name of the post-secondary program. Because the level of education in the pew had reached a higher level, especially in cities, it was thought that a two-year, college-level program was needed for the pulpit to keep pace. The Nigerian government insisted that all post-secondary institutions be affiliated with recognized universities. In 1988, NCBC became an affiliate of the University of Calabar, a federal university. Graduates of the affiliated program receive the Diploma in Religious Education, which enables them to teach Bible and one other subject in Nigerian secondary schools.

The University of Calabar had initial input into course offerings and annually reviews final exams, but never imposes its views on course content or doctrine. This arrangement suits ACSF and adds prestige to the three-year diploma program. Semester hours taken at NCBC are transferable to other universities within and out-side Nigeria.

Because leaders at NCBC were able to regain more influence over programs for youths at NCSS and because more room was needed for the two adult programs (ministerial and university affili-ated), the Bible college secondary programs were phased out in 1995. Annual adult enrollment at NCBC ranged between 160 and 200 in the 1990's, making it one of the greatest assemblies of Bible majors among Churches of Christ anywhere in the world. NCBC is on the verge of gaining approval through its affiliate to confer its own bachelors degree in religious studies.

A Greater Partnership is Emphasized

African Christian Schools Foundation has shown remarkable continuity over the years. Three of the first five board members; Elvis Huffard, Lucien Palmer and Roger Church (Chairman); are still on the board today. John Beckloff is very active administrative-ly. ACSF's twenty-two members average eighteen years of board participation. Five are elders and five others are former elders, all of different churches. In its forty-two-year history, ACSF has had only three presidents: Lucien Palmer, Willie Cato and Henry Huffard (Church, 2000). Those who have been on the board the longest marvel at the unity, cooperation and singleness of purpose which have characterized the organization from the day it was established.

While continuity and harmony produce stability, they can also bring about stagnation. Since ACSF's work started when Nigeria was a colony of Britain, it would have been easy for early pioneers to continue in a colonial mindset. Fortunately, this has not been the case. As Nigerians excelled in scholastic accomplishment and in leadership, the unequal partnership became more equal.

Just as some of the pioneering missionaries are still active in

ACSF's work, their early Nigerian co-workers are also still active on the field. Through the eighties, Nigerians were made the heads of all programs. Until 1997, an administrative committee of Nigerians and Americans ran NCBC. Then Dr. S. P. Ekanem was given the title Provost and made head of the school. Andrew Isiip moved west to pioneer again in 1999 as academic director of West Nigeria Christian College. Other key Nigerian personnel of the past, such as Dr. Timothy Akpakpan and Nelson Isonguyo, continue to head programs of the Bible college in Ukpom.

Nigeria has such a wealth of leaders that many organized successful Bible training efforts of their own without the help of ACSF. Graduates of the Bible college in Ukpom who became such leaders include Okon Mkpong (NCI, Nigeria), Samuel Obeng (GBC, Ghana), Stephen Okoronkwo (NCS, Nigeria), D. N. Elangwe (Cameroon), Fred Ayasa (RSOP, Nigeria), David J. David (CRS, Nigeria), Benjamin Ogbeifun (Nigeria), Koffi and Adjayi (Togo) and Prince Sylvanus, Chukwu Emmanuel, Chris Nnoduechi and Barnabas Okoro (ESSP, Nigeria). The educational efforts of these men have had a great impact for the Lord in the regions they serve(d).

There is no greater example of the shift from American control to partnership than ACSF's most recent school project. A group of planners from western Nigeria chose four governing board members and ACSF chose three for West Nigeria Christian College. The hopes and aspirations of the region are put forward by the local members, and the educational expertise is supplied by the ACSF members. All are committed to promoting the cause of Christ. The 2000-01 enrollment in this new school is thirty-one.

The mission statement of African Christian Schools Foundation is "to provide, through African partnership, centers of educational excellence to equip nationals for Christian service, leadership and evangelism in Africa."

With God's Help, Let Us Build on a Great Past

Over 1,300 ministers have graduated from programs at Ukpom. It is hoped that the new school in western Nigeria will yield comparable numbers with as great a positive impact on the growth of the church. Thousands attend Ukpom's annual lectureship, and hundreds attend their seminars each year. Hundreds obey the gospel each semester as student preachers put their coursework into practice. When students graduate, their zeal for evangelism continues.

As more churches are being planted throughout Africa at a rate as high as three per day, one wonders who will nurture them to maturity. At one time, it was thought by some that Nigeria would be the springboard for the conversion of the rest of Africa (Goff, 1964, p. 52). Nigeria is the most populous nation in Africa and has spread the gospel to many West and Central African counties. But successful schools in other countries are benefiting the cause of Christ, too, and have been for many years. In addition to all of these, more partnerships for Christian education may be needed to supply the great need for evangelists and church leaders. In a relatively new work, ACSF is helping John D'Alton conduct daily classes with several students in Namibia. In keeping with its mission statement, ACSF is seeking expansion into other African countries where church members have few Bible training opportunities. As the epicenter of Christianity moves from Europe and America to Africa, there is ample evidence that well-trained ministers of Christ are every bit as needed there as they are in the United States.

WORKS CITED

Berryman, Mark (May, 2000). *Status of Churches of Christ in Sub-Saharan Africa, May 2000.* Report compiled at the ACA conference, Johannesburg.

Broom, Wendell Wright (1970). *Growth of Churches of Christ among Ibibios of Nigeria.* Unpublished master's thesis, Fuller Theological Seminary.

Church, Roger T. (September, 2000). *A History of African Christian Schools Foundation,* Unpublished research from ACSF board minutes.

Goff, Reda C. (1964). *The Great Nigeria Mission.* Nashville, TN: Lawrence Avenue Church of Christ and Nigeria Christian Schools Foundation.

THE NAIROBI GREAT COMMISSION SCHOOL

William (Bill) Searcy

Bill Searcy has done mission work in the Soviet Union, Belize, and Kenya. He currently serves as both chairman of the board of directors and registrar of the Nairobi Great Commission School, wsearcy@africaonline.co.ke.

The vision for Nairobi Great Commission School (NGCS) began in 1988 when national leaders of the Kenya Churches of Christ together with some of the missionaries saw the need for further training church leaders. We realized that the church could not move forward into the 21st century without well-trained and equipped leaders. Excellent training had been done on the local church level and in provincial areas. Nevertheless, it was time to move a step beyond to a higher level of education in Bible, Missions, Church Ministry and Leadership that would balance quality academics with practical experiential training. This training would give national church leaders credibility as well as equip them for the task of planting and maturing new churches in Kenya, East Africa, the continent, and beyond.

These national church leaders and missionaries spent 1989 discussing these ideas with other church leaders and missionaries throughout the country. From those meetings what is now NGCS was established and opened in January of 1990. NGCS was legally registered with the Kenyan government in 1995 as a sub-branch of East African Development Ministries, a non-governmental organization. NGCS started the first term with ten full-time students and twenty-two part-time students. The school had an international student body from its beginning, with the first class of students coming from Kenya, Ethiopia, and Zaire (Congo). By December 1999, NGCS had had students from Uganda, Rwanda, Zambia, Sudan,

South Africa, Botswana, Ghana, Tanzania, and the USA as well. More than 125 students from 25 tribes have graduated in the six commencements exercises from 1991 to 1999. Most NGCS graduates are working effectively for the church or in church related ministries as elders, deacons, preachers, counselors, leaders teachers and missionaries. With such a geographic, ethnic, and linguistic spread combined with commitment to Christ, one can imagine the potential for the Kingdom of God as NGCS endeavors to fulfill its dream of equipping "Africans Claiming Africa" for Christ.

The Vision of NGCS

Imagine for a moment a church in Africa with no expatriate missionaries. Who will plant churches? Who will train others to do so? Who will evangelize the next tribe or the next country? The answer of course is National Church Leaders. The next question then is: Where will these leaders receive the training and equipping to carry out this task? It is the prayer of the NGCS that we will provide such training.

The vision of NGCS is to see Africans Claiming Africa For Christ! In April 1992 the school helped sponsor a missions conference with that title (see chapter 8). Two hundred and six church leaders representing 16 African nations and containing 6,564 Churches of Christ met for two weeks to discuss, pray, and plan concerning the growth of the Kingdom of God on the continent of Africa. It was then that the international significance of NGCS was realized. The task of claiming the continent for Christ is still enormous. Much of French Africa and Muslim Africa have not been penetrated with the good news of Jesus. Who will go? It is the conviction of the NGCS that this task will not and should not be Western expatriate missionaries; rather it will and should be African missionaries that carry on this task of claiming the continent for Christ. It is our dream that many of those missionaries will be trained and equipped at NGCS.

Many expatriate missionaries and NGCS personnel see the vision of when we are old and can hardly walk. Then we will hear the news of how our African brothers who were students at NGCS have faithfully spread the gospel throughout the continent of Africa because they obeyed their Lord's command in the Great Commission. Yes, when we are old we want to hear of how these students:

WENT...AND WENT...AND...WENT
PREACHED...AND PREACHED...AND PREACHED
AND MADE DISCIPLES...DISCIPLES...DISCIPLES

NGCS PROGRAMS

NGCS offers a number of different academic programs to meet the needs of the broad range of educational backgrounds and goals of African Christians.

Baccalaureate Degree Students

The baccalaureate degree program is operated in conjunction with Daystar University, Nairobi. The baccalaureate degree requires students to meet the minimum requirements for entering public higher education institutions in the country where their secondary education was completed. Students who earned the Advanced Diploma at NGCS transfer their credits to Daystar University. After earning the necessary semester hour credits at Daystar, they may be granted a baccalaureate degree.

Advanced Diploma Students

Students meeting the baccalaureate degree requirements but who do not wish to earn a baccalaureate degree, may conclude their formal education with the Advanced Diploma. Students who complete the Advanced Diploma complete a two-year residency at NGCS and a full-time curriculum that covers three traditional years of course work.

Advanced Certificate Students

Students who meet the general entrance requirements but who cannot meet the university entrance requirements may opt for the Advanced Certificate program. The certificate program follows the same procedure as the Diploma program, but with students who have not met university entrance requirements.

Extension Programs

One of the most important aspects of NGCS is the extension program. Not every Christian who wishes to have in-depth Bible and ministry studies can come to Nairobi for two or more years of residence work. Hence, the NGCS-extension program helps to fill this need near home by providing studies which may lead to: (1) an advanced certificate for those who speak English well and have a high academic ranking, (2) a basic certificate for those who do not speak English well and/or are not qualified academically for the advanced certificate (these classes are taught in Kiswahili or the tribal language of the area of the extension center), and (3) an audit certificate for those who cannot read or write and who must be tested orally. Currently, missionaries and a few nationals teach in the extension schools. The 2000-2005 plan is to cultivate graduates of the NGCS diploma program in Nairobi to teach the extension courses.

NGCS extension schools are located in the following countries and areas:

> In Kenya: Eldoret, Kisumu, Kitale, Malindi, Meru, Mt. Elgon, Ewaso Ngiru (Narok), Ngatataek, Kajiado District, South Nyanza, and Sotik with plans for additional extension sites in Kisii, Mombasa, and Nyeri
>
> In Uganda: Mbale, Jinja and Fort Portal.
>
> In Tanzania: Mbulu.

At any given time there are 300 to 1,000 students studying in the extension program.

Advanced Programs with US Universities

NGCS coordinates several of its academic programs with US based Christian universities. A primary health care curriculum was added in 1998 in collaboration with the Masters in International Nursing program at Harding University in Searcy, Arkansas. The NGCS primary health care courses, a street clinic, and counseling services are offered at the Rainbow Church of Christ in Nairobi as part of this arrangement.

In July 1998 NGCS and Abilene Christian University (ACU) began offering a Masters in Biblical and Related Studies degree under ACU accreditation. Each July students from countries such as Botswana, Ghana, Kenya, South Africa, and the USA come to NGCS to study in this program. The masters program is coordinated by Gailyn Van Rheenen (ACU) and William Searcy (NGCS).

"We Have a School in Africa, at the Foot of the Ngong Hills"

For seven years NGCS was housed in the Rainbow Church of Christ in the Nairobi West Shopping Center near Nyayo Stadium and Uhuru Highway. There were advantages to this arrangement because the Rainbow church building is located in downtown Nairobi in an area known locally as "Little Hell." There are more than a dozen bars around the building. Prostitution and drugs are rampant. Street children eat from trash heaps and sleep on the streets in the stupor of kerosene and glue-sniffed oblivion. The location provided a ready venue for practical ministry by NGCS students. As the ministries of the Rainbow church grew, however, both church and school realized that critical space issues would arise soon.

In 1997 the decision was made to move the NGCS campus to the site of the Kimbilio Guest House, a facility which had been built to provide transit housing for mission personnel who were traveling or staying in Nairobi for business. The Kimbilio house is located in Karen near the Ngong Hills and the Great Rift Valley at approximately 6,000 ft. above sea level. The campus is eight miles outside Nairobi city center in Karen/Langata, beside the African Fund for Endangered Species Langata Giraffe Center and Giraffe Manor. Students are warned that sometimes giraffes wander out of the estate to run up and down the road in front of NGCS at night. Also nearby is the Nairobi Game Park where lions, cheetahs, giraffes, hippos, rhinos, and other big and small game can be seen with the Nairobi City Center skyline in the background. Maasai herdsmen in their tra-ditional bright scarlet plaid skirts and ochre plastered, braided hair frequent the area and can sometimes be seen shopping at the Langata Grocery Store two blocks from the school.

The town and area of Karen are named after the Danish Baroness Karen Blixen (1885-1962) better known by her pen name: Isak Dinesen. Based on her life and book by the same name, the movie "Out of Africa" was filmed at her house just a few miles away from NGCS. The famous opening words in her book, "I had a farm in Africa, at the foot of the Ngong Hills" begin a marvelous description of this region in which the NGCS campus is situated.

The physical plant is a single building built in 1992. There are five boarding rooms which hold up to ten students each. The library contains approximately 6,000 books. There are two classrooms; the larger for diploma classes and the smaller for certificate classes. Three offices and an apartment occupy one end of the building. A spacious kitchen is linked to the larger classroom which doubles as a cafeteria. Future plans are to enlarge the library, build another office wing, and add classrooms and married student apartments.

NGCS Student Body

The NGCS student body is composed of church leaders, men and women, ranging in age from 21 to 70 years with at least a Form 4 (12th grade education). For the residential program in Nairobi each NGCS student must raise at least 10% (6,500 Ksh) of his/her support from the local church(es) in the area in which the student lives and works. Students have been known to sell the family cow in order to come to NGCS. The remaining 90% (58,500 Ksh) of the support comes from donations of interested individuals and churches in the USA.

NGCS Faculty and Administration

All of the NGCS advanced diploma teachers have at least a masters degree. Charles Akumu, a Kenyan national and former elder at Rainbow Church of Christ, was the principal (1994-1999) and a professor from 1994-1999. Charles is currently in the USA pursuing a Ph.D. in Intercultural Education. Dr. William (Bill) H. Searcy is the Chairperson of the board of directors (since 1997), Registrar (since 1997) and a Professor (since 1995). Other professors include Kenyan nationals as well as missionaries with many years of experi-

234

ence in Africa. Teachers in the certificate program in Nairobi or the Extension Program have at least a bachelors degree or they have completed the NGCS advanced diploma. A major goal of the school is to increase the number of qualified African professors at the masters and doctorate level.

Goals and Objectives of the Nairobi Great Commission School

The goal of NGCS is to provide academic and experiential training in the African context in order to equip men and women for ministry and missions in planting and maturing churches both locally and cross-culturally; "to go and make disciples of all nations..." (Matt 28:19) and "to build up the body of Christ until we all arrive at the unity of faith and understanding...that brings maturity...towards...the fullness of Christ." (Eph 4:12-13).

Objectives

1. To aid churches in Kenya and other African nations in their growth toward self-reliance by offering high-quality leadership training which recognizes and reinforces the unique and individual gifts of leaders and prospective leaders.

2. To promote evangelism and church growth on the African continent and beyond in the 21st century by equipping African evangelists and missionaries with ministry skills for planting and maturing churches both locally and cross-culturally.

3. To provide academic training that is enhanced with intensive field experiences.

4. To make graduate-level training a reasonable option for qualified students.

5. To emphasize the spiritual disciplines of repentance, confession, fasting, prayer and renewal, creating an atmosphere where the truly called can be recognized and empowered in the ministry of the Gospel.

SCHOOL FEES STRUCTURE

Kenya Shillings Per Year @ 1US$ = 72 Ksh rounded*

	Boarding Students		Day Students	
TUITION PER YEAR	15,000	$208	15,000	$208
BOOKS	3,000	$42	3,000	$42
ROOM AND BOARD	41,000	569	7,200 (lunch)	$100
STUDENT FEES	1,000	$14	1,000	$14
MEDICAL INSURANCE	2,500	$35	2,500	$35
PRACTICUMS	2,000	$28	2,000	$28
REGISTRATION FEE	500	$7	500	$ 7
TOTAL PER YEAR	Ksh	65,000	$903	
	Ksh	31,000	$434	

Admission Requirements

1. To be admitted to NGCS applicants must submit a written recommendation from a local congregation. The local congregation will verify that the applicant is a proven fruitful church member. Applicants are desired who have a high sense of calling.

2. Persons must be 21 years of age or older to be accepted.

3. Priority will be given to older married applicants.

4. Priority will be given to members of the Churches of Christ.

5. Those applying for either the Advanced Diploma or Advanced Certificate programs must be fluent in the speaking, reading, and writing of English.

6. Prospective students must pass the entrance examination.

7. Prospective students must be interviewed and accepted by the screening committee.

Applicants must provide evidence of ability to pay the school fees, plus room and board, or provide evidence that a church or other sponsor will guarantee such support.

Courses

Following are the courses taught in the residential program of the NGCS:

Bible
BIB 1013 - OLD TESTAMENT SURVEY
BIB 1023 - NEW TESTAMENT SURVEY
BIB 1033 - THE BOOK OF ACTS
BIB 2003 - HOW TO STUDY THE BIBLE
BIB 2033 - DOCTRINES OF THE BIBLE
BIB 2043 - CHURCH DOCTRINE
BIB 3033 - THE LIFE AND TEACHINGS OF CHRIST
BIB 3133 - HEBREW PROPHETS

Missions
MIS 1003 - INTRODUCTION TO MISSIONS
MIS 1031 - MISSION PRACTICUM I
MIS 1042 - EVANGELISM AND DISCIPLING
MIS 2031 - MISSION PRACTICUM II
MIS 2043 - EVANGELISM SEMINAR AND PRACTICUM
MIS 3013 - CHURCH GROWTH BASICS
MIS 3031 - MISSION PRACTICUM III

Ministry
CHM 1031 - PERSONAL DEVELOPMENT I
CHM 1043 - INTRODUCTION TO
                    CHRISTIAN COUNSELING
CHM 2031 - PERSONAL DEVELOPMENT II
CHM 3004 - CHURCH MINISTRY
CHM 3031 - PERSONAL DEVELOPMENT III

CHM 3043 - WORSHIP IN AFRICA
CHM 3053 - SPIRITUAL WARFARE
CHM 3133 - PRINCIPLES AND METHODS OF TEACHING

General Requirements
BIL 1002 - INTRODUCTION TO BIBLICAL LANGUAGES
COM 1001 - STUDY SKILLS
COM 2013 - COMMUNICATION AND CULTURE I
COM 2032 - PUBLIC SPEAKING
ENG 1000 - BASIC ENGLISH
ENG 1013 - ENGLISH I
FAM 2033 - MARRIAGE AND FAMILY IN AFRICA
HIS 2033 - RESTORATION HERITAGE
HOM 3013 - HOMILETICS I

THE INTERNATIONAL SCHOOL OF BIBLICAL STUDIES

The International School of Biblical Studies is based in Cape Town, South Africa, but operates worldwide under the direction of Roger E. Dickson. Interested parties in the School should write: International School of Biblical Studies, P.O. Box 1919, Bellville 7535, South Africa, or go online to www.isbs.org

The International School of Biblical Studies (ISBS) was established in 1980. From its beginning, the administration of the School has been dedicated to the development of quality printed biblical materials to fulfill the spiritual and intellectual needs of dedicated Bible students and church leaders throughout the world. The School originated from its American base in Hutchinson, Kansas USA, with the subsequent establishment of the first international base in the West Indies. In 1989 the international base was moved to Cape Town, South Africa.

From the inception of the International School of Biblical

Studies, it has always been the purpose of the director and staff to accomplish the apostolic directive of 2 Timothy 2:2:

> And the things that you have heard from me among many witnesses, commit these to faithful men who will be able to teach others also.

In order to accomplish the above directive of God, the administration of the School has continually worked toward the goal of developing the highest possible level of biblical distance training for faithful Bible students throughout the world. Through the opportunity of the internet, the School has added another dimension to the global availability of the courses of the School to preachers and Bible school teachers.

Distance Education through Mail and the Internet

In the development of the ISBS curriculum, it has always been the goal of the administration to develop courses to the highest possible quality for distance training in the field of biblical education. Though the ISBS is not at this time accredited through any state or regional system of accreditation, we have always sought to maintain the highest level of distance training by incorporating proven standards of programmed study that have been effectively used for many years by schools of higher education.

The internet has provided the opportunity for serious Bible students throughout the world to have the privilege of university level biblical studies in their own homes. Through this medium, the ISBS began in the year 2000 to offer Bible students of the global community the opportunity to participate in a curriculum of biblical studies that has been offered by the School in a printed format since 1980. Since the courses of the School are the "teachers" of the classroom in the student's home, the developers of the curriculum have sought to produce courses on those subjects that are both challenging, as well as applicable to the students' spiritual and intellectual needs as teachers of God's word.

The internet system of distance training has been carried over into interactive computer training courses for the internet department of the School. Each student receives the textbook and study manual material by downloading this material from the ISBS website. The study manual interactively guides the student through the textbook. The study manuals have a programmed format of graded questions that test the student's progress through each chapter of the textbook. Each chapter also contains a series of discussion questions to challenge the student's comprehension of key concepts. The discussion questions are completed and emailed or posted to the School for assessment. Once the student successfully completes each chapter test in the study manual, he or she completes a final exam, which is also provided with the study manual. Depending on the amount of credit a student desires to receive for any specific course, the final exam is completed either under the supervision of a moderator, or as an open book final test.

Student Enrollment

As a school of higher learning in biblical studies, the School seeks to aid those students who excel in three areas of spiritual growth. We seek to aid students who are mature, disciplined, and sacrificially committed to the study and teaching of the Bible. Mature students will approach their studies with great seriousness. Disciplined students will continue their studies while ministering what they learn to others. Sacrificially committed students will live what they learn in order to allow Christ to be manifested through their lives.

In order to enroll in the mailing department of the School, students must send a Letter of Application to the School. In this letter they must explain their work in the church and their reasons for wanting to enroll. Because this department of the School is tuition free, the School maintains the perogative as to who should be enrolled. The School maintains an active student body of about 1,500 students. Therefore, as students are graduated, new students are accepted for enrollment.

In order to enroll in the internet department of the School, students are required to have access to the internet via a web browser (eg. Microsoft Internet Explorer or Netscape Navigator). They must also have access to a computer that can run Adobe Acrobat Reader 4.05 software (MS Windows 98 or Mac OS). All course textbooks and study manuals are presented in Acrobat Reader format (PDF). In order to enroll in this department of the School, students are required to pay a fee for each course.

Curriculum

In January 2000 the listed courses of the ISBS were the following. In the year 2000, programming began in order to offer many of the these courses in a programmed electronic format. It is the policy of the School to continually add courses to the curriculum as they are developed.

101: Introduction to the Bible
102: Introduction to the Cross and the Church
103: Introduction to Biblical Interpretation, I
104: Introduction to Biblical Interpretation, II
105: Introduction to Law and Covenants
106: Introduction to the Sovereignty of God
108: Introduction to Baptism
109: The Church in Eternity
110: Satan and His Hosts
111: Old Testament History
112: New Testament Evangelistic Principles
114: Luke

115: Acts: Luke's Defense of Christianity, I
116: Acts: Luke's Defense of Christianity, II
119: The Doctrine of God, I
120: The Doctrine of God, II
121: The Doctrine of God, III
123: Christian Evidences, I
124: Christian Evidences, II
125: Christian Evidences, III
127: Servanthood Leadership
128: Revelation
129: John
130: The Theologies of Man
131: Hebrews
133: 1 Corinthians
134: 2 Corinthians
135: Romans
139: The Prison Epistles
142: James
145: Eschatology
146: The Christian World View
147: 1 & 2 Timothy, Titus
149: Personal Evangelism
150: Galatians
151: The Millennial Reign
152: Matthew
154: Introduction to the Seedline Promise
156: 1 & 2 Thessalonians
157: 1 & 2 Peter
158: 1,2,3 John & Jude

Administration

Roger E. Dickson is the director of the International School of Biblical Studies. Roger travels extensively in southern African conducting leadership training seminars for church leaders. Allan Holcombe is the administrator of the internet department of the School. Other local staff in our South Africa base include Martha Dickson (course processing and development), Denville Willie (Forum Moderator), Jim Hyde (media development), Jan Hyde (course processing and development), Triston Jacobsohn (multimedia development), and Marion Drury (course development).

SECTION 3

Mission Strategies and Issues

CHAPTER 11

East African Leadership

Stanley E. Granberg

Stanley Granberg served as a missionary in Meru, Kenya from 1983-1993. He holds the Ph.D from the Open University: Oxford Centre for Mission Studies. He taught as missionary-in-residence at Lubbock Christian University and is currently associate professor of Bible and Missions at Cascade College, Portland, Oregon. sgranberg@cascade.edu.

In the 19th century Africa was known in the western world as "the dark continent." In the 20th century Africa seems best known primarily as the cursed continent. Collapsing economies, frightful famines and bitter civil wars are the standard news reports from Africa. Often we westerners slip into the stereotypical understanding that the problem with Africa is its Africanness, typified in self-destructive leadership. In fact, one of Africa's own states that Africa is "making war on itself; African rulers are despots; politicians are venal, corrupt and violent; the state is a predatory monster..." (Chabal, 1992, p. 4).

Yet in this apparently bleak landscape of failure, a brilliant ray of hope is shining. Surprisingly, that hope is African leaders. All across the continent of Africa, God is raising up leaders for His church who demonstrate not only deep personal faithfulness, but a willingness to accept their leadership responsibilities and an evangelistic zeal that has contributed to the fastest growth among Churches of Christ on any continent in the world.

This chapter looks at leadership in East Africa. It explores the concepts of leadership and leadership emergence as they have occurred among the Gikuyu, Embu and Meru tribes (referred to as the GEM) of central Kenya. Our purpose is to gain a higher orbit perspective on the social context which influences African leadership in East Africa, then bring our new insights back into the way we understand leadership in African churches.

In this chapter we will identify first the social context, the moral economy, in which leadership occurs among many East African peoples. Then we will examine the way issues of authority are perceived by those who grant leadership and those who wish to wear the mantle of leader. Finally, with these two ideas as background, we will look at how leaders emerge and are evaluated as leaders among the Churches of Christ in Meru, Kenya, leaders who are fairly typical of those found in rural, village churches in many parts of East Africa.

Outlines of A Moral Economy for GEM Leadership

The framework in which leadership among the Gikuyu, Embu and Meru (GEM) peoples is best explored is that of a moral economy of thought (Scott 1976, Thompson, 1991). A moral economy consists of commonly held, invisible rules of life which direct the relationships among members of a society (Thompson, 1991). These rules are woven into a socially experienced "pattern of moral rights or expectations" (Scott, 1976, p. 6) which govern the expectations held about those who are stronger as well as the obligations required of those who are weaker, and which legitimate or bastardize the actions of individuals in the eyes of their community (Davidson, 1970; Scott, 1976). Lonsdale (1992) in *The Moral Economy of Mau*

Mau: Wealth, Poverty and Civic Virtue in Kikuyu Political Thought,
sketched the outlines of a moral economy for the GEM peoples by
linking the concept of a debated ethnic identity to the internal struggles for leadership which occurred among contenders for leadership
at various levels of the social hierarchy (p. 347). The task suggested
by Lonsdale is that by identifying the moral and intellectual context
in which leadership occurs in GEM society one might also learn the
principles of GEM leadership and the standards by which leaders are
evaluated.

The African Frontier: The Context for Leadership

The interpretative context for analyzing African leadership must
be derived from the environmental and historical contexts in which
African leaders lead. The most satisfying rubric for such an analysis
is that of the frontier (Kopytoff, 1987). Here we identify the characteristics of the African frontier—past and present—explain two primary themes of the African frontier—population and production—
and the values inhabiting those themes, values which African leaders
have adapted to and co-opted for their exercise of leadership.

The African Frontier

Early conceptualizations of the spread of the Bantu peoples
south of the Sahara described their movements in terms of a migra-
tion (Lambert, 1950; Munro, 1967; Oliver and Matthew, 1963).
The implication was that there had been a monolithic movement of
people, such as occurred on the frontier of the United States, which
spread from specific, populated dispersion points and moved across
definable boundaries into as yet unpopulated regions of the continent. The African frontier, however, was anything but monolithic.
Kopytoff (1987) and Iliffe (1995) demonstrate through archaeolo-
gy, economics and linguistics that the African frontier, rather than

247

being a wave of population movement, primarily consisted of small, uncoordinated bands of mobile frontiersman who moved across multiple, local frontiers. Iliffe (1995) says,

> Africa's colonisation was mainly an internal process, with innumerable local frontiers, and its cultures were chiefly formed in the frontiers. . . . Bantu-speaking colonists were not farmers slowly expanding cultivation by nibbling at the fringes of the bush; they were mobile pioneers, probably still reliant on foraging and hunting, who selected only the land best suited to their farming technology, . . . They selected micro-environments where they could utilize their skills ...When the surrounding fields were exhausted, the pioneers simply moved on to the next suitable micro-environment (pp. 3, 36).

The pre-colonial African frontier was constantly shifting, moving back and forth in spasms of human colonization, expanding and contracting in fluid movement as ecology, economy, and personal dictates required.

Life was precarious and harsh in these mobile frontier communities. Kershaw (1997) describes the conditions of Kikuyu frontier life as a forest economy (p. 21). The new forest settlers were often composed of small groups of men who joined in fictive brotherhood to pool resources to purchase and colonize the land. A Kikuyu pioneer could fell a single tree in two man-days (Lonsdale, 1992a). With axe and firestick, the tools of the pioneer (Fadiman, 1993), it required 150 man-days to clear the minimum three acres of land needed to provide a mother the space for an enclosed homestead, an acre of forage land for a few goats and cattle, and at least two-and-half acres for cultivation (Kershaw, 1997; Lonsdale, 1992). Seven cleared acres would provide auxiliary buildings and resources for wealth accumulation in livestock (Kershaw, 1997). Kershaw (1997) estimates that a pioneer family would likely require the working life of an entire buying generation before a household could regard itself as settled (p. 22). "The hard work, the dangers of pioneering, the uncertain outcome and the likelihood of an early death would have daunted anyone" (Kershaw, 1997, p. 31).

The chief problem confronting the colonizers of the frontier was "the construction and validation of authority over people and resources" (Lonsdale, 1988, p. 286) in a situation where those resources were the foundation for life but where authority was easily defied. Frontier life exhibited a fierce demand for population and an emphasis on the ability to produce. Population was required to provide labor in a situation where land was plentiful but labor was scarce. Production was required to ensure not only personal survivability, but also social mobility (Iliffe, 1995). Power was generated by wealth, and wealth was found in people. Together population and productivity formed a "labour theory of value" (Lonsdale, 1992, p. 333), the basis of the GEM moral economy.

Frontier Population

Men who would be leaders within African frontier communities had to prove their right to lead by demonstrating first their ability to attract and control people. Frontier leadership began with a concern on process, the process of acquiring and directing the human population necessary for production. Guyer (1995a) describes the concept of wealth embodied in the rights in people as a specifically African mode of accumulation that is close to the heart of African economic and social history (p. 84). The wealth-in-people concept recognizes that rights in people was the basis of accumulation, and that accumulation was the basis of power. But rather than being an additive concept, Guyer (1995b) argues that wealth-in-people is a compositional process describing "syndromes of interpersonal dependency and social network-building that clearly involves strategizing, investing and otherwise cultivating interpersonal ties at the expense of personal wealth in material things" (p. 106). As a compositional process, wealth-in-people is distinguished from pooled accumulation by a pursuit of multiplicity of productive forms. Where accumulation seeks to increase quantity, composition seeks to build patterns of production in alliances and networks. It pursues the multiplicity of productive techniques rather than mere production. Wealth-in-people recognized that people are assets by virtue of the knowledge and relationships that they possess. The result on leadership is that leaders must be able to attract and hold those who possess productive power. Guyer (1995b) summarizes her argument for the compositional nature of wealth-in-people saying,

> People were singularized repositories of a differentiated and expanding repertoire of knowledge, …We argue that social mobilization was in part based on the mobilization of different bodies of knowledge, and leadership was the capacity to bring them together effectively, even if for a short time and specific purposes. We refer to this process as composition and distinguish it from accumulation (p. 120).

The foundation for productivity, then, was the maintenance and use of population. Iliffe (1995) describes African societies as being characterized by a population protective stance. In a continent of plentiful land, the need has not been, until the recent twentieth century, to hoard land, but to have the wives and children necessary to cultivate the land. The ideal social organization was the household of the Big Man, a man "surrounded by his wives, married and unmarried sons, younger brothers, poor relations, dependants, and swarming children" (Iliffe, 1995, p. 94; Lonsdale, 1992a).

Iliffe (1995) demonstrates how the need for population resulted in the development of characteristically African ideologies focusing on fertility, the defense of civilization and the maximization of the population. Women were "bought" for sons by fathers who could accumulate the necessary brideprice, a recompense to the woman's family for the loss of her productive capacity to that social unit and the acquisition of property rights into the wife's family's holdings (Kershaw, 1977; Lonsdale, 1992a). Rich youths married young and often, achieving status for themselves and their families within the ruling councils. The poor man served the wealthy in hopes of scraping together enough accumulation of hoofed wealth through alliance with his patron so that he too might enter into self-respecting manhood (Lonsdale, 1992a). Civilization was cultivated out of the wilderness by the motivated labor of young pioneers seeking personal adulthood; men entered the wilderness with a hunter's audacity, violence and witchcraft, protecting the boundaries of civilization with magic articles which physically encapsulated the purchased knowledge and economic rights of the individual or family (Fadiman, 1993; Guyer, 1995; Iliffe, 1995; Mazrui, 1975). The maximization of population was demonstrated through a broad range of restrictions and penalties associated with childbirth, the taking and treatment of captives in war, and societal institutions such as the *gichiaro* in Meru which defined alliances between groups, serving as a means of preservation from violence, famine, and disease (Fadiman, 1975, 1993).

Another result of the need for and protection of population, particularly among the Kikuyu, was a highly developed form of land tenancy. Based around the Big Man ideal, the tenancy system provided opportunities for both the haves and the have nots. Those who controlled land and needed extra labor had the opportunity to attract around themselves tenants. Lonsdale (1992a) describes three tiers of tenancy. The most servile were *njaguti* (serfs, good-for-nothings), temporary agricultural laborers who were paid off in consumable food stuffs (Iliffe, 1987). The next tier were the *ndungata* (servants) were often employed as herdsmen and functioning as semi-permanent tenants. These men were often married to the landowners' daughter, but because brideprice was usually not paid, the offspring remained under the productive control of the householder (Kershaw, 1997, pp. 59-60). The upper levels of tenancy were populated by *ahoi* (tenants in friendship). Lonsdale (1992a) describes the *ahoi* as an "endogamous insurance policy" (p. 339); these were men of similar status as the householder who would care for unused land, make improvements on the land, and most importantly, provide opportunities for affinal relationships between the Big Man and other groups–enlarging the influence geography of the Big Man and diversifying his investments in fertility (Kershaw, 1997; Lonsdale, 1992a). The *muhoi* (friendship tenant), to his benefit, received the use of land for his herds, or from which, if he applied himself with diligence and wisdom, he might build up herds to use to purchase, land, wives and perhaps to become a full member of the *mbari* (clan) himself (Kershaw, 1997). The challenge was to close one's own door to the wilderness (Lonsdale, 1992a, p. 341), thus demonstrating the power of personal achievement and acquiring the obligations of others through the pursuit of multiple forms of fertility and alliances.

To enter into the ranks of leadership in African frontier society, men had first to conquer their own personal frontiers. This meant demonstrating their capability to harness the people who possessed the knowledge and capacity to create the structure and order that characterized civilization. Without this ability to attract and keep people, leadership was lost or never recognized in the first place.

Frontier Production Theory

The GEM moral economy was also concerned with end product, with wealth. Lonsdale (1992) explains the Kikuyu concept of wealth within the framework of a Kikuyu political maxim, *kuuga na gwika,* 'say and do' (p. 337). The concept of "do" involved the "direct investment of human toil" (Lonsdale, 1992, p. 334). The leaders of pioneering houses were those who successfully mobilized the productive capacity of the human resources of their households and turned that capacity into a usable commodity—wealth from which came power. The signs of wealth were very physical: lands, wives, and herds. Those who possessed these goods also possessed the means of survivability for their homes, an advantage which surely was enjoyed more by the wealthy than the poor (Kershaw, 1997). It was these "rich" voices who were heard most loudly within the community as the possessors of opinions which would provide advantage for the survival of the greater community in a violent world, just as they had already done for their own personal communities (Iliffe, 1995; Lonsdale, 1992).

The GEM, and similar East African societies, usually have been termed egalitarian, supposing a rather flat social structure. Kopytoff (1987) describes a very different reality of African cultures which are "suffused with a sense of hierarchy in social, political, and ritual relations" (p. 35). The result is a hierarchical ethic that accepts the recognized fact of life that seniors stood over juniors, patrons over their clients and the wealthy over the poor. "Despite their egalitarian ideologies,…people were highly differentiated by wealth…" (Iliffe, 1995, p. 120).

This inherent hierarchical ethic of the GEM societies resulted in a highly competitive climate where the common ambition was to found a household and acquire productive control of resources (Lonsdale, 1992a). This ethic also acculturated societal members into a relationship conscious society where inequality was understood and its terms negotiated. A language of class developed that is reflected in the rich vocabulary and literature describing both the wealthy and the poor (Iliffe, 1995). Lonsdale's (1992a) review of Kikuyu proverbs (Barra, 1960; Njururi, 1983) reveals that over six percent extol the virtues of leadership and organized cooperation as producers of public good: "wealth, cleanliness and satiety". Similarly, a Meru proverb recognizes the individual fortitude and skill of the hunter whose family eats meat while another berates the grasping of the poor who seeks a claim over that which they have not earned. The *athamaki* (leaders) of the community were those who not only had demonstrated the ability to control the human resources of their own personal frontiers, but they also had the wealth necessary to pay for their involvement in the high politics of their communities. A successful public career among the GEM peoples required the payment of at least 172 goats (Lonsdale, 1992, p. 342).

In GEM society personal status within this hierarchical world of thought was defined by the universe of relationships, superior and subordinate, in which people existed (Haugerud, 1995). Hierarchy was evident not only between groups but within family, kin, and political groups. Fathers held control over sons and the wealth they needed to define their own manhood. Elders controlled juniors through secrecy, ridicule and the use of "ancient" language that the young could not decipher. Patrons held sway over their clients. Patterns of superior-subordinate relationships also arose in this segmented world so that the firstcomer had priority over the latecomer, the wealthy over the poor, and where the achievement of rank was not lost (Kopytoff, 1987). Along with these patterns were mutually accepted, though continually negotiated, norms of sociality and patronage, as people of unequal position engaged in a continual press and pull of demands. Those who were less well off or in distress were expected to seek aid from the wealthy, who had to respond to requests for aid with good will, at the risk of losing their community reputation, though not necessarily with any largess (Haugerud, 1995; Lonsdale, 1992a; Scott, 1985).

Summary of the GEM Moral Economy

Leadership on the African frontier was both bought and earned; leadership was acquired by means of people. The African frontier was expansive but the historic underpopulation of the area made people and their stores of knowledge, skills, and abilities the backbone of production. Frontier leadership had to construct and establish its authority. Authority was not something that was easily taken or kept by force; with numerous frontiers escape was always a ready option if authority became too demanding. At the same time the necessity for wealth and an inherent hierarchical ethic not only allowed, but also expected, unequal social relationships. Those who worked towards acceptance as leaders had thus to engage in a compositional process which focused on creating patterns of relationship, networks of people and alliances. Leadership was predicated on the twin pillars of the ability to harness population and the wealth to pay for one's way through the social structures in which leadership was exercised. We now turn to consider the rules by which authority was perceived, gained and exercised in pre-colonial Kenya, and how those rules changed to arrive at their present state.

The Rules of Local Authority Relationships

The GEM peoples lived in loosely organized family and territorial units in which authority was distributed among temporary power holders within local councils of elders. There were no institutionalized groupings to identify permanent leader-follower relationships nor was executive authority concentrated in the hands of any single individual (Tosh, 1973). Leadership was conferred by common assent (Lambert, 1947, 1956; Kenyatta, 1953) on the basis of the personal qualities the leader displayed and success in life activities. The fluid social and political situation, particularly in the frontier zones, allowed outstanding individuals to rise into leadership positions, sometimes through quite innovative means (Clough, 1990). These conditions meant that the authority available to the leader was dependent upon his immediate relations with his family, neighbors, his fellow councilmen and his personal initiative. Tignor (1971) summarized the situation among these societies this way:

> They gave wide political influence to men of singular ability, but the influence of these men was not hereditary or authoritarian. Their positions depended on tendering good advice and having it accepted by their peers. …These men rose to prominence entirely on their own talented leadership (p. 342).

Leadership was exercised by the elders of each village who were organized into councils, called *kiama* by the Meru people, which were the administrative and judicial institutions of the GEM tribes. Every village or locale had its own *kiama*. Membership in the *kiama* was not optional, every man of appropriate stage in life was required to pay his goat as entry fee into the *kiama* in order to be married (Muriuki, 1974; Kenyatta, 1953). Kenyatta (1942) describes this governmental system as based on mutual responsibility: "In order to maintain harmony, it was decided that all the people, once they reached maturity, must have some responsibility in the government" (p. 18).

Characteristics of a Village Leader (Mugambi)

The leaders of the *biama* (councils) were called *agambi,* which in the language of the Meru people means "speakers". Among the Gikuyu they were called *athamaki.* Often these men had already distinguished themselves as warriors (Chege, 1993). But another layer of expectations had to be met within the *kiama* (council) of elders that went beyond those for a war leader. Recognition to the status of *mugambi* (speaker) was made on the basis of the possession of *ugambi* (no English equivalent exists, though 'leadership' or 'manliness' captures the general idea). Lambert (1947) describes the idea of *ugambi* as "a complex of intelligence, personality, good reputation, social and economic success, and a sound heredity... *Ugambi* is more than a mere appointment. It implies something of the 'common decency' of the English 'gentleman'" (p. 28). Typical descriptions of the *agambi* (speakers) and their qualifications for office focused on the personal characteristics of the individuals. Lambert (1947) said, "The word *mugambi* (literally, spokesman) implies a natural leader....A *mugambi* is so because of exceptional courage or intelligence or character, manifested in youth and maintained in manhood" (Lambert 1950, pp. 5, 7). Rimita (1988) identifies the *mugambi* as one who "had distinguished himself as a clever man or speaker during the hearing of cases" (p. 68). Cagnolo (1933) described the *athamaki* (speakers, leaders) of the Kikuyu as, "men with outstanding oratorical ability, physical strength, or wealth" (p. 121). Muriuki (1974) says that, "Self-assertion, courage, self-confidence and diligence were important assets for a warrior, while wisdom, tact, self-control and wide experience were some of the qualities looked for in an elder who aspired to be a *muthamaki*" (p. 132).

The candidates considered best meeting the expectations of a *mugambi* (speaker) were those "more charismatic individuals within each group of council members [who] would begin to emerge as spokesmen for their fellows in specific areas of mutual concern" (Fadiman, 1993, p. 26). There were no formal qualifications that had to be met. There was no election; selection was arrived at by public opinion, a "spontaneous public proclamation that the son of so-and-so had earned for himself this or that position" (Kenyatta, 1942, p. 19). Fadiman (1993) suggests that special expertise in some area was also a factor. An elder who had firsthand knowledge of a specific region, peoples, or situation would be selected to evaluate the topic as long as his expertise was needed (Fadiman, 1993). Wealth was also a major consideration as payments of goats, bulls, and millet or honey beer demanded as entry fees into the councils could often be more than an otherwise worthy individual was able to afford.

The agambi (speakers) did not hold a hereditary office nor did they possess any rights or privileges inherent in an office (Kenyatta, 1942). "The more qualities of leadership came together in one person, the higher was his authority and the wider the group that recognized it" (Wagner, 1940, p. 235). The *agambi* did not receive formal appointment or installation as the heads of family, sub-clan, or clan. They were the leading personalities of their age-sets, the *primus inter pares* who had gained a general consensus of opinion about their leadership from their peers and respective clans (Lambert, 1947; Muriuki, 1974).

British Administration

The British colonial administration had difficulty accepting the fluidity of this type of leadership situation existing in the many acephalous (leaderless) societies of East Africa. Government likes a more predictable–and controllable–situation. The British answer was to create a new administrative system (Vincent, 1977). The keystone for this system was to be the local administrative chief (Lonsdale, 1968). The first chiefs appointed were often the warleaders who were sent by their communities to meet the British invader entering their land, or they may simply have been those men who had failed to flee (Hawkins, 1996). The foreign administration tried to use the indigenous leaders where possible. These local men served as social communicators of the demands of the state (Lonsdale, 1968) and sometimes buffered their people from the more jarring administrative demands (Glazier, 1985).

The activity of the chief in the earliest years primarily was to represent the demands of the new rulers to the people; secondarily they were also expected to represent their communities to the administration (Berman, 1990). These first tasks were difficult, but not overly so. Warriors had to be controlled; labor was required to build the new roads connecting administrative areas or to develop settler farms; and taxes had to be collected (Clough, 1990). But, as the new system coalesced, the administration shifted emphasis from sufficient administration to effective administration (Lonsdale, 1968). The demands on the chiefs grew. Chiefs were later expected to run local courts, sit as representatives on the Local Native Councils, oversee local education, appoint lower level administrators (headmen and sub-headmen), and promote the agricultural reforms of the colonial state in addition to being "the law" on the local level. The chiefs fully became agents of the Conquest State, a role they continue to play in Kenya today.

The result of this superimposed administrative system on the pre-existing leadership system was to disassociate the externally posted chiefs from the natural selection processes of local authority. There was no role in traditional society that gathered so much power or authority into the hands of a single individual. The chiefs became the *de facto* lawgivers and lawmakers (Tignor, 1971). Removed from the control of the face-to-face authority of traditional society chiefs found their position a readily usable tool to acquire the traditional signs of wealth: wives, land, and cattle (Haugerud, 1997). They were also responsible for using their office to benefit their family lineage and clan (Glazier, 1985). Kinyanjui, paramount chief of the Kikuyu, claimed as much as 16,000 acres of personal land, which he used to reward his political supporters and underlings (Berman, 1990). Chief Kombo of Embu married thirty wives and made his family the dominant force in his location (Glazier, 1985). Because the chiefs lacked the traditional authority to impose their demands, they gathered around them small, personal armies of young men to be their enforcers (Lambert, 1947). Corruption and oppression was the fuel which fed the desires of personal ascendancy (Tosh, 1973).

The British administrative system imposed an entirely new authority system upon the formerly acephalous GEM societies. The chiefs were agents of foreign domination. They were removed from the local lines of authority distribution and placed within the larger authority network of the state. The chiefs represented a new form of leadership in East Africa, typically identified with domination and exploitation.

Changing the Rules of Local Power

Along with a change of authority, the construction of a system of chiefs also changed the rules of power for leaders. Traditional society gave preference to men of wealth and character, the visible evidences of the virtuous person (Lonsdale, 1992a), for their leaders. Those who demonstrated to higher degrees the ideals of society earned the power to influence. The key assets of traditional power, beyond the personal characteristics of the power holder, were land and the reproducible wealth it supported (Lonsdale, 1990). The more powerful men accessed labor resources beyond their families by developing relationships through trade, marriage, and social interaction, thereby reducing their exposure to catastrophe and expanding their access to power (Lonsdale, 1992a, p. 329). Politics were conducted within the arena of consumption; accumulation was limited by an early satiation point where the need to possess was transformed into the coinage of calculated largess (Mair, 1936).

> Fear of famine, labour shortage and the need to
> prove mastery over nature drove Kikuyu high politics to

compete in consumption rather than arms. A successful
life required an outlay of no less than 172 goats for cere-
monial slaughter and feasting at rites of passage and other
public occasions. Kikuyu history is about those who
could pay for a political life. We know almost nothing
about those who could not (Lonsdale, 1992a, pp. 342-
343).

The advent of the nation state and its superimposed administration radically expanded the field of competition for leadership
among the GEM societies. Along with that expansion of scope
came an entirely new source and type of power, a power which gathered around a monolithic center. The chiefs and big men in the local
arena were the access points to this centralized power. They arro-
gated this new power to support their drive for accumulation.
Where previously accumulation had been the means to achieve an
end, now it was the end for which the means of power was used.
Wealth now represented the result of the privilege of position, not
self-worth (Haugerud, 1995).

The new politics of power was defined by one's ability to access
the means of power. Intense rivalries within the local communities
emerged as contenders for leadership used their relationship with
powerful and wealthy outsiders to defeat their local rivals, thus
increasing their popularity and securing material and social advantages for their own constituents (Haugerud, 1995). Zero-sum politics ruled as the success of one group at accessing centralized power
excluded the losers from both the future decision-making process as
well as the rewards of office. Those who held power meant to keep
it while those without it tried to get it. The chieftainship became the
point of competition where victory meant self-enrichment and
defeat was potential impoverishment (Tignor, 1971). The rules of
power had changed.

The moral economy of the GEM peoples and the rules of the

local authority relationships provide the context in which the leadership in the village is played out. We now turn our attention to leadership as it is displayed by local, village church leaders.

Today's Village Church Leaders

The village church leader is the most common and probably the most important leader in the African church. The background for this discussion comes from the life of leaders of the Churches of Christ in Meru with supporting material drawn from other parts of Africa.

Expectations for Church Leaders

The expectations for village level church leaders springs directly from the tasks they perform in these churches. Their primary tasks are teaching, evangelizing, organizing church life, and providing pastoral care for the church members. Secondarily their tasks include activities such as record keeping, coordinating with local officials and project management.

Granberg (1995) investigated the positive and negative images by which these church members describe their leaders. When thinking about leaders accomplishing the above tasks, the church members of the Meru Churches of Christ prefer to talk of their leaders in terms of caregivers. The preferred positive image was that of Father (*ithe*), followed by that of Mother (*ng'ina*). Both these images share the underlying concept of the leader as a caregiver to the people. Good church leaders take care of their churches as a father or mother takes care of his or her children. They build the family, providing for the needs of the children (members) so they can do well. Two negative images were most preferred to describe bad leaders: poison (*urogi*) and darkness (*mugundu*). The image of poison was connected with the concept of the *murogi*, the sorcerer, who uses his poisons to dispatch his victims or to inflict suffering, pain, and loss upon them. Darkness represents the time when evil things are done. Bad leaders keep people in the dark. They teach their people bad things so that the people are led astray into personal destruction. When leaders are bad they act as poison, darkening the lives of their members with deceit and falsehood, destroying the life of the church and promoting the loss of its members. Good leaders, on the other hand, act in ways that promote truthfulness and goodness among the people, leading them to life and good things.

The image of the church leader as the *ithe* (father) figure for the church is related to the attitude and means the leader displays when doing the expected tasks, his style as leader. Granberg (1995) found the Meru church members view their leaders as authority figures, those who know what is right, what is wrong, and who are to be obeyed. As authority figures, these church leaders are relied upon to make good plans for the church and to communicate to the church what needs to be done. Cole (1982) and Harder (1985) found similar preferences for leader style among rural churches in Nigeria and Kenya. Among Nigerian village ECWA (Evangelical Conference of West African) churches, the pastor-leader was considered an authority teacher in the moral, ethical, and religious matters of life (Cole, 1982, p. 187). But the leader as an authority figure does not mean the leader is the domineering figure of command whose wishes are inviolate. Members of African Inland Churches in Kenya demonstrated a preference for a group-centered style of leadership (Harder, 1985). With a group-centered style, the church leader acts as the focal point for decision-making in the church. He is the one who defines the issues for the church, who guides the discussion among the leadership group, and who works within the group to develop a communal plan of action to which the whole church can give assent (Harder, 1985, p. 133). While members of the Meru Churches of

263

Christ expect their church leaders to be figures of authority and worthy to hear, these leaders cannot lapse into an authoritarian mode of leading without risking the desertion of their members, or at least the withdrawal of their active support.

Becoming a Church Leader

The Churches of Christ in Kenya are somewhat rare in the Kenyan Christian community in that there are no formal requirements for leaders or their selection. Men are not required to attend seminaries or other religious training forums to become leaders, though the people certainly expect their leaders to know the Bible and to live well the Christian life (Granberg, 1995). The result is that leaders emerge and are recognized in a fairly naturally-occurring system. We now look at how new leaders tend to emerge and then how this informal leadership is "routinized" into a more formally recognized state.

The emergence of new leaders is most clearly seen in the beginning stages of a new church. The earliest leaders in a beginning church are typically the one or two men who hold temporal primacy within the group; baldly stated, they were the first ones. Since such men usually generated the contact with the visitors (evangelists), they continue to negotiate the events by which a new church may form. As time passes, other leader candidates begin to emerge. Sometimes these later men establish their candidacy for leadership status by their stature in the village, by their educational achievements, or by their wealth. Others contend for recognition as a leader by dint of having the loudest voice, or maybe because they use it the most—they demand attention simply because they are there.

These initial periods of leadership emergence in a new church may last from a few months to a few years. Leadership is fluid as contenders rise and disappear, some by their own choosing, others when the blush of newness fades and new expectations arise. Eventually the leadership of the church routinizes as certain men meet the leadership expectations of the church through their good character, appropriate activities and successful accomplishments in the church. Through observation and experience the church develops a standard which it uses to differentiate those who would be their leaders from those who should be their leaders.

The selection of leaders is formalized first in small ways. Certain men are designated as teachers, as record-keepers, or as signatories on bank accounts. Others may self-select themselves into tasks carried out within the church. These aspiring leaders may begin working with young people in a church choir, they may organize work parties to share the task of digging the *shamba* (garden), or they may present ideas for the church community to consider. If these men meet with success in their initiatives, they too become recognized as leaders by the community and pushed to the fore in the life of the church.

Ultimately, as the churches mature in both their biblical and experiential understanding of what makes good church leaders, they publicly recognize their leaders as shepherds (the primary spiritual leaders), servants (deacons, recognized for their service to the church in specific areas), teachers, or evangelists. As long as these men maintain their respect in the church community and continue to meet with success in their tasks, they will retain their recognition as a leader. If they lose their personal integrity as godly leaders, lapse into patterns of personal tyranny, or fail repeatedly in their leadership tasks, the mantle of leadership is withdrawn through the unspoken consent of the people and ratified by the leader's exclusion from the church's leadership activities.

Village level church leaders have much in common with the traditional Meru *ithe* (father), but regarding the church they are the *ithe* of a community broader than their households. As *ithe* for the community of faith, church leaders are perceived as caregivers, those who look out for their members and encourage their growth. These leaders are also authority figures. They are people who know how to plan work, then to gain the co-operation of the people to complete that work. These two concepts, village level church leaders as caregivers and authority figures, reflect the primary understandings of the function of leaders among the Meru churches.

Conclusion

Leadership among the peoples of East Africa works from a very different base and set of rules than does leadership in the United States or other western countries. The moral economy of the GEM peoples is rooted in a frontier mentality characterized by the maintenance of a labor force of people and a hierarchical ethic that recognizes that people exist in unequal relationships. The intrusion of British administration, continued in the institution of modern government, has overlaid a new set of rules on the old economy. In the new economy, personal power is the currency of leadership, and wealth is the means to achieve that power. The economy of God's kingdom, however, continues to demand servant leaders. In a continent most typically described with adjectives of destruction, whose rulers often seem more like plagues than presidents, the amazing work of God is that the leaders in so many African churches are people of personal strength, integrity, and conviction. These men and women are God's gift to the church. They have exhibited a tenacious capacity to engage the task of Christian leadership while remaining within the expected economies of their people. We celebrate these leaders and watch them with great anticipation as they teach, preach, and lead their churches into the future.

Works Cited

Barra, G. (1990). *1,000 Kikuyu Proverbs.* London: McMillan.

Berman, B. (1990). *Control and Crisis in Colonial Kenya: The Dialectic of Domination.* London: James Currey.

Cagnolo, C. (1933). *The Akikuyu: Their Customs, Traditions and Folklore.* Nyeri, Kenya: Akikuyu Mission Printing School.

Chabal, P. (1992). *Power in Africa: An Essay in Political Interpretation.* London: Macmillan.

Chege, J. (1993). *Dynamics of Regulation of Sexuality, Gender Relations and Demographic Trends in Kenya: The Igembe Socio-Cultural Context.* Unpublished manuscript, Northwestern University.

Clough, M. S. (1990). *Fighting Two Sides: Kenyan Chiefs and Politicians, 1918-1940.* Niwot, CO: University Press of Colorado.

Cole, V. B. (1982). *Leadership Criteria and their Sources among ECWA Churches of Nigeria: Implications for Curriculum in Ministerial Training.* Unpublished doctoral dissertation, Michigan State University.

Davidson, B. (1970). *The African genius: An introduction to African social and cultural history.* London: Little, Brown and Company.

Fadiman, J. A. (1975). *Mountain Warriors: The Pre-Colonial Meru of Mt. Kenya.* Africa Series, no. 29. Athens: Ohio University Press.

———. (1993). *When We Began, There were Witchmen: An Oral History from Mount Kenya.* Berkeley, CA: University of California Press.

Glazier, J. (1985). *Land and the Uses of Tradition among the Mbeere of Kenya*. New York: University Press of America.

Granberg, S. E. (1995). *Curriculum Development Issues for types I and II Leaders for the Churches of Christ in Meru, Kenya*. Unpublished master's thesis, Fuller Theological Seminary, School of World Mission.

Guyer, J. (1995a). Wealth in people, wealth in things - Introduction. *Journal of African History, 36*, 83-90.

——— (1995b). Wealth in people as wealth in knowledge: Accumulation and composition in equatorial Africa, *Journal of African History 36*, 91-120.

Harder, K. (1985). *Kenyan Church Leaders: Perceptions of Appropriate Leadership Behaviors*. Unpublished doctoral dissertation, dissertation, Michigan State University.

Haugerud, A. (1995). *The Culture of Politics in Modern Kenya*. Cambridge: Cambridge University Press.

Hawkins, S. (1996). Disguising chiefs and God as history: Questions on the acephalousness of Lodagaa politics and religion. *Africa, 66* (2), 202-247.

Iliffe (1983). *The Emergence of African Capitalism*. Minneapolis, MN: UMP.

——— (1995). *Africans: The History of a Continent*. Cambridge: Cambridge University Press.

Kenyatta, J. (1942). *My People of Kikuyu and the Life of Chief Wangome*. London: Lutterworth Press.

——— (1938/1953). *Facing Mount Kenya: The Tribal Life of the Gikuyu*. London: Secker and Warburg.

Kershaw, G. (1997). *Mau Mau from Below*. Oxford: James Currey.

Kopytoff, I. (1987). *The African Frontier: The Reproduction of Traditional African Societies.* Bloomington, IN: Indiana University Press.

Lambert, H. E. (1947). *The Use of Indigenous Authorities in Tribal Administration: Studies of the Meru in Kenya Colony.* Cape Town: Communications from the School of African Studies, University of Cape Town.

———— (1950). *The Systems of Land Tenure in the Kikuyu Land Unit: Part I, History of the Tribal Occupation of the Land.* Cape Town, South Africa: University of Cape Town.

Lonsdale, J. M. (1968). Some origins of nationalism in East Africa. *Journal of African History, 9* (1), 119-146.

———— (1988). Review of Kopytoff, *The African Frontier: the reproduction of traditional African societies, African Affairs 87* (347), pp. 286-287.

———— (1992a). The Moral Economy of Mau Mau: Wealth, Poverty and Civic Virtue in Kikuyu Political Thought. In B. Berman and J. Lonsdale (Eds.), *Unhappy Valley: Conflict in Kenya and Africa, Book 2: Violence and Ethnicity,* pp. 315-504. London: James Currey.

Mair, L. P. (1936). Chieftainship in Modern Africa. *Africa, 9* (3), 305-316.

Mazrui, A. A. (1975). The Resurrection of the Warrior Tradition in African Political Culture. *Journal of Modern African Studies, 13* (110, 67-84.

Munro, J. F. (1967). Migrations of the Bantu-speaking peoples of the eastern Kenya highlands: A reappraisal. *Journal of African History, 8* (1), 25-28.

Muriuki, G. (1974). *A History of the Kikuyu: 1500-1900.* London: Oxford University Press.

Njururi, N. (1983). *Gikuyu Proverbs.* London: Macmillan.

Oliver, R. and Matthew, G. (1963). *History of East Africa.* Oxford: Oxford University Press.

Rimita, D. M. (1988). *The Njuri-Ncheke of Meru.* Meru, Kenya: Kolbe Press.

Scott, J. C. (1976). *The Moral Economy of the Peasant: Rebellion and Subsistence in Southeast Asia. New Haven: Yale University* Press.

———— (1985). *Weapons of the Weak: Everyday Forms of Peasant Resistance.* London Yale University Press.

Thompson, E. P. (1991). *Customs in Common.* London: Merlin Press.

Tignor, R. L. (1971). Colonial Chiefs in Chiefless Societies. *Journal of Modern African Studies, 9* (3), 339-359.

Tosh, J. (1973). Colonial Chiefs in a Stateless Society: A Case Study from Northern Uganda. *Journal of African History, 14* (3), 473-490.

Vincent, J. (1977). Colonial Chiefs and the Making of Class: A Case Study from Teso, Eastern Uganda. *Africa, 47* (2), 140-158.

Wagner, G (1940). Concerning the Logoli and Vugusu. In M. Fortes & E. E. Evans-Pritchard (Eds.), *African Political Systems.*, pp. 197-236. Oxford: Oxford University Press.

CHAPTER 12

The Formation, Training, and Transitions in Team Missions

Sonny Guild

Sonny Guild worked in Western Kenya with the Abaluyia people for 10 years. He preached in Tigard, OR for 14 years. Presently, Sonny teaches undergraduate Bible and Missions and directs the Institute for Missions and Evangelism at Abilene Christian University.

Formation of Teams

The task that Jesus Christ gave His followers was to "go and make disciples of all nations, baptizing them in the name of the Father and of the Son and of the Holy Spirit, and teaching them to obey everything I have commanded you" (Matthew 28:19-20). Such a work was daunting and not without opposition. Even so, evangelism was at the heart of the purpose and life of the church from its beginning. It was the overwhelming experience of the love of God in Christ that was the primary motivation for early Christian evangelism (Green, 1975, p. 236). Eventually, to accomplish Christ's commission, missionaries were selected and sent out on special missions.

Teams in the New Testament

The ministry of Jesus illustrates how God Himself accomplished His work through relationships. Jesus first invited His disciples into relationship with Him before He entrusted them with the task of preaching (Mark 3:14). Throughout His work, men and women were accompanying Jesus and this "working in relationship with others" pattern continued as He sent the disciples out in pairs on the limited commission (Luke 10:6).

Paul and Team Missions

Teams are not the only way to do missions, but the use of teams is the primary model found in Acts. One wonders if Paul's use of the team approach was deliberate or simply spontaneous. Because of Paul's proclivity toward working with teams, the use of teams seems to be deliberate (Sawatsky, 1988, p. 19), but does this make teams the scripturally approved method? Kenneth Mitchell, speaking from a contemporary setting, goes so far as to say that teams are not just man's preference but God's preferred way of working in our world (Mitchell, 1988, p. 28). It is interesting that, even though Paul's training and gifts equipped him for effective "solo" ministry, he was involved with various kinds of teamwork throughout his life. The New Testament church was primarily relational and its mission was best accomplished within the same matrix, relationships.

Missions has always included unique individuals who have worked alone and pioneered efforts in many places. We are thankful for such missionaries. Even so, there are strengths that come from working within the context of mission teams. In fact, it could be said that everything of significance is accomplished through relationship. Scripture is full of texts that illustrate the value of numbers. Ecclesiastes 4:9-12 explains the benefits of being in relationship with others, both for greater productivity and for personal well-being. 1

Corinthians 12 describes the church as a body with many members and that, without the multiplicity of members, with differing roles, there is no functioning body. The diversity of the body encourages the principle of synergy which ensures greater creativity. With multiple skills, talents, gifts, experiences and training, teams can outperform individuals acting alone, especially if they are able to capitalize on their diversity (Katzenbach and Smith, 1994, p. 14). Paul frequently gave thanks for the individuals who were his co-workers and, particularly, for the contribution they made to the work (Pocock, 1997, p. 13).

Worldwide Vision

Paul was drawn into working with teams because of God's leading through the Holy Spirit, but there was an additional compelling reality that kept his work team oriented. The global nature of the mission of Christ caused Paul to realize that to accomplish the mission the talents and energy of many people would be required. The teams found in scripture, especially those of Paul, are teams whose members complement one another in their gifts and ministries (Hesselgrave, 1980, p. 111).

Paul's own brief analysis of the value of differing roles and gifts is seen in 1 Corinthians 3:5-9. Paul and Apollos were laborers with God, each with an assigned task. Paul planted the seed, Apollos watered, and God gave the increase. The bringing together of team members with complementary gifts necessitated diversity. Paul's teams were, therefore, composed of diverse groups of individuals where leadership was frequently shared. Paul and Barnabas led at different times, and other team members had responsibilities of leadership as well (Philippians 2:19-24; Titus 1:5). Men joined them who were described as "leaders among the brothers" (Acts 15:22). Paul did not seem to wear the title of "team leader," but those who worked with him certainly recognized his leadership (Sawatsky, 1988, p. 17).

Paul's co-workers filled roles that included such tasks as planters of churches (Colossians 1:7), strengthers of churches (1 Thessalonians 3:1-2), stenographers (Romans 16:22), and messengers (Ephesians 6:21). Paul thought fondly all of his co-workers because of their contribution to the work. 1 Corinthians 16:15-18 is an example of Paul's feelings of devotion to such workers. He acknowledged their devoted service and that their work was worthy of recognition. The involvement of many people facilitated God's work to fulfill Christ's (and Paul's) vision of reaching the world with the Good News.

The Nudge Of The Holy Spirit

The book of Acts does not present only one method of bringing a mission team together. Even so, a consistent part of teams' forming was the work of God through the Holy Spirit (McQuilkin, 1997, p. 25). Acts 13 shows clearly that the choice of the first team was through the initiative of the Holy Spirit. The Holy Spirit was at work in the life of the church in Antioch and in the lives of the two men, Barnabas and Saul, whom He called out to team up for missions (Acts 13:1-3). At other times it was the suggestion of one worker to another to join together (Acts 15:36-41). This seems to have been a pattern of Paul's; he was always gathering others around him to help with the work. Even today, regardless of how the gathering of a team is done, the work of God in His people must be a primary part of the process of bringing teams together. The mission is God's, and he is the one to whom we pray for laborers for the harvest (Matthew 9:35-38).

The experiences of contemporary missionaries also show that there is not just one way to become involved in missions or to form

274

a mission team. Sometimes it is godly leaders at church who suggest the possibility of missions to individuals. Frequently it is long-time friends who explore the possibility of working together. At other times, individuals find themselves working with people they never knew before going to the mission field.

Two realities seem to be in the forefront of team formation. First, we should acknowledge the essential role of the church as the Holy Spirit lives in that community to mature lives and as he moves the church to bring teams together and send them. The church is missionary in nature and raising up and sending missionaries is one of her primary responsibilities, with the Holy Spirit as the guide for the missionary enterprise. Second, God works in the personal lives of his people, and these individuals often "shoulder tap" other godly people to consider working together in missions. While such a team is a group of individuals working together, their success as a team must continually flow from their relationship with Christ and with each other in Christ. In the final analysis, the Lord can further his mission only as both the church and individual Christians live under the call and control of the Holy Spirit.

The Challenge of Teams

Entering the world of teamwork is a new and exciting experience for many people. The initial excitement can bring some success, but success is not long-lived built on excitement alone. Entering the world of teamwork is much like entering a foreign culture. The new "team culture" is especially challenging to teams made up of Americans. America is described as a low-context culture, one that places more value on the individual than on the larger community (Elledge and Phillips, 1995, p. 241). A low-context perspective is counterproductive if one wants to work in teams. Some of the characteristics of a low-context culture are: individual

275

concern; a strong sense of competition; feelings are not as important as doing; and personal wants are more important than community or team needs. These descriptions of American culture necessitate a paradigm shift; from thinking about self to thinking about the good of the team and the ministry to which the team has been called.

When entering a new culture, the essential mindset the missionary must have is that of a learner. Likewise, when becoming involved with a team, there are new ways of thinking and acting to be learned in order to become a successful team. Learning the "culture" of teamwork is possible, but it takes the same kind of effort and dedication that the missionary gives to learning the host culture.

The Challenge of Scope

Mission teams present a unique situation that exacerbates the difficulty of learning the new team culture. Missionaries are often isolated and have less contact with people of their own culture. This isolation increases their interpersonal contact with other team members, thus increasing their degree of scope. Scope is the number of activities that individuals do together. Members of a mission team are involved in each others' lives in many ways: social activities, relaxation, work, worship, planning, children, etc. When there is such a high degree of scope, interpersonal tensions and difficulties are more likely to arise (Hardin, 1972, p. 1-4). The comparison of a mission team to a family, siblings in particular, illustrates how those tensions and difficulties can manifest themselves (Walker, 1992, pp. 16-17). Team members can becomes rivals, territorial, and simply disagreeable.

Cross-cultural living is stressful regardless of whether one's work has a Christian focus or not. The fact that mission teams are a group of Christians working together does not negate the impact of such stress on their relationships. Most significantly, mission teams are placed at the forefront of the war against Satan's kingdom of darkness. Satan will use every weapon he has to destroy them and their work and some of his easiest targets are their interpersonal relationships. Missionaries are not immune to sins of attitude such as hatred, discord, jealousy, anger, selfish ambition, dissensions, factions and envy listed in Galatians 5:19-21. Such sins are a common source of poor interpersonal relationships; therefore, promoting healthy relationships is vital to the life of a team.

The Challenge of Interpersonal Relationships

There are two important aspects of all teamwork: task and maintenance, also described as the task and social components of teams (Rees, 1991, pp. 41-42). Task relates to the work that a team does to fulfill its goals, and maintenance refers to the team environment which allows team members to work together effectively. Productive teams must function well in both aspects of teamwork. Often greater emphasis is placed on the tasks of missions and rightly so. Successful strategies are essential for the work of the team to produce the desired results. The social or maintenance side of teamwork, which relates to the interpersonal relationships of team members, is often neglected.

Both task and social (interpersonal) skills operate all the time. To the extent that a team does its work well, it will be productive. If a team manages its relationships well, members will have a strong commitment and will, therefore, increase productivity. Easier said than done! The lack of good interpersonal relationships is the most frequent sign of an unproductive team (Dyer, 1995, p. 81).

Research has shown that relationship maintenance is as important as being able to do the tasks related to teamwork. The secular world highlights how important interpersonal relationship skills are for team players. A study was done that ranked the importance of various training needs for Americans working in Asia. Americans and nationals both ranked human relations skills first in importance. Technical skill, the ability to do one's job, was ranked fourth by both groups (Johnston, 1973, p. 1-2). Both Americans and nationals felt that interpersonal relationship skills took precedence over task skills. A major concern for many employers today is to find employees who can work well with others.

Leslie Anne Moore wrote a master's thesis at Abilene Christian University studying reverse culture shock in Church of Christ missionaries. Her research indicated that interpersonal difficulties with team members were the most frequent problems missionaries experienced (Moore, 1981, 77). Steve Meeks (1987, p. 281) indicated that healthy interpersonal relationships are a key to having a successful mission team. Improving interpersonal relationship skills has been a neglected area of preparation in mission teams.

A survey done in 1996 of present and past Church of Christ missionaries explored what a mission team should learn before going overseas. Two important questions were asked: "What are the two or three most critical issues that teams should address?" and "What are the two or three most critical abilities a team should develop?" Fifty percent of the responses related to the need for good interpersonal skills (Guild, 1996, pp. 9-10, 115).

The presence of interpersonal problems among team members is not unique to Church of Christ missionaries. Conversations with leaders in Baptist missions and Wycliffe Bible Translators indicate that interpersonal conflict among missionaries is the major problem that most mission teams face. While training in interpersonal skills may seem less academic and perhaps less important than strategies, the lack of such skills is the major reason teams find themselves becoming dysfunctional and therefore must be addressed. Wendell Broom put it succinctly when, in a casual conversation, he said,

"Missions would be great if it weren't for people!" The challenge for missionaries is to learn how to get along with people, especially their fellow workers.

Advantages in the Midst of Challenges

We need not feel discouraged because there are significant challenges faced by missionaries involved in mission teams. There is great power through team corporate prayer. Multiple team members help the ministry avoid being personality centered. As a Christian community they provide support, encouragement, and accountability. New Christians, developing churches, and church leaders are blessed when they see a model of Christian community within the mission team itself.

Training of Teams

The most important factor influencing the success of teams is training. Becoming a mature team is a process. It is a process that is somewhat paradoxical. Human beings, on the one hand, have always worked toward common goals, as teams. But, on the other hand, often in formal organization, such teams can devolve into fragmentation, conflict, and dysfunction (Huston, 1999, p. 5). As a team begins to develop its relationships, interpersonal problems will arise. The same will be true throughout the life of a team. Hence, there is the need for team building, so that the fragmentation, conflict, and dysfunction will not destroy the team. Essentially, team building is helping a team gather data about itself and assisting them through a process of data feedback, problem identification, and action planning (Phillips and Elledge, 1989, p. 9).

Team building must go beyond teaching about certain skills. New information must be shared, but opportunities to practice new skills must also be experienced. The underlying assumption of team building is that individual performance affects the work of the team. Powerful team building occurs when team members rethink their team experience. Team building does not have to occur only when problems need to be addressed, but can be an effective way to help provide resources to deal with problems when they arise.

The team building experience is part of the process of developing the paradigm shift from a single-minded perspective to concern for the welfare of the group or team. Dealing with this shift in thinking, helping a team understand itself and the value of the diversity within the group, and developing good interpersonal skills will be part of creating a climate for a successful team experience.

The Basics of Team Development

Team building is not an event but a process. Particular issues must be addressed in this process in order to create a healthy team culture and to accomplish the mission of the team. Numerous authors provide lists of characteristics of healthy teams (Dyer, 1995, p.15; Harris and Moran, 1991, p. 182; Parker,1990, p. 31). Some of those characteristics are: clear purpose, informal atmosphere, listening skills, open communication, consensus decisions, and the ability to resolve conflict. Along with the input of these authors, the input of present and past missionaries can help determine the specific characteristics which ought to be addressed.

Definition of Team

A mission team must have an adequate understanding of what a team is. A team is more than a working group. A working group is involved in joint effort but does not necessarily view its work as interdependent, while a team is committed to collective, interdependent action. Teamwork and group activity do not necessarily add up to a team. Teamwork requires interdependence (Parker,

1990, p. 16). A mission team can work together as a work group, but the greatest productivity will come when the members are in relationship and work together within the context of those relationships.

Team Diversity

The concepts of teamwork and synergy are powerful because the team is made up of diverse individuals. Often people judge differences they see in others as wrong, simply because they are "not like me." Teams need to move from being judgmental about differences to understanding their diversity. From there they must come to respect and appreciate their diversity, and ultimately to value the diversity among them. Diversity can be measured in many ways: personality, behavior types, gifts, talents, training, experience, age, culture, gender...and much more. All of these diverse realities will bless a team which does not let their differences work against them.

Diversity can be dangerous if team members function with an individualistic perspective. In such an environment, diversity encourages conflict rather than teamwork. Valuing the team and the diversity of team members requires a certain amount of "letting go" of self and ego for the benefit of the group. Team members must believe that each individual has a valuable contribution to make and that the product of the group is better than that of any one individual.

Communication: Listening and Feedback

Communication is important within a team. In fact, one way to view the team environment is to see it as a communication network (Huston, 1999, p. 21). There are two important aspects of communication for teams: active listening and feedback. Glenn Parker suggests listening skills as the single most important factor distinguishing effective teams from ineffective ones (Parker, 1990, p.

37). Human beings spend forty-five percent of their time listening and only thirty percent of their time talking (DeVito, 1992, p. 54). While listening is done the most, the least amount of training is given in good listening techniques.

Active listening allows the listeners to check how accurately they have understood what someone else has said. Acceptance of the speaker's feelings can also be expressed. Because active listening facilitates understanding, it is an underpinning for all other determinants of team effectiveness (Parker, 1990, p. 37). Listening skills must be learned and encouraged. A team that listens well will have a better chance at success.

Dietrich Bonhoeffer developed a theology of listening in his book *Life Together* (Bonhoeffer, 1954, pp. 97-99). Listening is the first service one owes to another person. Our listening provides us with information about the needs of others and shows them that they are valued. God heard the cries of His children, He listened and responded to them (Exodus 3:7-10). We experience God's ultimate response to human cries through the cross. Good listening will help us become more like our Father in heaven.

As well as listening, team members must be able to communicate effectively. Verbal communication is essential: especially the giving and receiving of feedback. The purpose of feedback is to give or to receive help, but one of its challenges is to perceive feedback constructively. Team members need to trust each others' intentions and learn how to frame feedback properly.

Constructive Conflict Resolution

Conflict is a reality in human relationships. Dealing with conflict constructively presents a challenge to mission teams. Every individual has personal perceptions of conflict, most of which are negative. However, it is important to reframe our understanding of conflict. It is neither a necessary evil nor a sign of failure. Conflict is normal, and if it is handled well the results can be positive. Teams cannot avoid conflict, but they must learn to manage it.

Leadership

Effective leadership must be in place. Leadership can follow several models. It can be a designated leader, shared leadership, or leadership based on expertise. Who is leading is not as important as the fact that there is leadership. The realization that there are different styles of leadership is helpful. Also, as teams mature, there is less emphasis on one leader and greater emphasis on group leadership or group power. Mission teams must understand that Christian leadership is modeled after Jesus rather than the world. His style of leadership separated Him from the rest of the world. He employed a servant leadership style, which was illustrated when He washed His disciples' feet, thus serving His followers (John 13:1-17).

Decision Making

Good group process is essential to maintaining good relationships. The process of decision-making must be done well, or meetings can become destructive. These skills are developed through training, education, and experience. These skills must be used to attack a problem rather than attacking one another. The concept of consensus in making decisions that are lasting needs to be clearly understood.

Trust and Openness

Trust is built and derived from how the team members deal with each other and, as such, is the most critical factor in having a healthy team. Trust is not an immediate reality in a team. The lack of trust is at least part of the problem in almost every dysfunctional team (Elledge and Phillips, 1994, p. 51). Trust and openness naturally go together. Without trust, there can be no openness; without true openness, trust cannot be maintained. Teams that cultivate trust and protect the vulnerability created by openness are well on their way to success.

Transitions of Teams

A mission team goes through many transitions. In fact, its whole life will be one transition after another. Life is like that. Transitions are significant moments and need to be recognized as opportunities for team building. The process of becoming a team is the first transition to experience. It is important for the team to understand that this is a process and, therefore, can be survived effectively.

Becoming a Team

The process of becoming a team has been described in several ways. One description is: forming, storming, norming and performing (Tuckman, 1965, pp. 381-399). Another descriptive model is: getting started, going in circles, getting on course, and full speed (Wellins, Byham, and Wilson, 1991, pp. 191-213). A final model for describing the process of team development is: testing, infighting, getting organized, and mature closeness (Francis and Young, 1979, pp. 9-11). Whatever labels are used to describe this process, it is clear that a team moves through specific stages of team development.

Stages One and Two

The initial period (forming, getting started, testing) is a time of getting acquainted. Conversations are polite and surface level. As the team moves into the second stage (storming, going in circles, infighting), there is less concern for politeness. The concerns shift to the tasks of defining goals, roles, and other structures and strategies related to teamwork. This process brings out differences of thinking and personality. Some teams never enter this stage because they are fearful that "storming" will have a negative impact on the team.

Stage Three

The storming process leads to a third stage, a more secure stage of team development (norming, getting on course, and getting organized). Through the team-building process, guidelines are established for making decisions, dealing with conflict and interpersonal communication. Trust is increased because of their shared experiences and the new norms that have been agreed upon. Cohesion develops even in the midst of diversity, and relationships grow.

Stage Four

The goal of a team is to accomplish a task. The next stage (performing, full speed, and mature closeness) is where the team finally begins to do the work for which it was created. This stage has its own needs that are important for team development. Successful work provides opportunities for celebration, assessment, and readjustment.

Teams may move in and out of these four stages as changes in membership and leadership occur. The team building process will continue as long as the team exists.

Other Significant Transitions

A major transition is when the team arrives on the mission field. This presents a time that can create stress and test the relationships of team members. Language learning is part of this experience. Some team members may find language learning much easier than others. During this initial stage of acculturation teams need to be sure they are communicating. Questions should not just deal with the facts of what is going on but, also, with feelings: "How are you doing?"

All of the team members may not arrive on the field at the same time. When a new team member arrives, a significant transition moment has arrived as well. Team members always wonder how they will fit in. What will be their place in the team? Care must be given to incorporate the new member into the team. The team must be sure they make room in their busy schedules to give time and attention to team building, for the sake of the new team member and the team as well.

As the work matures, there will be new dimensions of how the team will need to function. Their relationship with mature churches will be different than it was with new Christians. This is a transition moment. The team needs to discover what the needs are and develop methods to address them, an opportune moment for team assessment and team building.

When teams come together there is the hope that their work together will continue for a significant number of years. Often, life brings realities that require some team members to leave the field sooner than expected, due to illness, death, needs of the family on the field or back home, or support difficulties. None of these are easy moments. Such a time is a significant moment for giving attention to the particular team members and to the team as a whole as well. Loss and the grieving process will be experienced. Team members should help each other with the specific realities and the impact of such loss.

Teams have a life cycle. There will come a time when the team will need to discover how they will end their work together called, planned disengagement. This will be a significant transition for the team and for the national church as well. Effective planning will need to be done so that the team's departure will not be haphazard but meaningful and productive. In fact, the ending of a team and teamwork may be more important than the beginning. The finish is what will linger in the mind and heart; therefore, it must be done thoughtfully and well.

Conclusion

Mission teams are the most effective method for planting new communities of faith around the world. They are not without problems and difficulties, but anything worthwhile is worthy of the effort to do it right. In the Churches of Christ, the training of mission teams has not always addressed the issues of interpersonal relationships sufficiently. Once we begin to address these issues in the training process, mission teams will be healthier and more effective. Beyond preparing the teams before they go to the field, teams must also be sustained once they are on the field. Churches who send and missionary trainers who equip must be dedicated to the task of continuing the job of building the teams we have sent. In this God will be glorified.

WORKS CITED

Bonhoeffer, Dietrich (1954). *Life Together.* New York, NY: Harper and Row.

DeVito, Joseph A. (1992). *The Interpersonal Communication Book.* 6th ed. New York, NY: Harper Collins.

Dyer, William G. (1995). *Team Building: Current Issues and New Alternatives.* 3rd ed. New York, NY: Addison-Wesley Publishing Company.

Elledge, Robin L. and Phillips, Steven L. (1994). *Team Building for the Future: Beyond the Basics.* San Diego, CA: Pfeiffer.

Francis, Dave and Young, Don (1979). *Improving work Groups: A Practical Manual for Team Building.* San Diego, CA: University Associates Inc.,.

Green, Michael (1975). *Evangelism in the Early Church.* London: Hodder And Stoughton.

Guild, Sonny (1996). *A Model for Enhancing Interpersonal Relationships Within Mission Teams.* Unpublished doctoral thesis, Abilene Christian University.

Hardin, Daniel C. (1972). The Missionary and the Concept of Scope. *Mission Strategy Bulletin 2:1-2.*

Harris, Philip R. and Moran, Robert To (1991). *Managing Cultural Differences.* 3rd ed. Houston, TX: Gulf Publishing Co..

Huston, J. T. (1999). *Truth About Teams: A Facilitator's Survival Guide.* Central Point, OR: The Oasis Press.

Johnston, Mary Boppell (1973). Training Needs of Overseas Americans as Seen by Their National Co-Workers. *Social Change, 4:1-3.*

Hesselgrave, David J. (1980). *Planting Churches Cross-Culturally: A Guide for Home and Foreign Missions*. Grand Rapids, MI: Baker Book House.

Meeks, Steven (1987). Successful Missionary Teams. *Gospel Advocate* 129 (10):281.

McQuilkin, Robertson (1997). The Role of the Holy Spirit in Missions. In C. Douglas McConnell (Ed.). *The Holy Spirit and Mission Dynamics*, pp. 22-35. Pasadena, CA: William Carey Library.

Mitchell, Kenneth R. (1988). *Multiple Staff Ministries*. Philadelphia: Westminster Press.

Moore, Leslie (1981). *A Study of Reverse Culture Shock in North American Church of Christ Missionaries*. Unpublished master's thesis, Abilene Christian University.

Parker, Glenn M. (1990). *Team Players and Teamwork: The New Competitive Business Strategy*. San Francisco, CA: Jossey-Bass.

Phillips, S. L., and Elledge, Robin L. (1989). *The Team-Building Source Book*. San Diego, CA: University Associates.
Pocock, Michael (1997). Missiology and Spiritual Dynamics: An Overview of the Issues. In C. Douglas McConnell (Ed.). *The Holy Spirit and Mission Dynamics*, pp. 9-21. Pasadena, CA: William Carey Library.

Rees, Fran (1991). *How to Lead Work Teams: Facilitation Skills*. San Diego, CA: Pfeiffer.

Sawatsky, Ben A. (1988). *A Team Approach to Church Planting in World Class Cities*. Unpublished doctoral thesis, Trinity Evangelical Divinity School.

Tuckman, B. W. (1965). Developmental Sequence in Small Groups. *Psychological Bulletin 63* (6): 384-399.

Walker, Rosalinda (1992). We are Family. *Journal of Applied Missiology* 3, (2): 15-20.

Wellins, Richard S., Byham, William C., and Wilson, Jeanne M. (1991). *Empowered Teams.* San Francisco, CA: Jossey-Bass Publishers.

finishing Well: Phase-Out or Partnership?

Monte B. Cox

Monte Cox served as a missionary among the Kalenjin peoples of western Kenya from 1982-1992. He is assistant professor of Bible at Harding University and holds the Ph.D. from Trinity International University.

Seven teams of missionaries of the Churches of Christ established churches in rural Kenya between 1969-1998. In keeping with a methodology widely accepted in the 20th century, these missionaries were all committed to the "three selves" strategy (plus one) that calls for the eventual "euthanasia of mission." That is, they believed their job was to establish "indigenous churches"–that is, churches that are "self-supporting," "self-governing," "self-propagating" and "self-theologizing"–then leave them as soon as possible to continue the work on their own.[1] The results of their efforts are impressive: together with their African colleagues, they have planted more than 500 churches in thirty years. And since 1992 all seven of these

---

[1] Paul Hiebert (1985) added this fourth phrase to the formula, suggesting that national churches must be taught to interpret Scripture themselves, without imposing upon them the imported interpretations of the missionaries.

mission teams have either completely or partially "phased out" of their respective areas according to their original plan.

Meanwhile, in wider evangelical circles, the call for the "euthanasia of mission" has been drowned out by the plea for "partnership."[2] Instead of leaving the field and handing over all responsibilities to young national churches, many missionaries and the churches sponsoring them are now looking for ways to partner with national Christians in the ongoing work of the church. The discussion usually raises four practical questions: (1) How should sending churches, missionaries, and national Christians work together organizationally? (2) How should the missionaries themselves—foreigners and nationals—work together? (3) How should sending churches and national churches cooperate financially? (4) How should sending churches, missionaries and national Christians work together in providing Bible training for local churches? These issues correspond to the "three selves" plus one that defined sound missions policy for two generations of missionaries. The debate about organization comes in response to the previous push for self-governance. The question of missionary personnel reflects tension carried over from the days in which "self-propagation" was the watchword. The emphasis in the past on "self-support" still raises concerns about the problem of financial dependency. And "self-theologizing" suggests to many a much lesser role for foreign "partners" than some missionaries (and national Christians) desire.

To be sure, partnerships between sending churches, missionaries and national Christians take many forms, but they usually involve

---

[2] For an historical review of the shift from "the three selves" strategy to "partnership," see Monte B. Cox, "'Euthanasia of mission' or `partnership'? An evaluative study of the policy of disengagement of Church of Christ missionaries in rural Kenya." Ph.D. diss., Trinity International University, 21-33. For similar but dated summaries of these same developments, the most valuable are those by Kasdorf (1979) and by Beyerhaus and Lefever (1964).

something less than the complete withdrawal of personnel and/or funds from abroad. Nevertheless, Church of Christ missionaries in rural Kenya have continued to "euthanize the mission" after ten to fifteen years of ministry, and effectively end any ongoing partnership. In the wake of their departure, there are some indications that the churches they established have declined in number, that morale among national church leaders is low, and that the informal organizational structures they left behind are not functioning well. The fundamental question addressed in this chapter and worded in biblical language is this: How can sending churches, missionaries and national Christians cooperate in shepherding, evangelism, giving and biblical training? To answer that question, I will first summarize the strategies of these seven mission teams in these four areas of church ministry—shepherding, evangelism, giving and biblical training—in light of the partnership issues outlined above. I will then describe these teams' "phase out" plans and evaluate them in light of the partnership literature and the opinions of African church leaders themselves.

THE STRATEGY OF THE SEVEN RURAL MISSION TEAMS

How did these seven teams operate with regard to shepherding, evangelism, giving, and Bible training in the churches they planted? The following summary is based on these teams' writings and personal interviews with team members.

Shepherding

These seven mission teams functioned in similar ways with regard to local church elders, the association of churches, and their interaction with national leaders. All of them said they were committed to appointing elders in each local congregation. Yet, with some exceptions, there is little evidence in their records or personal recollections of their teaching on the role of elders, training leaders to become elders, or instructing churches how to ordain them until just before they left the field. Instead, the focus of leadership training was on self-appointed, vocational evangelists. One common hindrance to the appointment of elders was the widespread practice of polygamy in these rural areas. Another was the missionaries' commitment to the "plurality of elders" and "local church autonomy" which made most of them nervous about the possibility of appointing elders over entire clusters of churches, a practice which would have enabled congregations with only one qualified elder candidate to appoint him to serve along with other qualified candidates from neighboring churches. Ironically, another hindrance to the appointment of elders in local churches was the missionaries' high level of involvement in the process whenever elders *were* appointed. Since the missionaries initiated and supervised the whole process, the mechanism whereby churches might appoint elders independent of the missionaries was not clarified. For the most part, missionaries seemed content with *de facto* leaders. Some suggested that God would show the churches how to organize after the missionaries left.

At the extra-congregational level, these missionaries unwittingly placed themselves at the center of the organizational structure in these seven rural church movements. Their travel from church to church for evangelism and teaching tied the whole movement together. The newsletters and other printed materials they produced were the main source of information exchanged between the churches in each area. Visitation between churches not in the same vicinity was usually facilitated by missionary vehicles.

The missionaries showed their dissatisfaction with being at the center of things organizationally by their attempts to shift the hub of the association to some other structure. Eventually, the cluster model of organization emerged as the preferred model. Churches in a given area, usually within walking distance of each other, were encouraged to gather once a month in a central location within their "cluster" for "unity" meetings. Still, most of them felt that the clusters alone were insufficient to foster the kind of cooperation and coordination that the movement needed. With their departure looming and no workable organizing structure in place, five of the seven teams opted to establish "training centers" which would do double duty as centralized leadership training facilities and as operational hubs for the whole association.[3]

Most of these missionaries aspired to a partnership model of interaction with African leaders, even referring to themselves in some teams as "church advisors" to stress the fraternal nature of the relationship. Missionaries and nationals worked together in church planting. But, with few exceptions, in the planning and facilitation of evangelists' meetings, the development of leadership training curricula, the construction and organization of the training centers, and the placement and replacement of foreign personnel, the missionaries made most of the decisions.

Evangelism

All of these rural mission teams stressed near-church evangelism by volunteer evangelists with informal or nonformal training as the best, most reproducible means of church growth. Unpaid preachers, after all, had the wherewithal to plant and nurture churches close to home which would also contribute to the development of clusters. Several missionaries organized more formal teams of volunteer

---

[3.] One team continued to build the association around an annual "preachers' meeting," while another established a loosely organized "advisory council" which met periodically whenever they–either the missionaries or nationals–felt the need. These two teams also built training centers.

evangelists to further encourage the establishment of churches "apart from the American missionary's influence" (Chowning, 1985, pp.36-37).

The missionaries themselves planted many churches that were far from their places of residence and far from each other geographically. Their vehicles and work funds made this far-flung evangelism possible. But no team devised a strategy for how evangelism to distant parts of the tribe and beyond would continue without them. It should also be noted here that while all but one of these teams planted at least one church in the town where they lived, by their own admission these urban churches function like rural ones on the edges of the city.

Giving

Most of the teams in rural Kenya during this period held to a strict no-subsidy policy in keeping with their commitment to self-support. This does not mean that the missionaries never gave money to Africans. Generally speaking, they responded to individual requests or to church building projects, but only as personal benevolence or as personal contributions to churches during *harambees*, or public fund-raisers. At the same time, all but one team admit that they spent little if any time teaching local churches about giving or tithing.

Their rigid adherence to self-support brought criticism from nationals along the way. In one area, the missionaries were derisively labeled "*wenye mikono tupu*," "the ones with empty hands" (Merritt, 1980, p. 44). Missionaries occasionally bowed to the pressure and experimented with paying national evangelists with American funds. But the few experiments on record caused tension and division and were quickly abandoned. Then, during a period when the government became suspicious of the missionaries because of the lack of visible physical development in the churches, most of the teams chose to subsidize the construction of local church buildings to one degree or another. Later on, when teams began to phase out, most of them changed their tune on self-support. The most visible and common departure from the previous policy is seen in the proliferation of the training centers mentioned before, which five of seven teams have established. Without exception, these centers were built, maintained, and staffed entirely with American funds. When asked about this change in policy, most of the missionaries expressed reservations about the financial arrangements, but justified the move by defending the need for an ongoing training program in a central location.

Bible Training

Most of the missionaries from these seven teams agreed with this "central thesis" of the "Kenya Church Growth Philosophy" as stated by Gailyn Van Rheenen, a thesis which reflects their commitment to "self-theologizing" in particular and to the other "selves" in general:

> Our central thesis has been that we must raise up self-sufficient evangelists, not evangelists dependent on us....[They] should not be dependent upon us for finances, for the making of plans for evangelism, and for the making of theology for the Kipsigis. We must feel that Christ who is the head of His church can mature evangelists to support themselves, to make plans for evangelism, and to work out God's will from a biblical base for Christians of Kenya (Van Rheenen, 1983b, p. 37).

All of these missionaries wrestled with the tension between the constant push for planting new churches and the need to stabilize existing ones through leadership training. Some of them believed that the best theological education occurred in the context of evangelism. As Van Rheenen explains:

> Our emphasis was first church initiation and maturation and secondarily leadership training. We believed that leaders develop naturally in a growing, vibrant fellowship. If leaders are trained before a church develops cohesiveness, a distinction is typically made between the clergy and the laity. If, on the other hand, many men are simultaneously matured in the context of a vibrant body of believers, many more men evolve into evangelists, elders, and deacons. Thus, we initially matured churches and only at a later time trained leaders who grew out of these fellowships (Van Rheenen, 1985, p. 83).

The priority of evangelism led most teams to choose a nonformal mode of theological education which they could implement as "on-the-job" training for evangelists without sacrificing evangelistic momentum to do it. In contrast to this model, which could be called "theological education *through* evangelism," one mission team opted for what could be called "theological education *before* evangelism." This team began systematic leadership training with a much smaller base of churches, leaving church planting to the nationals early on.

Time exposed the weaknesses of a lack of balance on this issue. The teams that chose 'theological education before evangelism" wondered later if the decision had stunted church growth in their area. Those that preferring the "on-the-job-training" approach began to hear African church leaders call for more formal modes of education, especially as educational standards in Kenya began to rise. Their requests often met with resistance from the missionaries. But, as the time for disengagement drew near, many of them became more amenable to the idea of formal theological training centers, both as a positive answer to the nationals' request and as a possible solution to the organizational dilemmas raised by their imminent departure from the field.

Disengagement

Two restatements of the classic "euthanasia of mission" philosophy, written by former missionaries from these teams, reflect the attitude of most of these missionaries toward disengagement.

> The role of American church advisors (missionaries) is seen as temporary. They are here to establish and assist (not to rule or to legislate for) the church for a limited time in hopes that the national congregations will continue with no ill effects after Americans relocate, hopefully at the end of the 1980s (Hemphill, 1980, p.47).
>
> There comes a time when the initial evangelists from another culture must leave the work in the hands of the Lord. We want to prepare for that time instead of letting it catch us unaware. The church should continue to grow even when we are away. We must teach them that the most urgent task before them is evangelism. They need to be doing that now and not wait until they feel forced to do it since we are no longer here to do it for them (Barr, 1980, p. 107).

Again, the majority of these missionaries entered Kenya with the intention of disengaging after ten to fifteen years. But, with the exception of one team that wrote a sixty-page phase-out plan, there was no clear disengagement strategy. Until last year, none of these teams had conducted an objective analysis of the impact of disengagement on their churches. Anecdotal evidence suggested to them that churches have struggled just to retain the growth they achieved when the missionaries were present. The missionaries interviewed during a study in Kenya in 1998 offered these recurring bits of advice on disengagement from the vantage point of hindsight: (1) involve nationals in decision making from the start; (2) introduce formal training sooner than most of them did; (3) don't cling to rigid phase out time tables, but rather appreciate the "mystery" of the timing of disengagement and the movement of God's spirit in the lives of people; (4) establish urban churches, too.

African Church Leaders' Evaluation of the Strategy

The conclusions in this chapter are supported by research I conducted in 1998 to assess the impact of missionary disengagement on the churches, particularly those in Eldoret, Kenya (Cox, 1999).[4] Leaders there were asked specific questions critiquing the missionaries' policies on shepherding, expansion, finances and theological education. Regarding elders, the leaders said that the lack of formally recognized leaders has contributed to low member retention, and that recent moves to expedite the appointment of elders in local churches were already helping correct the problem. Still, they said, many of the elders who have been appointed need more training to understand their role. At the cluster and association level, few elders are meeting together to coordinate their efforts as they were encouraged to do. They blamed this failure on the departure of the missionaries who had pushed for such meetings. They also cited confusion surrounding the elder selection process that has prevented more churches from appointing elders since the missionaries left.

Regarding expansion, the leaders were less critical of the missionaries, though they were saddened by their impression that while our evangelists start churches quickly, they do not know how to care for them once they are planted. They also perceive that expansion

---

[4] For complete quantitative and qualitative data, see Cox (1999).

has slowed considerably since the missionaries began to disengage. Even near-church evangelism has been hampered by the poor economy which forces volunteer evangelists to spend more time making a living. Also for economic reasons, far-flung evangelism has slowed to a standstill with the departure of the missionaries.

The leaders saved their strongest criticisms for the missionaries' financial policies. Most of the leaders who spoke out were troubled by the missionaries' insistence on self-support from the start when the churches were young and small. The subsequent lack of church buildings negatively affected the morale in the churches and tarnished the churches' image in the eyes of the public. Their comments showed that the missionaries' policies had also eroded the trust between the nationals and the missionaries, especially as the leaders became aware of missionaries in other regions who were not as strict on self-support. Some Kalenjin church leaders concluded that these missionaries in Eldoret were blocking the flow of funds from the States, funds that should have been given to the nationals. The leaders did assume some responsibility for the poverty of the churches, admitting that their own giving was anemic at best, but blaming the missionaries for neglecting to teach them about tithing from the start.

While the leaders appreciated what these missionaries had taught them through informal and nonformal methods, they agreed that these approaches were no longer adequate. They praised initial attempts at extension programs and requested still more formal training.

The leaders' evaluation of the missionaries' disengagement policy can be summarized in four phrases: too soon, too hurried, too haphazard and too hidden. It came too soon, they said, because the church was still small and weak with too few members who were too

301

poor to assume the responsibilities of the missionaries. Their disen-gagement was also too rushed and too haphazard, as if the mission-aries had not planned for the transition at all. And, they were per-turbed by what they perceived to be a lack of openness about the whole process.

It was clear from the comments of these church leaders in Eldoret that the "four selves," and even the terms translated for shepherding, evangelism, giving and Bible training needed to be replaced in future discussions about the same issues with categories that made more sense to them, namely: *ripset* (protecting) *amdaet* (preaching), *tesetab tai* (development), *somanet* (education) and *kipagenge* (unity), which refers mainly to the cooperation necessary to making improvements in the first four areas of the churches' life. These were the categories that were used to outline specific changes recommended in subsequent meetings between the nationals, the missionaries, and the U.S. elders that sponsored them.

Implications

Based on the experience of these missionaries in general and the evaluative study of the Eldoret disengagement in particular, five broad implications of this data stand out as most significant. They all relate to the need to clarify the confusion associated with: (1) organizational ambiguities; (2) the authority of the missionary; (3) the transition period that precedes missionary disengagement; (4) the definition of an "indigenous church"; and (5) the tendency to over-correct mistakes of the past.

Clarifying Organizational Ambiguities

It is obvious that the organizational ambiguities in the Churches of Christ in rural Kenya, both at the local and association level, have at least dampened morale and perhaps stunted the growth of the church, not only in Northern Kalenjin, but perhaps in other mission fields as well. The questions that must be asked are structural ones: What are the structures of shepherding, evangelism, giving and Bible training? Or, in Kalenjin parlance, how can churches show *kipagenge* (unity) and cooperate for the sake of *ribset* (member care), *amdaet* (evangelism), *tesetab tai* (development), and *somanet* (education)?

Unfortunately, too many missionaries defend a "hands off" approach to these basic organizational questions, claiming that it is "healthy" for nationals to work these things out for themselves or believing that the Holy Spirit will eventually resolve these issues. The missionaries need to hear not only the complaints of these nationals, but the warnings of eminent missiologists and sociologists about the failure of "antistructural movements" like this one. Paul Hiebert, for one, writes, "The transition from charismatic founder to bureaucratic leader is crucial for the survival of the institution. If it does not take place, the institution dies" (Hiebert, 1983, 159).

With that warning in mind, missionaries and nationals need to give more attention to what one missionary calls "infrastructure development" at both the local and association level. In local churches, leaders and missionaries must devise a mechanism whereby elders are appointed, one which is not dependent on the presence of the missionaries. Prerequisite to that agreement, some of these missionaries must set aside their preference for *defacto* leaders. Even in churches where there are no qualified elder candidates (according to the biblical criteria), the organizational structure must still be taught early in the life of the church.

At the association level, missionaries and nationals must clarify the relationship between churches, replacing the concept of "local church autonomy" and its negative connotations of separateness and isolation with a healthier understanding of the interdependency of churches in Kenya and beyond. To do that, those involved must ask hard questions about their commitment to strict congregational polity. Is this commitment rooted more in the democratic spirit of the founders than in clear biblical teaching? Does Scripture really prescribe only the sorts of interchurch cooperative efforts that are accepted by Churches of Christ in the United States? Is there any room for innovation on the mission field? I am not suggesting that is it necessary to introduce structures that are radically different from those in the United States, structures which would likely weaken rather than strengthen the ties between these rural Kalenjin churches and their counterparts abroad. But I do believe churches could appoint elders over entire clusters of churches and that elders–American and foreign–and missionaries–American and Kenyan–should meet regularly as the council that shepherds the whole body. Such a model is based on positive biblical precedent (namely, the Jerusalem conference of Acts 15 which included both elders and apostles).

Clarifying the Role of the Missionary

The missionaries in this study need to clarify their role in terms of their authority, the relationship between themselves, the churches they plant and the churches in the States that sent them to Kenya, and their length of service on the field.

These missionaries typically rejected the authority that the Kenyans tended to ascribe to them in favor of a more fraternalistic self-understanding after the fashion of Roland Allen and the "Nevius Plan." Were they wise to do so? Jim Reppart argues that,

> The missionary needs to assume the role that the African gives him. He looks at you as bishop. And biblically, in the book of Acts, you are an apostle, you are sent out. So behave that way. Take the authority (Reppart, p. 1998).

Reppart adds an example of how a missionary who accepts this "apostolic" role might be involved in the selection of church leaders:

> If you think that guy [an elder candidate] is the wrong spiritual person, say, "That's the wrong guy." I know that goes against the grain. We used to think, "No, let the nationals choose." . . . But as a missionary with spiritual judgment, I believe we ought to take a deeper role in developing those spiritual leaders . . . from the beginning. None of this "let them decide." How are they going to decide? What spiritual equipment do they have to make that decision (Reppart, p. 1998)?

I do not agree that the missionary should have veto power in the nationals' leader selection process nor would I support a return to a paternalistic model of interaction between missionaries and nationals. But role clarification would mean that the missionary would act with more authority than these missionaries did, especially when it comes to establishing organizational structure. At the same time, they would avoid placing themselves at the hub of the whole association, as these missionaries inadvertently did. To do so, they would explain from the beginning how they were sent to the field, who is responsible for them, and how the churches they are planting should be organized. They would not leave the fundamental organizational issues for nationals to decide.

Missionaries should also serve as the initial link between the churches they plant and the churches that sent them. But, as soon as possible, the leaders of those sponsoring churches should form a relationship with local leaders so that the missionaries do not act as middlemen indefinitely. In the Eldoret case, this meant a face-to-face meeting between American and Kalenjin church elders. Such a move (a) reinforces the church-centered organizational model the missionaries want to put in place rather than a missionary-centered model; (b) reduces the feeling of isolation expressed in various ways by the Kenyan leaders in this study; and (c) minimizes the risks of a loss of trust between missionaries and nationals over various decisions which nationals often think the missionaries make on their own. Wise missionaries will learn from the Kenyan experience and open the lines of communication sooner than these missionaries did.

Still under the heading of role clarification, missionaries in these circles need to think through the issues related to increasingly brief terms of service including the roots of this shift in missionary tenure and the importance of replacement teams. First, most of the missionaries in this study left the field for personal reasons, usually the education of their children. But most were convinced that they could disengage without injuring the churches they left behind. The missionaries need to reexamine the notion that they can "get in and out in a hurry," and check for ways in which their culture's obsession with productivity and efficiency has influenced their view of the missionary task. Although it is impossible and unprofitable to establish rigid time tables for disengagement, the evidence suggests that ten to fifteen years is simply not enough time in most mission fields to establish a new movement of churches, then leave them on their own. These missionaries need to think of ministries that last at least two or three decades. That means that either they reconsider on-the-field alternatives for the education of their children or reconcile themselves to the need for replacement teams and plan accordingly.

Preparing for Transition

The record shows that, generally speaking, the mission teams in this study did not prepare for a smooth transition from missionary leadership of the church to national leadership. Their training did not prepare them for a "collaboration stage," to use Van Rheenen's

terms, in which missionaries and nationals work side by side in anticipation of the missionaries' departure, paying special attention to
what he calls "the structures of continuity" that enable the churches to advance after the missionaries leave (Van Rheenen, 1998).
Tyler compares this gap in training to NASA sending astronauts on
a mission to the moon with no idea of how and when to bring them
back (1998). This needs to change, he suggests, since transition is
really a mind set that missionaries should maintain throughout their
ministry.

There are two realities that missionaries preparing for transition
may have to reckon with, at least in rural Africa. One stems from the
African view of the future. In the words of Jim Reppart,

> The problem in African culture is that reality is never
> reality until it is past tense. So if you are going to do a
> phase out, they are not going to work towards that per-
> centage [of their responsibilities] until it comes up and
> they say, "Oh, it has happened." (Reppart, 1998).

A second possibility that missionaries discussing transition must
face is that church growth will slow down, even decline for a while,
following missionary disengagement. The potential damage caused
by both of these problems could be minimized by missionaries who
establish structures of organization and work alongside them as partners far in advance of disengagement.

From "Indigeneity" to "Ownership"

Missionaries in these teams made some strategic mistakes in the
name of indigeneity. For one, the term inclined them toward the
either/or distinctions that Tite Tiénou criticizes (1990; 1992). To
many of them, "indigenous" meant traditional. In theological education, for example, the Eldoret missionaries (among others) clung

to the informal approach because it was "indigenous" (that is, traditional), not "Western" (meaning imported) like all other approaches seemed to be. Their definition of "indigenous" ignored the elasticity that enables people in all cultures to adapt to their changing environment. Similarly, the missionaries' notion of "indigeneity" bound them to rigid interpretations of the four selves to the detriment of the Kenyan church.

The inculturation of the gospel is essential everywhere. But I propose that the word "ownership" conveys more accurately what the missionaries wanted to inculcate in the churches in the name of "indigeneity." As Glenn Schwartz describes it, a church that displays a sense of ownership not only controls the paperwork (legal ownership) and fills the leadership positions (functional ownership), it is a church whose members believe that its future depends on them (psychological ownership) (Schwartz, 1996, p. 6). The four selves are still appropriate measures of ownership; churches that are "locally owned and operated" are churches that assume primary responsibility for shepherding, evangelism, giving and Bible training in the church. But the term "ownership" raises new questions. Two are especially important to consider in this space: (1) What is the relationship between ownership and partnership? (2) Is it possible to speak of ownership and financial partnership at the same time? If so what are the principles that safeguard such a partnership between a national church and its outside supporters against the hazards of dependency?

Ownership and Partnership

To missionaries with "indigeneity" on the brain, "ownership" and "partnership" may sound like a contradiction in terms in the same way that "indigenous" and "foreign" are antonyms. But ownership and partnership are not either/or distinctions. A church can be both "owned" by nationals and partnered with internationals. A key ingredient in such a partnership is "participation," which inspires ownership. Missionaries must involve nationals in decision-making early in their work together, finding the right balance between fulfilling their apostolic role and empowering local leaders. There must be regular forums in which the missionaries explain their policies and solicit the input of the nationals.

Ownership should be the main criterion by which missionaries and nationals determine the timing of disengagement. The missionaries should not withdraw until the church is owned by the nationals. In the case of the Churches of Christ in this study, that means especially that the organizational structures must be clear and operational *before* the missionaries leave.

That does not mean that missionaries must leave in order for nationals to "own" the church. I am assuming that disengagement is inevitable. Most missionaries will come and go for terms that last less than the two or three decades necessary to establish a self-sustaining movement of churches. Some of them will not find replacements when they leave, if only because of a lack of missionary personnel in the Churches of Christ. But regardless of the disengagement plan, there must be an intentional transition from missionary leadership to national leadership that begins the moment the missionaries set foot in the new mission field! If nationals want missionaries to work alongside them and within their structures until the Lord comes, that is theirs to decide together. Depending on the history between the missionaries and nationals, the working arrangements after transition may seem awkward at first. But ownership is not *necessarily* violated by the ongoing presence of missionary partners.

Ownership and Financial Partnership

The relationship between ownership by the national church and financial partnership with the international church requires special attention as a particularly thorny problem. Stated as a question which borrows vocabulary from development debates, can outside funds ever really "build capacity" locally or do they always create dependency?

In some ways the popularity of "interdependency" is sweeping the issue of financial dependency under the rug in a wave of missiological correctness, despite the warnings of the likes of Glenn Schwartz, John Gatu and Jonathan Bonk. But chronic dependency is harmful to churches in the long run. One of the sources of tension that perpetuates the dependency problem is the tug-of-war between the legitimate desire–shared by missionaries and nationals alike–for respectability and the harsh economic realities of life in a poor country. On the one hand, no one involved wants the Churches of Christ to be seen as a "fly-by-night," temporary movement because they lack the "marks of authenticity" (Schrage, 1998). Church buildings and schools are legitimate symbols of stability and permanence and enhance the church's credibility among potential members. On the other hand, even with generous donations from abroad, the Churches of Christ cannot compete financially with the larger and older denominations that preceded Churches of Christ in East Africa. Furthermore, some financial partnerships, especially those which include some form of gradualism with its decreasing levels of funding, are based on the assumption of future prosperity in Kenya. It is as if the national churches simply need a boost in the beginning to build the same expensive structures that have characterized the church in the North and, over time, they will be able to maintain them themselves. But this assumption ignores both the last thirty years of economic history in post-colonial Africa as well as pessimistic prognostications about the future based on the evidence that affirms the "limits of growth," a sober realization that is gaining ground among development experts. It also overestimates how indispensable the expensive structures are as opposed to more affordable, scaled-down versions.

The dominant voice in discussions about these two issues–the push for respectability and the economic plight of people–must come from Scripture. The biblical teaching on materialism versus contentment must temper the whole debate lest the church reinforce the notion that buildings, schools, hospitals and the like are even close to the most important "marks of authenticity" for the people of God. The biblical "theology of enough," as John Taylor labels it, is relevant in every culture including the poorer ones (Taylor, 1975). Financial partners must let it permeate every conversation about money.

Based on the experiences of these teams and the literature on the subject, I recommend the following principles for financial partnerships between national and international churches which can help regulate the flow of funds in such a way that a sense of ownership is fostered and dependency is minimized. These principles also provide criteria by which requests for funding may be evaluated.

1. *Funds should only be given for projects that can be maintained locally.* This "sustainability" test is a good one. Nationals may solicit funds for help in establishing a particular program or project, but if they cannot maintain the same program or project on their own resources, they are getting ahead of themselves. This guideline commends the preference for one-time capital donations from abroad over regular monthly contributions.

2. *Aid given by foreign partners should be tied to what locals have already given.* The principle highlights the importance of teaching tithing in the local church from its inception. This is not a blanket

endorsement of contracts in which the local church that contributes a certain percentage to a project is entitled to a predetermined amount from her partners. That arrangement tends to depersonalize the relationship. But local initiative is encouraged when partners respond only to requests for financial aid that reflect sacrificial giving by those submitting the requests.

3. *Financial partners should be open about the nature of the local accountability structure, trust that structure, and give funds to specific projects without excessive earmarking.* Those who contribute the funds have a stewardship obligation to inquire about the local accounting system: Does the recipient church or committee have a bank account? Who are the signatories, how many are there, and did the church choose them? What are the concrete plans for how the money will be spent—architectural drawings for a building, for example—and how did the church agree to these plans? Churches abroad can and should contribute money without asserting the control that often accompanies earmarking.

4. *The financial partnership is best served if the missionary is not the middleman receiving and disbursing funds.* Of course, it is the missionary who serves as a bridge, at least initially, between the national church and the missionary's sponsors abroad. But the potential for friction between the missionary and the nationals and other negative consequences of such a precedent justifies this general rule. It is better for national church leaders to deal directly with their counterparts in the churches that send them funds. In the case of Churches of Christ, that means that African elders should deal directly with American elders in discussing these matters.

Avoiding Over-Corrections

As these missionaries and nationals critiqued the missionaries' disengagement policy and the four selves strategy that inspired it, they needed to resist the tendency to over-correct. Many of their original emphases were sound and should be imitated by others who minister in similar settings. With regard to shepherding issues, churches do well to build organizationally around unpaid, volunteer shepherds who are chosen by the local church and supervise the paid leaders. Likewise, with regard to evangelism, a new emphasis on hiring paid evangelists in the Kalenjin churches cannot be allowed to drown out the appeal to "the priesthood of all believers" and the goal of a mobilized membership as one of the main keys to growth. Concerning giving, stakeholders should not be prompted by a relaxed position on self-support to exchange large sums of money without considering the issue of local ownership and thereby create the dependency they have tried so hard to avoid. In the same vein, they should not let the new emphasis on development become a source of the wrong sort of this-worldly pride and obscure what matters most in the life of a healthy church. Finally, the new push for formal theological education for a few leaders must not diminish the significance of the informal discipling for all members that the missionaries tried to model.

Conclusion

Near the end of his life, the apostle Paul planted churches on the island of Crete. For reasons that are not revealed to us, Paul left the island before the work was done. Fortunately, the missionary contingent was not withdrawn entirely, for Paul's missionary protégé, Titus, stayed behind. Titus' mission, as Paul reminded him in the letter that bears his name, was to "straighten out what was left unfinished and appoint elders in every town" as Paul had previously directed him (Titus 1:5).

Two millennia later, the missionaries who planted hundreds of congregations of the Churches of Christ in rural Kenya over the last thirty years find themselves in a similar situation. They pursued a strategy that they attributed to Paul himself as his methods were understood by influential missiologists of the last century and a half. Yet they and the leaders of those churches agree that the work was left unfinished and that the missionaries withdrew prematurely. What was it exactly that was left undone? What adjustments can be made now to finish the task and shore up the churches? This chapter was written to address those questions and presented with the realization that, though we are obligated to work as "expert builders," employing all the skills and knowledge God provides, ultimately only God can make his church grow.

WORKS CITED

Allen, Roland (1927). The use of the Term Indigenous. *International Review of Missions 16*: 262-270.

———— (1962a). *Missionary Methods: St. Paul's or Ours?* Grand Rapids, MI: Eerdmans.

———— (1962b). *The Spontaneous Expansion of the Church.* American edition. Grand Rapids, MI: Eerdmans.

Anderson, Gerald H. (1974). A Moratorium on Missionaries? *Christian Century, 16*, 43-45.

Barr, Lawrence (1980). God's work among the Luo of South Nyanza. In the Kenya Mission Team (Eds.), *Church Planting, Watering, and Increasing in Kenya: The Study of Church Growth among Churches of Christ in Kenya, 1965-1979*, pp. 102-107. Austin, TX: Firm Foundation.

Beyerhaus, Peter, & Lefever, Henry (1964). *The Responsible Church and the Foreign Mission.* Grand Rapids, MI: Eerdmans.

Bonk, Jonathan J. (1991). *Missions and Money: Affluence as a Western Missionary Problem.* American Society of Missiology Series, No. 15. Maryknoll, NY: Orbis.

Bosch, David J. (1991). *Transforming Mission: Paradigm Shifts in Theology of Mission.* American Society of Missiology Series, No. 16. Maryknoll, NY: Orbis.

Butler, Phil (1994). Kingdom Partnerships in the '90s: Is there a New Way Forward? In William D. Taylor (Ed.), *Kingdom Partnerships for Synergy in Missions*, pp. 9-30. Pasadena, CA: William Carey.

Chowning, Richard (1985). Kipsigis Evangelists and Church Planting. In the Kipsigis Team (Eds.), *Church Growth among the Kipsigis: A Statistical Picture of the Church of Christ among the Kipsigis in South West Kenya, vol. 5*, pp. 35-67. Sotik, Kenya: Privately published.

Corwin, Gary (1995). Howdy, Partner. *Evangelical Missions Quarterly 31,* (4): 402-403.

Cox, Monte B. (1999). *Euthanasia of Mission or Partnership? An Evaluative Study of the Policy of Disengagement of Church of Christ Missionaries in Rural Kenya.* Unpublished doctoral thesis, Trinity International University.

———. (1994). *The Missiological Implications of Kalenjin Concepts of Deity, Sin and Salvation.* Unpublished master's thesis, Harding University Graduate School of Religion.

Davis, J. Merle (1945). *New Buildings on Old Foundations.* Studies in the World Mission of Christianity, No. 5. New York: International Missionary Council.

Dodge, Ralph E. (1964). *The Unpopular Missionary.* Westwood, NJ: Fleming H. Revell.

Faircloth, Samuel D. (1991). *Church Planting for Reproduction.* Grand Rapids, MI: Baker.

Gatu, John (1997, August). Dependency in Africa. Speech to All Africa Missionary Conference of Christian Churches/Churches of Christ, Limuru, Kenya.

Gration, John Alexander (1974). *The Relationship of the Africa Inland Mission and its National Church in Kenya between 1895 and 1971.* Unpublished doctoral dissertation, New York University.

Hamm, Peter. 1983. Breaking the power habit: Imperatives for Multinational Mission. *Evangelical Missions Quarterly 19* (3): 180-189.

Hemphill, Preston (1980). Church Growth in Western Kenya. In the Kenya Mission Team (Eds.) *Church Planting, Watering, and Increasing in Kenya: The Study of Church Growth among Churches of Christ in Kenya, 1965-1979,* pp. 47-67. Austin, TX: Firm Foundation.

Hesselink, John (1984). The Role of the Missionary in an Indigenous Church. *Reformed Review 37* (3): 137-150.

Hiebert, Paul G. (1985). *Anthropological insights for missionaries.* Grand Rapids: Baker.

——— (1983). Missions and the Renewal of the Church. In Wilbert R. Shenk (Ed.), *Exploring Church Growth*, pp. 157-167. Grand Rapids: Eerdmans.

Hodges, Melvin L. (1972). Are Indigenous Church Principles Outdated? *Evangelical Missions Quarterly 9* (1): 43-46.

Ilogu, Edmund (1955). The Biblical Idea of Partnership and the Modern Missionary Task. *International Review of Missions 44* (176), 404-407.

Kasdorf, Hans (1979). Indigenous Church Principles: A Survey of Origin and Development. In Charles H. Kraft and Tom N. Wisely (Eds.), *Readings in Dynamic Indigeneity*, pp. 71-86. Pasadena, CA: William Carey Library.

Maluleke, Tinyiko Sam (1994). North-south Partnerships: The Evangelical Presbyterian Church in South Africa and the Department Missionaire in Lausanne. *International Review of Missions 83* (328): 93-100.

McGavran, Donald A. (1980). *Understanding Church Growth.* Rev. ed. Grand Rapids, MI: Eerdmans.

Merritt, Hilton (1980). Kisumu: A Team Effort. In the Kenya Mission Team (Eds.), *Church Planting, Watering, and Increasing in Kenya: The Study of Church Growth among Churches of Christ in Kenya, 1965-1979*, pp. 39-46. Austin, TX: Firm Foundation.

Nevius, John L. (1958). *The Planting and Development of Missionary Churches.* Philadelphia: Presbyterian and Reformed Publishing.

Plueddemann, James A. (1983). Beyond Independence to Responsible Maturity. *Evangelical Missions Quarterly 19* (1): 48-55.

Reppart, Jim (personal communication, March 13, 1998).

Sawatzky, Sheldon (1996). From Mission to Church: A Careful Look and Sensitive Observation of the Mennonite General Conference Transition to National Leadership. *Taiwan Mission 6* (2): 22-31.

Scherer, James A. (1964). *Missionary, Go Home!* Englewood Cliffs, NJ: Prentice-Hall.

Schrage, Mike (personal communication March 12, 1998).

Schwartz, Glenn J. (1996). *Dependency among Mission-Established Institutions: Exploring the Issues.* Lancaster, PA: World Mission Associates.

Shenk, Wilbert R. (1994). From Mission to Church: A Response. *Brethren in Christ History and Life 17* (2): 157-172.

——— (1983). *Henry Venn: Missionary Statesman.* Maryknoll, NY: Orbis.

Smalley, William A. (1958). Cultural Implications of an Indigenous Church. *Practical Anthropology 5* (2): 51-65.

Taylor, John V. (1975/1977). *Enough is Enough.* Minneapolis, MN: Augsburg.

Tiénou, Tite (1990). Indigenous African Christian theologies: The Uphill Road. *International Bulletin of Missionary Research 14* (2): 73-77.

——— (1992). Which Way for African Christianity: Westernization or Indigenous Authenticity? *Evangelical Missions Quarterly 28* (3): 256-263.

Tippett, Alan R. (1987). *Introduction to Missiology*. Pasadena, CA: William Carey.

Tyler, Shawn (personal communication, February 28, 1998).

Van Rheenen, Gailyn (personal communication, April 25, 1998).

———— (1996). *Missions: Biblical Foundations and Contemporary Strategies*. Grand Rapids, MI: Zondervan.

———— (1985). Looking back. In the Kipsigis Team (Eds.) *Church Growth among the Kipsigis: A Statistical Picture of the Church of Christ among the Kipsigis in South West Kenya, vol. 5*, pp. 69-89. Sotik, Kenya: Privately published.

———— (1983). Leadership Training. In the Kipsigis Team (Eds.) *Church Growth among the Kipsigis: A Statistical Picture of the Church of Christ among the Kipsigis in South West Kenya, vol. 5*, pp. 37-55. Sotik, Kenya: Privately published.

Wagner, C. Peter (1975.) Colour the Moratorium Grey. *International Review of Missions 64* (254): 165-176.

———— (1971). *Frontiers in Missionary Strategy*. Chicago: Moody.

Williams, C. Peter (1990). *The Ideal of the Self-Governing Church: A study in Victorian Missionary Strategy*. Studies in Christian Mission, Vol. 1. Leiden: E. J. Brill.

CHAPTER 14

Humanitarian and Development Work in Africa

Don Yelton and Dan McVey

*Don Yelton is program Director of Relief Ministries
for the White's Ferry Road Church of Christ, Director of
AMEN Ministries which serves military personnel in the
Churches of Christ, and board member of Healing Hands
International. Don and his wife Harriette live in North
Carolina. donyelton@wfrchurch.org.*

The continuing disaster relief and humanitarian work in Africa
is an ongoing great blessing to the mission work of the churches of
Christ. During the last twenty years churches of Christ have contributed approximately $20 million for various projects in Africa in
more than fifty countries. Together with the hands-on leadership of
national Christians and missionaries, this work has saved thousands
of lives and reduced human suffering; it has also enhanced evangelism. The good will produced by these acts of love and concern lives
in the hearts of average people and many governments and as well.

The experience of missionaries in Kenya in 1989 clearly
illustrates one aspect of humanitarian work. In a surprise move by
the Kenyan government, more than 30 church of Christ missionary
families received notices directing them to depart the country with-

in 30 days. One of the reasons listed on the expulsion order was the lack of work benefiting the development of the country. When this reason became known, a list of the humanitarian activity of the churches of Christ was compiled and delivered to the appropriate government authorities; nobody was deported. These humanitarian works and development projects were later described and illustrated in a pictorial booklet for distribution to government officials (Labnow and Granberg, 1992).

Another similar instance, occurring in Ethiopia during the years of a ruthless communist regime, shows that humanitarian acts done in cooperation with governments can reduce or eliminate some governmental restrictions. From about 1973 until 1986, the communist government strictly controlled travel outside the capital city Addis Ababa. Behailu Abebe, Demere Chernut and other national church leaders in Addis Ababa were not able to visit and encourage churches in remote areas. Also, printing and/or distributing religious materials was forbidden. Leadership training for church leaders was not permitted and evangelism was stifled. After the famine relief work of 1985 – 1986, new ways to print and distribute leadership materials and other religious materials were found, with minimum interference from the Ethiopian Government. Since the government was encouraging humanitarian projects, church leaders could travel for famine relief projects and visit churches at the same time; because we were following the government plan, our brothers were not criticized or hampered to the degree they had been previously.

Humanitarian and relief works have helped better relationships with governments in many ways. First, obtaining a residence visa only for the stated purpose of evangelism is a major obstacle to mission work in many countries. If a family is actually in residence, visas must be renewed often and other bureaucratic requirements satisfied. Having a reputation for doing good can move a missionary to the "head of the line" in getting paperwork done. Second, in most countries permission must be obtained to buy land, build buildings, and sometimes even to teach and preach in a public assembly. Missionaries involved in humanitarian or disaster relief work make friends in high places who are then sympathetic to such requests. Also, in countries where the rule of thumb is "what is not permitted is forbidden," lack of governmental good will toward missionaries can seriously hamper the preaching of the Gospel.

Dan McVey, a missionary to Ghana, West Africa since 1983, details the history of disaster relief work in that country and some of the lessons learned. In a World Relief Conference in Germany in 1999 he says in part:

> "Compassion opens doors. It opens hearts. It speaks to the soul. To hear of suffering and shed a tear is laudable. To hear of suffering and sacrifice to relieve it is godly. The confidence that we have won in the hearts of many due to relief efforts, particularly among Islamic people, is based upon the fact that we share with everyone, regardless of tribal or religious background. They know we care, so they listen when we speak of spiritual things."

Churches of Christ from all around the world have delivered an estimated $50 million dollars in humanitarian assistance since 1983, delivered through African Church of Christ leaders or missionaries. Tens of thousands of lives were saved, and thousands of souls now know Jesus because of the ensuing evangelism. The following brief descriptions provide a partial account of the aid provided to Africa over the past twenty years.

Ghana

In 1983 Ghanaian World Bible School teachers, missionaries,

and national church leaders in Ghana, West Africa appealed to the White's Ferry Road Church of Christ for food. We were grateful to be asked, and Churches of Christ in the United States and Canada contributed over $2 million to deliver food to Christians in Ghana.

As funds poured in, missionary Jerry Reynolds immediately ordered several hundred tons of flour, corn meal, and beans. Jerry and I then traveled to Ghana to plan the distribution with church leaders there. Churches in Ghana, working closely with their government, provided transportation for the distribution.

These brothers weren't waiting around. Already they had held a national meeting of church leaders and agreed that the food we had shipped would be distributed to the needy prioritized as follows: 1) Christians and their families, 2) villages and neighbors of Christians, 3) national organizations. A more complete report of the relief work in Ghana can be found in Dan McVey's report provided below.

Ethiopia

A famine of "biblical proportions" hit Ethiopia in 1984. Even my experiences as a combatant during the wars in Viet Nam and the Dominican Republic, and relief work during six other wars did not prepare me to face the massive starvation I witnessed in Ethiopia. More than one million people died, and tens of millions suffered beyond description as they watched their children die, their farms turn to dust, and their families attempt the long walk to refugee camps.

In response to the Ethiopian tragedy, and through the request of the church in Ethiopia, the White's Ferry Road Church of Christ established the African Famine Relief Fund to reduce some of the suffering in Ethiopia and other African countries during this period. Churches of Christ in the United States and fifty other countries contributed more than $8 million to this fund. Other nationally based and United Nations relief organizations, both secular and religious, contributed an additional $10 million in cash and goods to the effort of our churches in Africa. The bulk of these funds were used to build and supply feeding centers in Ethiopia where tens of thousands of people received food regularly during the famine. As the famine broke these same people were provided farming supplies to help them reestablish their lives. The donations made to the African Famine Relief Fund allowed us to promote humanitarian projects in Africa for fourteen years; we helped Christians and their neighbors in hundreds of large and small humanitarian projects to God's glory.

The benefit of the relief projects to the church in Ethiopia is inestimable. Even the communist leaders of Ethiopia, who had limited many freedoms of their people including forced mass migrations within the country, commended our work and relaxed the restrictions placed on our churches. After the government publicly recognized the Churches of Christ in Ethiopia for their compassion, the church was allowed to openly train preachers for the first time in over a decade. There has been steady church growth since that time.

Another clear illustration of the power of humanitarian projects is the result of our three schools for the deaf in Ethiopia, for many years the only deaf schools in the country. Under the communist restrictions, our brethren could not print Christian tracts, songbooks, or leadership training materials. However, in 1986-1987, while Ethiopia was still ruled by the communists, we were able to locate some special computer software that would print Ethiopian characters. We purchased computers, printers, and software and took them to Ethiopia. Since then our brethren have printed thousands of tracts, correspondence courses, and leadership training documents for their school of preaching. The only way the communists

would allow the importation of the computers and printing equipment was because we had three deaf schools in the country, and the
equipment could be also used to help these children in a non-reli-
gious way.

With the monies from African Famine Relief Fund, we have
been able to help with relief and development projects in more than
ten other African countries. In many areas, seed or matching funds
encourage national Christians to contribute their time and their
money. Additionally, and with the permission of the contributors,
10% of the funds were used for direct mission work. These funds
were also often used as matching funds, sometimes on a 1 for 3 basis,
creating even more funds for preaching of the Gospel in Africa. The
African Famine Relief funds were not depleted until 1999.

Botswana

In Botswana, funds in a remote desert community helped feed
both hungry Bushmen and Christians who lived in the towns. We
also helped with water and agriculture projects.

Uganda

Missionaries in Kenya informed us that a civil war in Uganda
might be opening doors for mission work. We were able to provide
$100,000 for medical relief to help the national churches and to pre-
pare for missionaries to enter the country. Additional funds were
provided to several missionaries for war relief, including medical care
for landmine victims.

Kenya

Droughts and poverty are common in Kenya, and missionaries
have often asked and received help with their humanitarian projects.
We have helped with drought and flood relief work and with many

humanitarian projects. We helped the Eastleigh vocational training school, Ethiopian and Sudanese refugees, a preacher's training school, and the care of street children.

Also in Kenya our brothers helped build houses and established a training center to improve the lives of Kenyans. We also have made small grants to establish a loan fund to help poor people establish businesses to pull their families out of extreme poverty.

Zambia

A drought hit Southern Zambia in 1987, and we were able to help with food, transportation, re-digging of water wells, and ongoing water projects for several years. Our brotherhood also supports ongoing schools and many other humanitarian projects in Zambia.

Tanzania

In Mbeya our brothers have long supported a hospital and school to train preachers. With funds from the African Famine Relief Fund we were able to contribute to the revitalization of their water supply. We also sent medications and helped with other medical work.

Malawi

A major flood in Southern Malawi destroyed the homes of thousands of people and hundreds of Christians. Monies from the African Famine Relief Fund purchased and delivered food and helped rebuild homes.

Mozambique

Unable to actually enter Mozambique, brethren in the Zomba area of Malawi first helped Christian refugees with food and other emergency supplies. Later they risked their own lives to cross the landmine-infested areas to preach Jesus and deliver supplies. In recent years flood relief work has been supported by our brotherhood.

Sierra Leone

Funds on two different occasions helped deliver food that was distributed through local churches of Christ.

Liberia

Civil war has torn this country apart. Missionaries have been unable to live there for several years, but have received funds to ship and/or buy food locally to help Christians and others. Refugees from this country have been helped by Ghanaian churches and many Liberians have been baptized.

South Africa

A number of relief projects have been assisted in South Africa where there is much poverty in normal times. Many Christians in this country are helping some people in the squalid refugee and worker camps.

Zaire

Christians in Europe have led several relief projects in Zaire, but civil war continues to prevent close contact with Christians in this country.

It is not possible to mention even a fraction of the missionaries, brotherhood humanitarian organizations, and churches involved in major efforts to relieve human suffering and preach the Gospel of Jesus Christ. Hundreds of African Christians have volunteered their time to work in life threatening areas to demonstrate God's love. We salute each one who lives to the glory of God.

The following article by Dan McVey discusses humanitarian work in Ghana. It is worthy to note that the Ghanaian Christians are doing considerable amounts of relief work without help from outside their country. Ethiopian and churches in other African countries also first received help now fund their own programs to help their needy neighbors.

The Impact of Relief Efforts on the Growth of the Church of Christ in Ghana, 1983-1999

Dan McVey

The following transcript was presented at the World Relief Conference, Germany, November 18-19, 1999.

Introduction

Relief work among the Churches of Christ in Ghana has always been based upon the extreme needs found in a particular situation to which we have been compelled to respond. We have found that relief work can be described as the expression of God's grace via compassion in the hearts of his people. His grace is seen in the actions and attitudes of his children as they demonstrate some of the most noble of Christian characteristics, namely honesty, purity of heart, and sacrifice. As our Lord Jesus taught us so many years ago, love is the defining characteristic of discipleship. This love must be seen in the abundant outpouring of compassion from his Kingdom as we see others in need.

Over the past 17 years, we have been blessed in Ghana to take part in several relief efforts from which we have seen a great variety of developments in the church's growth and leadership. I will try to draw some vital lessons which we have learned from four relief efforts and their resulting impact on the church. These four major relief efforts are:

1. Famine relief of 1983-1984 - Ghana was struck by a severe drought which forced repatriation of over 2,000,000 Ghanaians from Nigeria. Churches in the United States put together over $2,000,000 in food, medical, and general aid for the brethren and public. The aid was distributed and the relief projects overseen by a committee of brethren in Accra, the capital, along with another distribution center in Kumasi, the second largest city. This project developed into other long-term relief programs like clinics and water well drilling.

2. Refugee relief - The civil war in Liberia brought over 25,000 refugees to Ghana in 1990-1991. Food, medical, and general aid was given from some sources in the United States as well as many Ghanaian congregations over a 5-year period. A church was started in the refugee camp near Accra (15 miles distant) which resulted in the conversion of over 2000 refugees. This relief effort was overseen for the most part by the Nsawam Road Church of Christ, Accra.

3. Food relief in a time of economic collapse - Political turmoil in the nation of Togo, east of Ghana, from 1991-1993 caused the economy of that country to suffer terribly with Lomé, the capital, witnessing over one half of the population fleeing to the countryside in search of food. We had one congregation of around 100 members in Lomé at that time, so with some help from the USA, brethren in Accra began sending monthly contributions to purchase food and medical supplies for those brethren remaining in Lomé. Some refugees also came to Ghana, and there were some efforts to donate food, clothing, and other needs from churches in Accra.

4. Relief in times of war - In 1994, the Northern Region of Ghana was blasted by a terrible tribal war. It occurred in an area

where we had started church planting and a water well drilling project. The devastation and lack of security, not to mention threats against us by Muslim tribesmen, caused a great pause in our church planting efforts; however, with some sources of help in the USA, and abundant help from churches in southern Ghana, we were able to aid both sides of the conflict with food, medicine, clothing and other needs. The church served as a great catalyst to bring the two warring tribes back together as we had churches between both tribes.

There have been other relief projects through the years within Ghana, but these four constitute our substantial experience in this area of service. We are greatly indebted to many fine brethren in the USA and the UK who have helped with these various efforts, particularly the White's Ferry Road Church of Christ and the Traverse City Church of Christ.

Classification of Relief Projects

It is possible to classify these projects along three general lines:

1. Short Term Projects – These projects deal with immediate needs in a situation that is of limited duration. The projects in Togo and the war in northern Ghana fall under this classification because the contributing factors to the disaster were rectified within a relatively short period of time. Moreover, the actual relief given was of a limited, narrow scope—food and medical aid.

2. Long Term Projects with a Limited Scope – These types of projects deal with need over a longer period of time, but the needs are limited to a specific location and easily identifiable group. The project at the Liberian refugee camp fits this category because the time period was long, five years, but the recipients were basically confined to the camp where United Nations relief programs were focused as well. Food, medical, evangelistic and other forms of relief were thus limited to supplying what the UN and other donor

agencies did not supply, and were focused on helping the Liberians prepare to return to their homes or be assimilated into Ghanaian society.

3. Long Term Projects with a Broad Scope – This type of project is marked by relief efforts of large proportions which are extended over a long period of time developed into specific projects that have a long life of service, or become permanent fixtures in the life of the church. The famine relief project of the early 1980's fits this classification. What began as famine relief later developed into the establishment of clinics. From this heightened awareness of physical need and the establishment of networks of donors also came a water well drilling project for northern Ghana. Thus, the two base clinics (one in the South and one in the North), dozens of village clinics, and the two branches of our well drilling project (again, northern and southern Ghana) are directly linked in history and in structure to the original famine relief.

Impact on Church Growth

From 1982 to 1999 the number of congregations in Ghana grew from 100 to over 950 congregations. The thousands of converts at the refugee camps, the survivability of the church in Togo, the opening of doors to an Islamic tribe, and the opening of hundreds of villages to the Gospel, not to mention thousands of lives saved due to medical care and pure drinking water, are growth realities in some part or in large part, due to relief projects. While the ultimate impact of these relief efforts can only be measured in terms of eternity, there are some outstanding, tangible impacts upon church growth:

1. Open Doors - Compassion opens doors. It opens hearts. It speaks to the soul. To hear of suffering and shed a tear is laudable. To hear of suffering and sacrifice and to relieve it is godly. The

confidence that we have won in the hearts of many due to relief efforts, particularly among Islamic people, is based upon the fact that we share with everyone, regardless of tribal or religious background. They know we care, so they listen when we speak of spiritual matters. They know we love them, so they respond to our reaching out to them. Recently, the king of the Dagomba people, an Islamic tribe among whom I work and where we have clinic and well drilling projects, told us that no church has ever penetrated his people like we have. He went on to add that he regards us as "his church," Meaning he has taken us to be the ones who can lead his people in spiritual matters. One of the most difficult and resistant areas to the Gospel is now being opened. The key to this lock is compassion.

2. Broadened Perspectives - No one benefits more from relief projects than those who organize and oversee them. Church leaders have their perspectives of human nature and human need broadened, as well as their understanding of prevailing conditions. Relief projects, especially those on a large scale, have a unique way of opening one's eyes to the realities of what we are facing in this spiritual war we call evangelism. Satan's corruption and cursing of this earth goes unchecked unless we step in with the compassion and message of Christ. Everything from cultural, social, economic, educational, political realities to the spiritual conditions that exist in a people will be more readily seen and understood by those who are working in a combination of relief and evangelism. Personally, I can testify to the fact that the first two years I spent in Ghana were worth ten or more years in terms of what I learned about the church, people, culture, needs and socio-economic situation, all because I was coordinating the famine relief project.

3. Focus on Priorities - There is a natural tension that exists between relief efforts and evangelismbecause most relief efforts focus on the material needs which are deemed less important than the

spiritual. However, I am of the view that relief efforts can actually aid us in keeping proper spiritual focus by constantly putting us in the situation where we must assess our church planting programs and relief projects in terms of balance. We are always thus exhorting ourselves to be sure that our relief efforts not only have the tangible results of relief from physical suffering, but also that they are geared toward opening doors for evangelism. When evangelism is done among a people who need relief and that need is ignored, or left unattended in at least the most basic effort, then our message may ring hollow in the ears of the hearers. Also, when we balance relief and evangelism, we are constantly measuring the progress of the two; thus we are assessing our progress on several fronts at once. The competing demands that relief and evangelism place upon our resources, strengths and time result in this tension of which we are speaking. One may surrender to the strong demands of relief projects and allow them to swallow or overshadow evangelism; but this is not inevitable. Our experience in Ghana is quite the contrary. I learned from the Ghanaian brethren long ago that their view of meeting man's physical as well as spiritual needs is much more biblical than the other view that spiritual needs outweigh physical so much so that even the tension between the two should be avoided. A simple look at the ministry of Christ will dispel that view—he met both needs, and most often met the physical before he addressed the spiritual needs. Therefore, our experience goes to support the view that relief projects actually aid in properly focusing our priorities when we have the correct spiritual outlook upon which all church projects are based to begin with—compassion and sharing.

4. Networks - Relief projects require advancements in communication, thus aiding in establishing networks. These networks will function within the country where the project is based as well as between that country and donor sources. I need not say much on

this topic since the world is an ever-evolving village in terms of communication. Relief projects simply require accountability, networking and intensified communication. Our experience is that where brethren communicate and plan together, there is greater fellowship and opportunity for growth.

5. Developing Church Leadership - Relief projects are excellent training grounds for mature church leaders to grow even more in their service and leadership skills. The strong character needed in relief leadership in terms of honesty, purity, compassion, and diligence provide a learning and maturing opportunity beyond compare. We have seen many brethren involved in relief leadership and service who were actually being prepared by the Lord for something even greater that he had for them in the future. Accountability and faithfulness are always good qualities to develop. Thus, properly managed relief projects serve as examples to growing churches. In Ghana, much of our relief work has been overseen by the Nsawam Road Church of Christ in Accra; in my years with them, I have never found a more responsible, dedicated leadership than that which has emerged in that church. Their growth from 150 to over 1800 members is in no small part due to the experience we the leaders received from being tested and proven faithful in handling large sums of money and many responsibilities in terms of relief projects. Our broadened perspectives and constant evaluation of our priorities aided us in reaching great heights in church growth and development.

6. Injection of Compassion - Relief projects inject compassion into our faith systems. Some of our most lofty ideas and theories of mission work and church growth are based upon some quite faulty thinking. On the one hand, there are those of us who insist on absolute rigid adherence to modern mission theories that any form of institutional or traditional relief mission work is a hindrance to

national church development. Thus they refuse to get involved in or even allow relief efforts among the churches where they work. I believe this is not only short sighted, but also can even be a form of racism. How can we who come from lands of little or no physical deprivation prevent or hinder the expression of compassion by God's church? I find that this view is usually based upon academic theories rather than spiritual maturity or spiritual discernment, often resulting in very deeply felt resentment on the part of national church leaders and members. Relief projects can inject an unselfish compassion into our faith systems by putting us into contact with the real needs of people, demonstrating a compassion and concern for their suffering. On the other hand, some resist involvement in relief projects because they do not have much compassion to begin with; in fact, legalists do little relief work. Their faith system does not allow room for the fact that situations determine courses of action; they see every nation, town, village, and household in terms of their own narrow perception of need. Thus their lack of flexibility in theology is reflected in their very limited interest in getting involved with the real needs of people. They do not want to "get down into the dirt and disease and chaos," so to speak in which many people are forced to live because it may force them to realize that some things in life are more important than their own predetermined set of doctrines. Again, relief efforts inject, yes, inject, compassion into our faith systems until they become a part of us.

The Drawbacks of Relief Work

As with all forms of church growth, there are some drawbacks to relief work that we have seen in Ghana. I will mention a few with limited comment.

1. Time and Resource Consuming - Yes, relief projects do consume much time and resources. The challenge here is to learn to

balance the relief work with evangelistic goals. If the relief work is kept subservient to evangelistic goals, then the investments will be worthwhile. Relief for the sake of relief is not worthy of the Kingdom, for we have a message that all people must hear. However, sometimes relief is the only way we can get in the door for someone to hear the message.

2. Attraction of Those with Impure Motives - Material aid can attract people to the church out of purely physical motives. If that is seen as a beginning point from which we then evangelize, then we are simply following the example of Jesus in John 4 with the Samaritan woman. Relief work may also attract some who wish to use the church's generosity for purely selfish gain. Jesus faced this problem in John 6 and solved it by taking the people to a higher level of learning. Those who could not meet the demands of faith turned back. Yes, relief work can face us with the problem of less than pure motives in people. I believe an awareness of the problem is the greater part of solving it. Did all of the 5000 who ate from Jesus' miraculous feeding have pure motives? Time and emphasis on discipleship and accountability will aid in keeping this problem to a minimum. We cannot reject people because of their moral weaknesses; that is why we are approaching them in the first place. In the words of Charles Hodge, " Is the church a hotel for saints or a hospital for sinners?"

3. Promotes Secular Views of Christianity - The world has its own perceptions of what churches are all about. In most developing countries, this view has been established long before we arrive on the scene. Relief aid is expected from Christian churches by many populations. If we engage in such relief, some say we are confirming a secular view of the church as a relief agency. Again, if we do relief projects along the pattern of many denominational agencies, then we can expect much the same response. However, we will do

it differently if we emphasize evangelism. We do not see relief as an end in itself; therefore, we do not fit the normal definition of most church-related relief agencies.

Suggestions:

I would like to offer a few suggestions for the successful involvement of the church in relief works.

1. Let all personnel working with relief projects be proven, faithful believers, preferably those who have demonstrated not only faithfulness in financial matters, but who have also shown great concern for evangelism and church planting.

2. Let there be full partnership between national and foreign leadership. Let the relief project be a growth opportunity for the national church.

3. Always demand accountability. Maintain a very limited overhead in terms of national staff and infrastructure—enough to do the job—but do not only allow the project to be seen as an employment opportunity. Let there be as much volunteer service from national brethren as possible.

4. Let there be partnership between the church on one hand and the governments and other NGO's on the other hand. Let us not duplicate a lot of services or "reinvent the wheel." Relief work requires a lot of liaison with others who have already learned many lessons we need to learn.

5. Keep all relief projects supportive of evangelism and require that they show a direct impact on church growth. Are church planting or other evangelistic opportunities being created?

6. Recognize that in some cases relief projects come before substantial church growth and in some cases they come after. Relief projects may be a door opener where the church does not exist or has limited presence, or they may be an outgrowth of general church

development. We must look carefully at the prevailing circumstances to see whether a relief project is necessary, what mechanics and infrastructures are needed, and what is the potential for other projects to emerge from it. In areas where there is no church presence or it is very limited, we must examine how a relief project should be designed so as to maximize evangelistic results.

Conclusion:

When we look at the vast areas of need in the world and at the immediate opportunities we have to demonstrate the love of Christ, it is no surprise that with all the technology informing us so quickly about the world's needs also has come the immense wealth of the Western democracies to finance relief projects. I do not think we should do Satan the honor of allowing him to blind us with flagrant materialism, which keeps us focused on our own investments and ease of life while the rest of the world suffers. I believe the unsurpassed wealth and overabundant economies of the last decade are very much an attempt by Satan to divert the church in the Western world from looking outward at the ripened fields. Why should we allow Satan to toy with us, for we are not ignorant of his devices? As Augustine commented when contemplating whether the Israelites should have taken gold from the Egyptians at the time of the exodus, "Gold from Egypt is still gold." Government agencies, international agencies, and the overflowing pockets of our own brethren give us rich wells from which to draw resources for relief. It is time to capitalize on the vast amount of prosperity in the Western world through diligent appeals and faithful stewardship to demonstrate the compassion of our Master and open doors for lost souls to enter the Kingdom. I believe this may be especially true in the Islamic world. Argumentation does not convert Muslims; compassion and the overwhelming divinity of Jesus does when people are given a chance to see Jesus as he really is, and not as their religious leaders have depicted him.

The growth of the church in Ghana has been positively and powerfully impacted by relief projects, and we fully expect this to continue in the future. Within Ghana, almost every congregation is involved in some form of benevolent relief to its own members, to church projects like an orphan's home, schools, and clinics. The relief projects of the past and present have helped condition in the spirits of the Christians a concern and willingness to show that concern to those in need, even though ninety percent of all our members in Ghana are far below anyone's definition of a poverty line. From Ghana, the Gospel has gone into several other African countries. Also, Ghanaian Christians are revitalizing the church in places like Italy and Canada, as well as making impacting countries like Israel, Belgium, the UK and the USA. Almost without exception, these diaspora Christians remember their brethren and the evangelistic work back in Ghana and send back finances and material aid. Relief projects stir up attention and resources that allow us to penetrate the darkness. Let us intensify our efforts. May God bless those who have made this their focus. May God bless us all to spread the Kingdom until Jesus comes.

CHAPTER 15

The Gospel and the Spirits

Shawn Tyler

*Shawn and Linda Tyler are veteran missionaries.
They have worked in Mbale, Uganda since 1995; prior to
that they worked in Kitale, Kenya from 1981-1994. They
are sponsored by the Quaker Avenue Church of Christ in
Lubbock, Texas.*

The Gaps Between Cultures - Why is it Hard To Understand?

Nigel Barley (1986) in his humorous book, *The Innocent
Anthropologist*, talks about his anthropological research among the
Dowayos of Cameroon, West Africa. Barley's response to the local
rainchief is a classic illustration of the gap between Western cultural
beliefs and that of many Africans. After he worked hard for months
to convince the rainchief to let him see his rain stones (the rainchief's
most prized possessions), the rainchief finally agreed. Barley speaks
of an arduous climb to the top of a bitterly cold mountain where he
finds a waterfall. He writes:

> A watercourse issued from above and beneath the icy
> spray was a hollow in the rock. Within were large, lumpy
> clay pots like water jars; inside these were stones of
> various colors for male and female rain. The rainchief
> splashed them with the same remedies he had spat on me

and held the rocks out for my inspections. There was one more thing. We splashed through the water to a large, white rock. This was the ultimate defense of the Dowayos. If he removed this the whole world would be flooded and all would be killed (Barley, 1986, p. 160).

Upon their descent, the rainchief asked Barley if he was happy. Barley said he was, but that he still wanted to see the rainchief make it rain. The witchdoctor asked if he did not see the remedy that he splashed on the rocks. The rainchief confidently predicted it would rain on them before they reached home. Again Barley writes:

> The storm hit us at the very worst point of the descent where we were executing goat-like leaps across the fissures. Granite becomes slippery when wet. At one point I was reduced to crawling on all fours. The rainchief was sniggering and pointing to the sky. Had I seen now? We were shouting above the storm to be heard. 'That's enough,' I cried, 'you can make it stop.' He looked at me with a twinkle in his eye. 'A man does not take a wife to divorce her the same day,' he replied" (Barley, p. 161).

Barley's visit to the mountain, his secret glimpse of the rain stones, and the heavy downpour on the way home did not convince him of the rainchief's powers; in fact, he admits, "I, of course, would never believe anything so against the grain of my own culture without much better evidence than this. I – like they – see what I expect to see" (Barley, p. 161). Barley's response illustrates one of the fundamental obstacles in understanding the spiritual world in/of another culture. Our own culture conditions and trains us to see and interpret events through our own cultural framework. We consider our conclusion to be true, but people of another culture may experience the same event and come to a different conclusion. Which is true?

A Matter of Holiness

Relating another incidence, Barley speaks of his first glance at the tools of the local rainchief. His response highlights another misunderstanding among Western cultures concerning objects dedicated to witchcraft. He writes:

> The rainchief showed me his portable rain kit…. He took me off into the bush and we crouched down behind a rock with much extravagant looking around and scanning of the horizon. Inside was a plug of ram's wool. 'For clouds,' he explained. Then came an iron ring. This served to localize the effect of the rain: if, for example, he were at a skull festival, he would make it rain in the middle of the village until the people brought him beer. Next came the most powerful part of all. This was a great secret that he had never shown anybody. He bent forward earnestly and tipped up the horn. Slowly, there rolled into his hand a child's blue marble such as one might purchase anywhere. I made as if to pick it up. Horrified, he withdrew his hand: 'It would kill you'" (Barley, p. 157-158).

To help understand the difference between typical Western understanding of witchcraft and that of animists, let us consider what makes an object holy. The Hebrew root words for holiness mean: to separate, divide, earnestly dedicate, devote, put under a ban, and consecrate (Wright, 1992, p. 237). Holiness is not inherent in creation. It comes by God's dictate (Wright, 1992, p. 237). God sanctifies or sets apart someone or something such as: the Sabbath (Exodus 20:11); Israel and its priests (Exodus 29:44; 31:13; Leviticus 21:8, 15; 22:9, 16); firstborn (Numbers 3:13; 8:17); and sanctuaries (Exodus 29:44; 1 Kings 9:3, 7; 2 Chronicles 7:16, 20; 30:8; 36:14), and they become holy.

In the Old Testament, objects dedicated to the Lord or for his purpose were designated as holy. Some such objects were: the

343

temple furniture (Exodus 30:26-29), priestly clothing (Exodus 28:2), real estate (Leviticus 27:14-25), money (Leviticus 27:23), animals (Leviticus 27:9), oil (Exodus 30:22-33), incense (Exodus 30:34-38) and water (Numbers 5:17). Achan's sin in Joshua 7 was to take something dedicated to God from the spoils of Jericho. The spiritual significance of Achan's theft is spelled out with devastating clarity in Joshua 7:10-12 where his entire family was executed because of distributed guilt.

Barley makes the mistake of evaluating the rainchief's tools by their form and substance and not by their dedicated purpose. As a western anthropologist, Barley recognized the common form of a child's marble, but he failed to realize the marble had been dedicated to the spirits and work of rain making. Sometimes missionaries fall into the same trap. Because we can see that a certain witchdoctor's medicine is simply a piece of bark, some powder, a shell, a tree root, or some other seemingly innocuous thing, we too are quick to dismiss both the object and the witchdoctor as bogus. We overlook these objects' significance as having been consecrated to demons for some particular task while we concentrate on its external form and substance.

Turn this around for a moment and consider how Africans sometimes respond to the form and substance of Christian rituals. Baptism, a spiritually significant washing away of sins (Acts 22:16), is humorously viewed by some as merely submerging a person in water with all their clothes on. Prayer is nothing more than closing the eyes and speaking to no one! Communion, an important remembrance of fellowship in the death of Christ (1 Corinthians 11:23-26), is an unsatisfying meal of bread fragments and sips of wine. In the 2nd century AD some unbelievers made the malicious claim that Christians were cannibals who ate the flesh of their savior (Mattox, 1961 p. 67); unbelieving Africans have made the same charges today. The form and substance in these events seem inconsequential to the unbeliever, but they have tremendous importance and power to the believing participant and severe consequences when neglected (1 Corinthians 11:27-32).

Does consecration work both ways—to righteousness and to evil? More specifically, can a simple object dedicated to evil spirits bring harm? Consider God's commands to the Israelites in Deuteronomy 7:25, 26:

> The images of their gods you are to burn in the fire. Do not covet the silver and gold on them, and do not take it for yourselves, or you will be ensnared by it, for it is detestable to the Lord your God. Do not bring a detestable thing into your house or you, like it, will be set apart for destruction. Utterly abhor and detest it, for it is set apart for destruction.

This passage indicates that even the silver and gold dedicated to making the idols carried a punishment for its possessor. In fact, God uses the phrase "set apart for destruction" as an antithesis for something set apart for righteousness. Paul uses a similar argument in his teaching to the Corinthians about things devoted to idols. Paul said,

> The sacrifices of pagans are offered to demons, not to God, and I do not want you to be participants with demons. You cannot drink the cup of the Lord and the cup of demons too; you cannot have a part in both the Lord's table and table of demons. Are we trying to arouse the Lord's jealousy?" (1 Corinthians 10:20-22).

A missionary should not underestimate the significance or the power behind charms, shrines, idols, talismans, or tools of the witch-doctors. What may only look like a root, or feathers, or powder might actually be "something set apart for destruction." Might a

345

person become a participant with demons by having or using such an object?

Is the Supernatural Real?

The ultimate question which we must answer is how are we to view the supernatural? Americans view the supernatural through one kind of lens while Africans view it through another kind of lens. What constitutes these lenses, and is there still a third lens which comprises a biblical view?

American View

Americans have, at best, a confused idea of the spirit realm and witchcraft. Social scientists from the late 1800's and early 1900's developed views that the practice of magic and belief in spirits was simply a model of "evolutionary development (from magic, to religion to science), a psychological coping mechanism, a prelogical explanation of natural events, or a sociological phenomenon that helps define and sustain community roles" (Kuemmerlin-McLean, 1992, p. 470). These views still heavily influence contemporary thinking. In fact, the social scientific view has had its greatest impact in the medical, judicial, and educational systems of America.

Many Americans consider people who conduct seances, read palms or Tarot cards, or make astrological predictions as phony. Westerners tend to think belief in spirits as primitive, prelogical, or unscientific. The media often represents witch covens as eerie kooks and social misfits who perform secret animal sacrifices. Yet many of our classic children's tales involve magic. Supermarket tabloids often scream headlines of ghostly or angelic encounters. And many of our popular movies contain themes based upon demons, Satan, angels, curses, or witchcraft. Perhaps the result of such a confluence of thoughts, is that witchcraft, demons and the supernatural have become interesting and even entertaining topics, but not real enough to merit a place of serious thought by the American public.

American Christians have an even more difficult time reconciling their belief in the supernatural world and modern scientific theories. They profess belief in Biblical accounts of demons, angels, and the supernatural. However, to integrate these beliefs with academic and scientific theories, American Christians often try to limit such supernatural experiences to Biblical times. Currently, a growing number of American Christians are embracing a belief in contemporary supernatural activity. This belief, however, still tends to be undefined and often mixed with popular thought and social science views.

These conflicting views are often held consciously or unconsciously by American missionaries entering African mission work. It is part of the unseen cultural baggage that American missionaries have to understand to become effective cross-cultural evangelists.

African View

In Africa, strong animistic beliefs provide the cultural framework for most people. Animism has a "strong belief in the presence and power of 'spirits' and other supernatural forces in the world" (Kuemmerlin-McLean, p. 470). In this view, the spirit world definitely exists and interacts with the physical realm. Sickness, death, crop failures, business successes, and many other things are seen to be affected by the spiritual world. Animism provides the lens through which many Africans see all experiences, events, and values. Witchcraft is an important part of this system as a means to control the spirits and supernatural forces. Each tribe may have special spirits guiding and protecting them. Often there are clan spirits and prescribed sacrifices for everything from rain, crops, livestock and children to personal protection from evil. The Bagisu people of Uganda keep a special shrine for the rain spirit (*Nabende*). The neighboring Bagwere people make small holes in their huts so the child spirit (*Mukama*) can come and go freely. The Sebei people living on the Ugandan slopes of Mount Elgon put a special tree branch over their doors to protect them from measles. Each clan and tribe often has dozens of spirits and activities that these spirits require them to do. Some spirits may even have the same name from place to place. The *Jinn* spirits of the Berbers in Morocco (Beckwith, & Fisher, p. 82) are called *Jini* among the Swahili of the Kenyan coast, and are called *Majini* among the Bagwere of Uganda.

This animistic world view is even accepted by African government courts. In 1987, the Luo people of Kenya petitioned the government to return a large python taken from their area to Nairobi for treatment. The clan elders claimed the snake's absence would hinder their communication with the spirits and bring disaster upon the area. The government not only agreed to return the snake, but did so in a private plane.

Also in the 1980s, a famous Luo lawyer, S. M. Otieno, died. When his wife (a Kikuyu of central Kenya) announced plans to bury him on the family farm north of Nairobi, the Luo clan elders sued Mrs. Otieno for the body, claiming the clan spirits would be angry if he were buried outside of their homeland. The case took 52 days in the court, which ruled in favor of the husband's clan.

Biblical View

The Bible presents still another view of the spiritual realm, about which it is very clear. The supernatural is real. God, angels, Satan, and demons are realities. Human interaction with the supernatural is guided by spiritual laws given by God within the Bible itself.

Throughout the Bible there are terms which refer to practices of the supernatural and magic. The most specialized vocabulary appears primarily in the Pentateuch when God commands the Israelites not to adopt the evil practices of the nations they would conquer (Deuteronomy 18:10-11; Leviticus 19:26, 31; 20:1-6; and Exodus 22:18). "The most basic and inclusive list is found in Deuteronomy 18:10-11" (Kuemmerlin-McLean, p. 469).

Instead of teaching that the practice of magic is fake, the Bible assumes it is real and prohibits its use. The Egyptian magicians had the power to duplicate by their secret arts three of the signs that God commanded Moses to do before the Pharaoh (Exodus 7:11-12, 22; 8:7). On another occasion, the Bible records King Saul's consultation with a witch who summoned Samuel's spirit for guidance (1 Samuel 28:3-25). Simon the sorcerer of Samaria had great power that amazed the people of his area (Acts 8:9-24). Ephesus was a center for learned practitioners of witchcraft who produced scrolls of their art (Acts 19:19). The essence of the biblical view is not denial of evil power, but the insistence that God's power is greater (Exodus 7:12; 8:18,19; Acts 8:13; 19:17-20). Throughout the Bible, Scripture encourages righteous people to trust in God's strength, and warns them of punishment and separation from God if they indulge in practices associated with witchcraft and idolatry (Deuteronomy 18:10-11; Leviticus 19:26, 31; 20:1-6, 27; Exodus 22:17; 1 Samuel 28; Isaiah 8:19; 57:3; Ezekiel 22:28; Malachi 3:5; Galatians 5:20; Revelation 21:8; 22:15).

Why Is Witchcraft So Attractive?

Witchcraft maintains an astonishing hold over many Africans. The person who would grudgingly give the smallest coin to the Lord on Sunday might travel 200 miles over several days and spend two month's wages to seek relief from a personal problem from a famous witchdoctor.

On the island of Lufu (Lake Victoria), a witchdoctor instructs a person with family problems to take a goat in a canoe and paddle out to a distant, isolated island and sacrifice it to the island spirits. This person will sell his possessions to purchase a goat, undertake the long and arduous journey to the island, and spend several days performing all the tasks given by the witchdoctor. But this same person will not attend a *free,* two-hour church meeting on biblical principles for family unity 100 yards from his house.

Why will people willingly submit themselves to travel long distances, dig deep holes, swallow unknown substances, build costly shrines, burn and sacrifice good food, bury clay pots, hide expensive powders, run around naked in their neighborhood at night, and do all manner of odd activities to satisfy a witchdoctor's prescription, but not lift a finger to fulfill even the slightest obligation put upon them by the church? Such people make excuses and go to great lengths to justify their laziness in Christian matters, but they are the champion of witchcraft practice. Why are people attracted to witchcraft? What is its appeal?

First, witchcraft releases the user from numerous personal responsibilities. If a child gets sick, the favorite soccer team loses, a driver has an accident, or a thief is caught stealing, either the charm they used simply was not strong enough or perhaps others had stronger medicines.

For the wife who thinks her husband is interested in another woman, she can buy a charm to fix the problem. She herself has to do nothing to change. She does not have to look any nicer; she does not have to behave any more respectfully or show more honor to her husband; she does not have to work any harder in the house; in short, she does not have to do anything herself to keep her husband around. That is the work of the charm! She can continue to be lazy, disrespectful, dirty, quarrelsome, sexually cold, or whatever other action/attitude with which her husband finds her difficult to live If the husband runs away, it is the charm's fault!

For the man who fails in his business, the charm he purchased was not strong enough to attract customers. He does not have to admit that he tried to cheat customers with price increases. He does not have to say that he was rude and showed little concern for customer satisfaction. He does not have to tell anyone that he did not restock his store and that he misused all the money that came in. It is not his fault for mismanaging the business. The charm simply wasn't strong enough. A stronger charm will help him succeed in some future business.

To be relieved of personal responsibility is a powerful attraction of witchcraft: "I am no longer the cause of my troubles and misfortunes. I do not have to do anything to change. I can continue living as I want. I simply buy charms to ensure that I can do as I please. And if a problem does arise, then it is the charm's fault. I am free of blame".

Second, witchcraft gives the user the power to manipulate people, spirits, and circumstances around him. With a sacrifice or little bit of medicine, the user can cleverly bend everything to his wishes. He becomes the master of his universe. He sees himself as smarter and more clever than others because he has secretly made people do his bidding. He has greater power. He can do more. He is in control of his life. He has to answer to no one else.

Yes, that person will admit that there is a spirit world and that God and spirits do exist. But with witchcraft, she can manipulate the spirits to do her will. She can gain protection from evil or even curse others. Witchcraft can "appease" the spirits and turn their anger away. A sacrifice, a promise to do good, praise, or a contribution at church will make God happy and allow the witchcraft user to continue with her own lifestyle. In fact, she will ask for prayers for her sick child and then buy a charm thinking that she has cleverly covered all the bases and provided maximum protection for her infant.

The powerful attraction here is that the person becomes his or her own god. He sets things up to do his bidding. She bends and manipulates everything else to her wishes. She has to conform to nothing but her own desires. He cleverly controls all things. Perhaps this is why witchcraft and idolatry are so closely related in the Bible (2 Kings 9:22; 1 Samuel 15:23; Micah 5:12-14; Nahum 3:4; Galatians 5:20).

Why Is It Hard For Africans To Renounce The Spirits and Witchcraft?

The following examples are by no means exhaustive. They are a composite picture of African life experiences from the Bukusu, Luo and Kabras peoples of Kenya, the Bagisu, Sebei, and Bagwere peoples of Uganda, and the Lomwe people of Malawi. These stories illustrate how many Africans are exposed to witchcraft in every stage of their lives.

Many African women purchase charms to help them get pregnant. Among the Bagisu people there are special waterfalls called *nabeke* where barren women bathe. The washing ritual is supposed to increase the woman's chances of getting pregnant. Once she is expecting, she will eat a special mixture of animal blood, milk, and pumpkin to make her healthy and protect the baby. In some cases, special ceremonies are conducted as soon as the baby is born. If previous children have died in a Bukusu home, as soon as the baby is born it is passed out of a window and laid upon the trash heap. A grandmother will pick up the child, bring it through the front door and ask if anyone in the house wants to care for it. This ritual is meant to confuse the spirits who caused the death of previous children. If the child lives, he is named *Makokha* (the Bagisu name is *Kuloba*) meaning trash heap. Kabras mothers put charms called *eyindukhulu* on infants to ward off sickness. The babies may be completely naked but wear a string around their waist, a necklace, or a bracelet (*hirizi*). Before a child can walk, a Gwere mother will dash from her house and lay her infant in the tracks behind a passing vehicle. She believes the energy from such a vehicle will be transferred to her child. The Kabras lay their infants upon the back of a black cow or strong dog for the same reason. If a Bukusu child wakes up with nightmares from evil spirits, he is fed *kimikalo*, a special herb mixture to ward off spirits. Bukusu grandmothers conduct special name-calling ceremonies (*khutuma visambwa*) over a child to identify which ancestral spirit has come back in the form of this child.

Growing up in the home, children see and hear about the spirits that live around them. They learn the names of clan spirits and what each one does. When they are sick they are taken to witchdoctors for treatment. Among the Bagwere, cuts on the chest or arms of a child are a sign of such treatments. Gwere children will watch as their fathers sacrifice a chicken and break it up into a small clay pot which he buries in a strategic spot in the compound for protection against all kinds of evil. Additional medicines may be buried at the door step into the home. Some Sebei families place medicine for protection above the doorway to keep evil spirits or harm from entering with a visitor.

At circumcision time when young men begin their rite of passage, the Bukusu and Bagisu make special shrines called *namwima* for the ancestors to sit in and watch the proceedings. The blood of a sacrificial chicken is smeared on the circumcision knife and special herbs (*etiang'i*) are eaten by the initiates to make them strong during the ritual so that they won't cry out and shame their families.

Students may purchase charms to better their performance in school or athletics. Is the town's soccer team or the national team playing poorly? The witchdoctor prescribes a special medicine that is put into the shoes of the athletes. This medicine is designed to attract the soccer ball and to help the athlete kick accurately. Additional, stronger medicine will make the opponent's goalie see more than one ball coming at him. This will make the goalie jump to block mirages and allow the real ball to pass. African newspapers acknowledge that many soccer teams on the continent hire their own team witchdoctors. The Kenyans even claim that one of their witchdoctors was recently hired by a German team. One wonders how many competitors wear charms at the Olympics to enhance their performance and abilities?

When Africans are older, they may purchase small roots/charms for their wallet to help them secure a job. The charm costs about two months' wages, but as long as they keep the charm in their wallet, they cannot lose their job. The fact of the charms' existence must also be kept secret. If others know about it, the charm may lose its power. A Lomwe woman notices her husband is spending too much time away from the house; she fears he has a girl friend somewhere. The witchdoctor instructs the wife to catch a gecko and take its tail which she burns, crushes, and secretly adds to her husband's food. This will make him stay at home. If a Lomwe man is gone from home very much, most assuredly he eats gecko tails in his food. Charms (*eyisimbishila*) purchased by a Kabras bride will enhance her ability to keep her husband faithful.

Whole communities will also participate in spirit-pleasing sacrifices at funerals. Every activity of the funeral from where the grave is dug to how the body is prepared reflects beliefs in spirits. The family honors the spirits of the dead who are now able to bless or curse them. Shrines are built in clan areas and designated as sacred spots. The Balangira clan of the Gwere tribe collects the skulls of ancestors and keeps them in special shrines. The community reinforces such beliefs by the prevalence of these ceremonies.

Thus, from birth to death, spirits and witchcraft cover every major event in an African's life. If there is a problem with the spirits, troubled relationship, enemy, fear, or curse, the witchdoctor can sell something to take care of it.

The pressure to conform to these beliefs and practices is intense. The clan and extended family can withhold numerous privileges from any uncooperative member. Dennis Okoth, a Kenyan Luo, upon his confession of Christian faith, was tied up by his father, beaten, and starved for several days, in an effort to make him renounce his new faith. Mung'ono, a clan priest among the Bagwere, lives on clan land, in a clan house, and receives his entire income through clan donations. If he renounces the clan spirits and becomes a Christian, he will become destitute. Such harsh punishments and family repudiations await many who seriously consider confessing faith in Christ. Death is not an uncommon punishment in the most extreme situations.

What Should a Missionary Do?

It is into this environment of life-long conditioning, fear of spirits, and family and community pressure that a missionary comes, often unaware of the social, familial, and economic choices he asks an African to make by confessing Christ. The most tightly knit, traditional communities tend to resist the Gospel. Syncretism is the only way many Africans can find to appease the spirits, their family, and their missionary friend; this is a difficult position for the missionary to be in as he or she begins their work.

What Does Not Work

Denying the existence of demons and spirits and the power of witchcraft is not the way for a missionary to begin. The lone voice

355

of the missionary, calling within a vast community of Africans who have years of traditional experiences, will be judged by his hearers as a fool. He will undermine his credibility as an ambassador of Christ. Think how Paul approached the Athenians in Acts 17:16-34. He did not begin by condemning their idolatrous practices. Instead, he commended them for their religious interest and then spoke of God by using one of their own altar inscriptions. Missionaries will get much farther if they begin by acknowledging the existence of spirits and demons, but then go on to explain where the greatest power of protection and blessing lies. Missionaries and African Christians would do well to preach on Biblical texts that show Jesus' power over evil spirits. Jesus casting out the Gaderene demon named Legion (Mark 5:1-20) will make an African audience take notice. Casting out demons, healing sicknesses, raising people from the dead, performing miracles, all these proclaim the power of Jesus Christ in terms that Africans can relate to. Preaching about those who confess Jesus as the Son of God (including demons and Satan, in his tempting of Jesus) makes an impact on African listeners as to who is really in control. Jesus promises freedom from the bondage of evil spirits, fear, and curses. This is an "Athenian" opening we missionaries must not neglect.

Reasoning does not work either. I have tried to reason with people who use charms by asking the following questions: "What kind of an explanation can you give if your soccer team, which wears charms to win, is beaten by a team that does not use charms? If you use charms to help you succeed in business, then why is Uganda one of the poorest countries in the world with an annual per capita income of less than $400 per person? If your children wear charms for protection against sickness, then why do people in Uganda have a life expectancy of 48 years of age and its infant mortality rate ranks among the highest in the world? If your women truly buy charms to keep their husbands faithful, then why do Ugandan newspapers estimate that adultery affects over 70 percent of the households in the country?" Their answer is always the same. Either the medicine was not strong enough, or, they say, "Just think what things would be like without the charms working so hard."

What Does Work

The first and most important step is becoming a Christian. Responding to the Gospel is the greatest step in an African's move away from the bondage of the spirits. Dying to sin (Romans 6:1-14), being washed clean and free of sins (Acts 22:16; John 8:32), and receiving the Holy Spirit (Acts 2:38) and his empowerment (Ephesians 3:16) are necessary to crush the influence of evil spirits in an African's life.

The implications of confessing Christ as Lord should be explained and enacted much more specifically than what we have usually done in America. The Greek word for "confess" literally means "to speak the same as" (Vines, p. 226). To confess Christ would then mean to speak as Christ would speak. We would speak against the same things he would. We would bless the same things he would. The African Christian should publicly speak his allegiance to Christ only and renounce all past association with evil including clan spirits, witchcraft, and traditional spirit practices. The more detailed and extensive this confession and renouncing is, the clearer his allegiance to Christ will be. Witchcraft-related cultural practices that may have happened to him while in the womb or as an infant should also be included in the renunciation. Do not neglect to address generational curses, sacrifices, and beliefs (Exodus 20:4-6).

A complete cleansing must take place in the new Christian's home and life. The missionaries and church leaders must lead the new Christian in burning all objects associated with the spirits.

Remove and destroy all symbols and charms of witchcraft, shrines, sacrifices, and objects of protection. This may involve digging up buried charms, pulling up special plants, cutting off amulets from the body, ripping out charms sewn into clothing, and uncovering all manner of talismans hidden in the roof, bedroom, kitchen, grain storage, and compound. The public confession of evil deeds and burning of scrolls for witchcraft in Ephesus provides an important example for such cleansing (Acts 19:18-19).

There is great need to fill up a person's life with good now that he or she has emptied him or herself of evil. Jesus' parable of the evil spirit going out of a man and returning to find the house swept clean, put in order, and empty graphically illustrates the vulnerability of new African Christians (Matthew 12:43-45). Teaching on spiritual disciplines and a Christian life are crucial for the new convert. Jesus commanded his followers to "make disciples," and this included teaching new converts to obey all of Jesus' commands (Matthew 28:18-20). Replace the passive confidence in charms with an active participation in the fruits of the Spirit. Teach new converts the power of prayer, fasting, Scripture memorization, praise, and fellowship.

New converts should not be left without an encouraging support group. They should be incorporated as quickly as possible into a body of believers who will see to each others personal and spiritual needs. The new Christian will need strength to withstand the family and cultural pressure to return to his or her old practices. If God's people will do this the local church will be a strong place of refuge as new Christians gain a new spiritual identity, family, and way of life.

The missionary's main weapon from a distance will be prayer — constant and vigilant. Paul mentions Epaphras in his letter to the Colossians. He says that Epaphras worked hard for the Colossians by "wrestling in prayer that they stand firm" (Colossians 4:12-13). Even from a distance, the missionary can work hard for new

Christians. In fact, a missionary's greatest work is not teaching seminars, holding Bible studies, writing and printing tracts, but knee-bending prayer. Mission committees, sponsoring churches, friends, and family should all be recruited for focused prayer covering the work.

Conclusion

The effects of belief in the spiritual world and the practices associated with witchcraft are pervasive and powerful in the lives of many Africans, unbeliever and believer. As western Christians we must open our eyes to the difficulties African Christians face as they attempt to live out their faith in Jesus in a pagan context. If Christianity is to be wholly and appropriately lived out by African people, they must be allowed to ask and taught how to answer the questions of life which they face every day.

WORKS CITED

Barley, Nigel (1986). *The Innocent Anthropologist*. Middlesex, England: Penguin Books.

Beckwith, C. and Fisher, A. (1999, November). African Marriage Rituals. *National Geographic Society*.

Keummerlin-McLean, Joanne K. (1992). Magic. *Anchor Bible Dictionary*.

Mattox, F. W. (1961). *The Eternal Kingdom*. Delight, AR: Gospel Light Publishing.

NIV Study Bible (1985). Grand Rapids, MI: Zondervan.

Vine, M.E. (1979). *Expository Dictionary of New Testament Words*. McLean, VA: MacDonald Publishing Company.

Wright, David P. (1992). Holiness. *Anchor Bible Dictionary*.

SECTION 4

Concluding Thoughts

CHAPTER 16

The Future of Missions in Africa

Sam Shewmaker

Sam and Nancy Shewmaker have been missionaries their entire careers. Sam was born to missionary parents in Northern Rhodesia, now Zambia. They have worked in Zambia and Kenya, as well as criss-crossed the continent to promote the ACA conferences and develop communication networks among the African churches. They currently reside in Searcy, Arkansas. sshewmaker@earthlink.com.

The continent of Africa is one of the largest in area as well as one of the most linguistically and culturally diverse regions of the world. Africa contains 1,918 languages and more than 2000 people groups in some 57 nations; Africa's population now exceeds 800 million. And, in spite of one of the highest incidents of HIV in the world, Africa continues to have one of the world's highest birth and population growth rates.

But the negative side of Africa's ledger is also full of number one positions. Africa is the only region of the world with a decreasing cumulative gross domestic product in real terms. Negative economic and social forces are contributing to make Africa increasingly a continent of hopelessness and despair that is growing in its dependence on foreign aid. In many countries, a culture of 'grab whatever you can any way you can' and 'live for now because there is no future,' is causing the breakdown of basic moral values, increasing materialism, and heating up old tribal hatreds.

In spite of, or perhaps because of, high levels of poverty, disease and illiteracy, the people of Africa in general are very dissatisfied with the inadequacy of their traditional religious beliefs and practices. This is making them more receptive to the gospel of Jesus Christ, to Islam, and to other religious faiths as never before, if only as a possible solution to the problems of every day life, where their old religions have failed them.

The State of the Churches of Christ in Africa Today

According to David Barrett, renowned church statistician, there are about 350,000,000 people in Africa who consider themselves Christians today. Africans are becoming Christian at a rate of about 20,000 per day; Barrett projects that by 2025 more Africans will be Christian than any region of the world.

What have the missions of the Churches of Christ accomplished in Africa? In the year 2000, the Churches of Christ in Africa will surpass the United States in the number of congregations in existence. This is a milestone indicating fertile fields blessed by God with a bountiful harvest. But to look at the situation another way, the membership of Churches of Christ represents only one tenth of one percent of the population of Africa. More than 90% of that church membership is found in only 10 of the 57 countries of Africa. From this perspective, we have barely had any impact on the continent.

What is the situation in terms of missionary personnel? The number of full-time western missionaries resident in Africa peaked at about 230 in 1994. The figure in 2000 is about 165. For example, in 1990 there were approximately 80 Church of Christ missionary personnel in Kenya. In 2000, there are about 35. Is this good or bad? The good news is that this change reflects a maturing mission work in Kenya and a move toward fielding missionaries in 'newer' frontiers among unreached peoples. The bad news is that attrition, the net loss of overall numbers of western missionaries, is draining the missionary force in the field. We are simply not fielding enough new missionaries as older missionaries withdraw or retire.

The Unfinished Task of Missions in Africa

What remains to be done in the missionary task in Africa? Many people groups remain unreached in sub-Saharan Africa in both urban areas and in the countryside. Little has been done in such war-torn countries as Angola, Rwanda, Burundi, Liberia and Sierra Leone. More survey work needs to be done to discover the most receptive peoples in West Africa whom we should target for field teams of missionaries. In some places where churches do exist, little growth is happening even where people are receptive because of inappropriate missionary attitudes or approaches.

But by far the greatest challenge facing Christianity in Africa is the Muslim world of North Africa. Scores of people groups throughout the Saharan and Mediterranean-bordering countries have little or no witness of the gospel of Christ. This part of Africa must become the focus of much of our mission efforts and resources in the years ahead.

What Will it Take to Complete the Task?

As in every field of endeavor, continued success depends on rec-ognizing changing conditions and adapting to new realities. No less is true of missions. In the churched areas of Africa, nationals are beginning to take up the reins of responsibility and leadership. With this development, the roles of missionaries and nationals need to change. As a friend of mine is fond of saying, "missionaries need to learn to be comfortable in the back seat."

Where are Western Missionaries Needed?

Missionaries must adapt to the changing situation and needs of the African church if we are to continue to promote the growth and maturing of the African church. The changing roles of the missionary will encompass the following areas:

1. Missionaries are still needed in new works and in pioneering situations. American missionaries operate best in roles that call for new challenges, innovation, adaptation, initiative, ingenuity and the desire to make a difference. Our 'can-do' spirit coupled with a 'take charge' attitude serves to make many well-trained American missionaries best at being starters of a work.

Ideally, though, missionaries should quickly begin discipling, training, and delegating the primary work of evangelism and church planting to local maturing Christians. In contexts where churches have begun to mature, missionaries must begin early to prepare for and initiate an evolution of roles.

2. Western missionaries are needed in roles that support the local churches as they expand and mature. These include printing and publishing, theological training, translation projects, and other support ministries.

3. Western missionaries are needed in service ministries that are designed to express the love of Christ through a holistic approach to the gospel. These might include medical, agricultural, social ministries and vocational training.

4. Western missionaries, especially those with some years of field experience, are needed in broader service to the churches across the continent. African Christians long for a sense of connection and solidarity with fellow Christians. Teaching seminars on various topics, reporting and consulting are functions vital to the health of the church.

5. Former missionaries who may be called to other fields or areas of service need to remain available for consultative and encouragement roles with people where they have worked. Africans grieve over the departure of those who have brought them the gospel and greatly impacted their lives, and they need the continued connection to nurture their faith and courage and to challenge their vision. That need can seldom be met by a 'replacement' or 'second-generation' missionary.

New Roles for African Christians

As missionaries hand over the reins by trusting more and delegating more responsibility to the national church, the roles filled by the national Christians and church leaders will also change. These changes will be seen most readily in the following areas:

Local Christians need to take on roles of leadership and planning for the future of their churches, depending less on missionaries.

African leaders need to do more of their own theologizing. That is, they need to learn the skills of getting deep into the Word of God, understanding and applying it in their cultural contexts, both for their churches and in message formulation for the lost.

African Christians need now to become the primary witnesses of the gospel to the lost of Africa. In the years ahead they will be the missionaries to the unreached tribes of sub-Saharan Africa. They will also be the businessmen and women, the teachers and other professionals who will bear witness to Jesus of Nazareth among the peoples of North Africa from the Horn of Africa in the east to the mouth of the Gambia River in the west.

New Strategies for the Use of Available Resources

Some of our old paradigms of missions need to be reexamined and in some cases scrapped and replaced with better ones. In almost

367

every sphere whether politics, economics or international relations, the trend is to think and act globally. This is a reflection of the recognition that significant events and developments in one part of the world tend to impact the whole world. We need to think and act globally in missions too.

Most missionaries in the Churches of Christ in Africa have opposed the use of 'American money' in missions except for the support of American missionaries and the programs and institutions that these missionaries believe are appropriate. Missionaries have tried to insulate the emerging churches in Africa from any connection to American missions-supporting churches out of a fear that the misuse of money would spoil the work. While there is a sound basis for this concern, the policy of insulation has been frustrating to many Africans. It is often viewed with suspicion and seen as greed and protecting self-interest on the part of the missionary. Other than implementing a flat 'one-size-fits-all' policy, little has been done to understand and resolve the cultural, spiritual, and ethical issues surrounding this question. It is a troubling irony that wealthy American Christians cannot find enough missionaries among their own people to use that wealth effectively in missions, while literally thousands of committed African Christians would gladly and effectively serve as missionaries on a small fraction of that wealth. We need some creative ideas to seek fair and workable solutions to this impasse in ways that will avoid dependency and false motivations while encouraging true, balanced partnership.

Paul taught us to view Christians as members of one another and of the whole body of Christ locally. Our emphasis on local church autonomy has tended to make us usually think locally, seldom globally. We need to view all segments of the church as part of the universal Body of Christ. Just as Paul taught that we are all members of one another and that all gifts accorded to the members are for the benefit of the whole body, so too, I believe, we need to see the spiritual gifts and other resources of the different segments of the church as belonging to, and for the benefit of, the universal Body of Christ. Now this principle is much easier to express than to put into practice. It is fraught with all kinds of possible dangers and problems. On the other hand, I believe there are serious ethical issues here if we refuse to deal with this principle.

The body principle also has within it great possibilities for synergy, cooperation and partnership that can revolutionize missions in the 21st century. Imagine, for instance, two churches committed to missions, one in North America and one in Africa. Imagine that between them they shared the biblical spiritual gifts of evangelism, administration, faith, leadership, languages, giving, mercy, and service. In addition, they would share at least two cultural perspectives on the Word and will of God. With great measures of love, commitment to understanding one another and how to present the gospel in a new mission context, and with able people willing to follow Christ's lead, one can hardly imagine what God could do with these people in missions.

New Kinds of Mission Approaches?

To meet the new demands of the new century we are going to need new approaches to missions in Africa. There are numbers of new approaches available to us, but the following ideas seem to hold out the greatest promise.

Intercultural Missions Teams

In the last 30 years there has been a strong emphasis on the development and fielding of teams of missionaries. Some of the early teams were disasters in terms of relations between the missionaries as doctrinal, personality and methodological conflict took their toll on

369

the missionaries as well as the people they went to win to Christ. But overall, as we learned how to build teams effectively, the results in terms of church growth were good.

Some of the issues and questions that missionaries face include, "How can I best learn the language?" "How can I truly identify with these people?" "How do I know who I can trust?" "How do I overcome these cultural misunderstandings?" "Are people coming to me out of wrong motives?" These and many other questions are issues that the western missionary often struggles with for a long time to find answers.

A new configuration of mission teams needs to be considered that might contribute to better and quicker solutions for these and other perplexing questions. We might call these 'intercultural' missionary teams. Imagine a team of missionaries that included both westerners and Africans. Such a team might include people gifted in language who could teach the other members more quickly and effectively. Africans on such a team would be able to understand the mind-set and motives behind responses in another African context. They would bring the ability to adapt to the situation more readily. Americans, for example, would be able to bring gifts to the team that would represent the best characteristics of western culture: breadth of education, Bible knowledge, missions training, vision and motivation.

Would there be problems to overcome with this concept? Certainly. There would be issues of potential cross-cultural conflict and values differences. There would be issues of team-building, of lifestyle, the means and structure of financial support and many other challenges. But if we believe that missions is no longer either the prerogative or the sole responsibility of the western churches, we must work together to devise bold and innovative configurations of mission structures that will forward the missionary task in this new era.

Urban Strategies

Most of our mission efforts in Africa have focused on rural peoples. This may be because our background in the United States was largely rural and we find the rural culture simpler and easier to understand than the complex urban culture. But with the poverty and other negative factors of the rural areas increasing, African urban populations continue to grow. It is imperative that we devise effective strategies to win to Christ the diverse peoples flooding into the large urban centers of Africa-economic and political refugees, the unemployed and the unemployable, those seeking education and a better life.

Reaching the Muslim World

While there are yet millions of unreached peoples in sub-Saharan Africa, the last great frontier for the gospel in Africa is the Muslim world of North Africa. Islam has attempted to make inroads into the 'Christian' south of the continent through the building of mosques and the funding of educational and other benevolent programs underwritten by Middle Eastern oil profits. Religious and political conflicts in Sudan, northern Nigeria, Algeria and other hot spots have fomented clashes between Muslims and Christians. So far evangelistic efforts in Muslim areas have proven largely ineffective or very slow. Notable exceptions to this are found in northern Nigeria, northern Ghana and Ethiopia where significant inroads of evangelism and church planting are being done among largely Muslim peoples.

Professional missionaries cannot enter and openly proselytize in most North African countries under Islamic governments. So new, different kinds of approaches must be devised to make it possible to offer the gospel to those in the darkness of Islam.

371

Tentmaking Ministries

Tentmaking ministries are an alternative to traditional, professional missionary approaches. Tentmaking in the context of missions refers to a person or group using a secular vocation as a means of support and/or as a cover for being in a position to share the gospel where they might not otherwise be able to.

To respond to the challenge of Islam in Africa we need to change our paradigms of proclaiming the gospel. We must broaden our definition of 'missions' and 'missionary' or get rid of the term altogether, especially where missionaries are regarded with suspicion. In our recruiting for missions we must recognize that we need far more people working for the cause of the gospel than will ever be professional missionaries.

Missionary Training

Our Christian universities have traditionally been a source of many missionaries. There are at least two things we need to change in our Christian university training that have great potential to add to our Christian impact in the world in general and Africa in particular. First, we need to overcome our natural cultural tendency as Americans toward ethnocentrism and isolationism by encouraging all of our Christian college students to think of themselves as 'world Christians.' We must lead them to be citizens of the kingdom of God, first, but also to be citizens of the world. We need to encourage them to engage the world and to believe that they can make a difference.

Second, we need to be harvesting many kinds of workers for the gospel from among our university students. For example, we need to find political science majors who have a heart for God and who can be encouraged to join the Foreign Service and work in American embassies and consulates. We need agriculturists and veterinarians

372

who can work with USAID and other non–governmental organizations. English majors and teachers can teach English in African universities and do training for multinational companies. I have an American friend, for example, who is a trainer for an oil company in Angola. She doesn't see herself as an evangelist or church planter, but she could be a 'strategic agent' or a contact person for a new work there. Business majors should be challenged to be entrepreneurs to open companies or work for companies with branches in North Africa. The possibilities are almost limitless if we could break out of what Donald McGavran called "the prisons of previous patterns"– in this case thinking largely in terms of the professionally–trained traditional missionary. After all, when the church in Jerusalem was persecuted, the 'professionals' remained there, while "those {ordinary disciples} who had been scattered preached the word wherever they went" (Acts 8:4).

Third, in Africa also, we need to be calling faithful men and women into the service of Jesus Christ by training them for vocations in which they can support themselves while sharing the gospel where 'missionaries' are not allowed. Already some of this training is being done in southern Zambia, Northern Nigeria, Kenya and other places, but often without visions and strategies for finding the lost in new areas. Businessmen and government officials who are Christians travel all over the continent, but often without a sense of urgency about sharing their faith or encouraging the brethren where they go. These people need to be infused with a missionary vision and a burning desire to let their light shine as they travel.

Conclusion

These are but a few of the ideas, methods and strategies that will be needed in the decades before us. I fully expect that it will not be long before there will be hundreds of African missionary families serving Christ cross–culturally within the continent and beyond.

At the dawn of a new century, Africa is in the sunrise of its Christian experience and its potential Christian impact on the world. Our prayer is that God will give us more men and women with the heart and vision of Wendell Broom, to carry the flame farther into the darkness, that there may be light in dark places, and that every tribe and nation will find the path that leads to the true Light.

CHAPTER 17

A Challenge to Meet in the Middle

Reported by Sam Shewmaker

In a volume dedicated to African missions and to a man who has given his life for the cause of doing missions as well as teaching and inspiring others to missions in Africa, we would be remiss to conclude the book without describing one of Wendell Broom's great visions for mission in Africa. Some years ago Wendell conceived the idea of challenging East African Christians to turn their eyes west toward the great expanse of territory in Central Africa as yet unreached with the gospel: to pray, to plan, and to act for the spread of the good news of Christ among the lost there. In August 1997, Wendell found his opportunity to complete the outline of this vision in a presentation to his brethren in Nigeria. At a lectureship meeting of evangelists and church leaders he presented the following covenant for those present to consider and commit to do.

Covenant to Meet in the Middle

We, the undersigned preachers of the Gospel of Jesus Christ have met together at the Huffard Annual Lectures of 1997, at the Nigerian Christian Bible College. We have read, studied, and prayed in these meetings about Africans Claiming Africa for Christ. Especially have we been impressed by the unreached people and the nations between East Africa and West Africa that lie unevangelised between us.

We have learned of the role that Africa must play in God's plan to plant churches of born again believers in all the world. We have seen that our countries will double their numbers of church in the next ten years or less.

We have also heard that some of you have made a covenant with some of us to march toward each other in preaching, teaching and planting churches, with the goal and dream to meet in the Central Africa Republic by the help of God's power and in the will of God for the faith of Jesus in all nations.

We therefore put our hands to this epistle in pledge before God:

> that all of us will pray for such a march and meeting;
>
> that some of us will begin to plant churches in northern Cameroon, Chad and Central African Republic;
>
> that some of you will begin to plant churches in Western Ethiopia, Western Uganda and Southern Sudan;
>
> that we will train our brothers to plant churches that plant churches that plant churches until we meet together in love, faith and victory some day soon as God wills;
>
> that we shall study the maps, find the towns that will link together to form the chain that will lead us to the meeting point;
>
> that we shall unite our tribes and nations in brotherly love between Christian believers in honor, integrity, and purity of character, that Africa may rise up under the hand of God to bring peace, prosperity, brotherhood and eternal

life to the vast millions of Africa and the world, so help us God.

Therefore, on this the 11th day of August, 1997, in gathering at Ukpom, Abak, Nigeria, we sign our names and pledge our prayers and labour to Christ for His Glory.

[Note: Of those present at the meeting that day, 178 preachers, church leaders and evangelists signed the declaration. Such is the missionary zeal and leadership of Wendell Broom, a man we consider it a privilege to know and to honor.]

CHAPTER 18

An African Bibliography

ACU Missions Dept (1994). "World Survey Charts. *Journal of Applied Missiology 5* (2) [on-line], http://www.bible.acu.edu/missions/Journals/jam/vol_05_2/wrldsur2.htm.

Alexander, Frank (1969). *Missions in Malawi.* Unpublished masters thesis, Fuller Theological Seminary, School of World Mission.

Allison, Fielden (1977). *Church Growth Among the Kipsigis of Southwest Kenya.* Unpublished manuscript

———— (1978). The National Evangelist. *Christian Chronicle 35* (4), 8.

Allison, Janet (1996). An Intern and AIDS. *Journal of Applied Missiology 7* (2) [on-line] http://www.bible.acu.edu/missions/Journals/jam/vol_07_2/aids.htm.

Avery, Allen (1969). *African Independency.* Unpublished masters thesis, Fuller Theological Seminary, School of World Mission.

————. (1971) *Church Growth in Southern Zambia, Volume 2.* Privately published

Avery, Allen (1995). *A manual on spiritual warfare for use in tribal Africa.* Microform, Harding University, Searcy, Arkansas.

Barr, Lawrence (1978). A Circuit Preacher in South Nyanza. *Christian Chronicle 35* (4), 3.

Beckloff, Kenneth Edward (1972). *Building the Church in Mende Traditional Society.* Guided research paper, Harding College Graduate School of Religion.

Benson, George S. (1987). *Missionary Experiences.* Phil Watson (Ed), Edmond, OK: Gospel Light Publishing.

Bolden, Kenneth (1994). *The Relevance of Covenant Concept in Developing a Strategy for Christian Ministry Among the Luo People of Kenya.* Unpublished master's thesis Wheaton Graduate School and Daystar University, Nairobi, Kenya.

Boyd, Glenn (1988). *A Model Program for Primary Health Care Delivery in Ghana, West Africa, for The African Christian Hospitals Foundation (Churches of Christ).* Unpublished dissertation, Trinity Evangelical.

Brewer, Charles R. (1964, 1966, 1968) *Missionary Pictorial.* Nashville, TN: World Vision Publishing Co.

Broom, Wendell (1958-1961). Nigerian Newsletters. Brown Library, Abilene Christian University.

——— (1970). *Growth of Churches of Christ among the Ibibio of Nigeria.* Unpublished masters thesis, Fuller Theological Seminary, School of World Mission.

——— (1972). Eight Keys to Church Growth in Cities. *Mission Strategy Bulletin 1* (6).

——— (1975). About that Visa Squeeze. *Mission Strategy Bulletin 2* (5).

——— (1975). Why some Churches Grow and Some Don't. *Mission Strategy Bulletin 3* (2).

——— (1976). Church Growth Principles. In G. Gurganus (Ed.), *Guidelines For World Evangelism,* pp. 81-104. Abilene, TX: Biblical Research Press.

Chenault, Bessie Hardin (1986). *Give me this Mountain, The Work in South Africa.* Winona, MS: J. C. Choate.

―――― (1989). *All the Children: A Collection of True Stories from Around the World for Junior and Intermediate Age.* Winona, MS: J. C. Choate.

Chowning, Cyndi (1978). Woman's Role in Kipsigis Churches. *Christian Chronicle 35* (5), 5.

Chowning, Richard (1984). Hyena, walking sticks and missionaries. *Mission Strategy Bulletin. 11* (4).

Chowning, Richard (1987). Mature Leader. In *Advancing The Kingdom: Church Growth Through Leadership Development*, pp. 77-84. Unpublished manuscript, Cascade College.

―――― (1990). Mission Opportunities in Communist Africa. *Journal of Applied Missiology 1* (1) [on-line] http://www.bible.acu.edu/missions/Journals/jam/vol_01_1/comafric.htm.

―――― (1991). An Urgent Need for Evaluation. *Journal of Applied Missiology 2* (1) [on-line] http://www.bible.acu.edu/missions/Journals/jam/vol_02_1/needeval.htm.

―――― (1991). Bibliography on Africa. *Journal of Applied Missiology 2* (2) [on-line] http://www.bible.acu.edu/missions/Africa/africbib.htm.

―――― (1992). A Field Selection Model For Use At Academic Institutions. *Journal of Applied Missiology 3* (1) [on-line] http://www.bible.acu.edu/missions/Journals/jam/vol_03_1/fldsel.htm.

―――― (1995). Missions Among the World's Suffering Masses. *Journal of Applied Missiology 6* (1) [on-line] http://www.bible.acu.edu/missions/Journals/jam/vol_06_1/suffmass.htm.

Cishak, Luther D. (1985). *Relationships Between Church and State as They Affect the Church of Christ in Nigeria.* Unpublished masters thesis, Fuller Theological Seminary, School of World Mission.

Connally, Claudene (1995). *I Walked by His Side.* Seagoville, TX: Connally Publications.

Cox, Monte B. (1987). The Developing Leader. In *Advancing The Kingdom: Church Growth Through Leadership Development,* pp. 62-65. Unpublished manuscript, Cascade College.

———— (1994). *The missiological Implications of Kalenjin Concepts of Deity, Sin and Salvation.* Unpublished master's thesis, Harding University Graduate School of Religion.

————. (1999). *"Euthanasia of Mission" or "Partnership"? An Evaluative Study of the Policy of Disengagement of Church of Christ Missionaries in Rural Kenya.* Unpublished doctoral thesis, Trinity International University.

Curry, Michael (1972). *Mission Institutions of the Churches of Christ in Southern Tanzania.* Unpublished thesis, Fuller Theological Seminary, School of World Mission.

Davenport, Dewayne (1965). *Animism in West Africa.* Unpublished master's thesis, Harding College Graduate School of Religion.

———— (1972). *Communicating Christianity to the Ashanti Tribe: A Study in Cross Cultural Communication.* Unpublished thesis, North Texas State University

Dickson, Roger. *The Call of World Evangelism.* Winona, MS: J.C.Choate.

Dickson, Roger (1994). *Namibia.* African Open Door Series. PO Box 1919 Bellivelle 7535, South Africa.

———— (1995). *African Missionary Pilot.* Winona, MS: J.C. Choate.

————— (1996). *Angola.* African Open Door Series. Bellivelle, South Africa.

————— (1998). *Preaching Through Africa.* Capetown, South Africa: International School of Biblical Studies.

Dodd, Carley (1978). Insights into Church Growth in Ghana. *Mission Strategy Bulletin 5* (4).

Drumbeat. See Sam Shewmaker.

Echols, Eldred (1989) *Wings of the Morning- The Saga of an African Pilgrim.* Fort Worth, TX: Wings Press.

Eichman, Phillip (1999). *Medical Missions among the Churches of Christ.* Gallipolis, Ohio.

Elkins, Philip W. (1964). *Toward a More Effective Mission Work.* Dallas, TX: Christian Publishing.

————— (1969). *Missions among Churches of Christ.* Unpublished masters thesis, Hartford Seminary.

————— (1974). *Church Sponsored Missions.* Austin, TX. Firm Foundation.
————— (1981)."A Pioneer Team in Zambia, Africa. In Ralph D. Winter and Steven C. Hawthorne (Eds.), *Perspectives on the World Christian Movement,* pp. 682-688. Pasadena, CA: William Carey Library.

Elliston, Edgar J. (1968). *An Ethnohistory of Ethiopia: A Study of the Factors Which Affect the Planting and Growth of the Church.* Unpublished masters thesis, Fuller Theological Seminary, School of World Mission.

Evans, Shelly R. *Mental Health Among Missionary Repatriates.* Unpublished master's thesis, Abilene Christian University, 1992.

Gilliam, Doyle D. (1967). *Certain African Concepts of God.* Unpublished masters thesis, Abilene Christian College.

Goree, Glenn Haddon (1975). *Dynamics of Urban Evangelism Among the Southern Bantu.* Unpublished master's thesis, Harding College Graduate School of Religion.

Granberg, Stanley Earl (1987) The Emerging Leader. In *Advancing The Kingdom: Church Growth Through Leadership Development*, pp. 54-61. Unpublished manuscript, Cascade College.

———— (1989). Biblical Foundations for Development. *Kenya Church of Christ Brakenhurst Men's Meeting 1989*, pp. 12-32. Unpublished manuscript, Cascade College.

———— (1989). Entering Your Target Culture by Bonding. *Evangelical Missions Quarterly 24* (4), 344-350.

———— (1992). Stages in the Life of a New Church. *Church Planter 1* (2).

———— (1993). Alumni Spotlight...Stan Granberg. *Harding University Graduate School of Religion Bulletin 34* (1).

———— (1993). *Behailu Abebe, Called to Serve: Leadership Emergence in Ethiopia, 1943-1993.* Unpublished manuscript, Fuller Theological Seminary.

———— (1995). *Curriculum Development Issues for Types II and III Leaders for the Churches of Christ in Meru, Kenya.* Unpublished masters thesis, Fuller Theological Seminary, School of World Mission.

———— (1999). *A Critical Examination of African Leadership and Leadership Effectiveness among the Churches of Christ.* Unpublished doctoral thesis, Open University: Oxford Centre for Mission Studies.

———— , Pritchett, Roger K. & Trull, Richard E. Jr. (1987), *Church growth among the Meru: Ministry of the Churches of Christ in Meru, Kenya–1987.* Unpublished manuscript, Cascade College, Portland, OR.

———, McLarty, Bruce, & Trull, Richard E. Jr. (1984). *Church Growth among the Meru, 1983.* Unpublished manuscript. Meru, Kenya.

———, Nicholas, Mark, Pritchett, Roger K., Trull, Richard E. Jr. & Williams, Keith (1992). *Church Growth among the Meru, 1992.* Unpublished manuscript. Meru, Kenya.

Greek, Stephen (1985). Predicting Missionary Effectiveness: A Personal View. *Mission Strategy Bulletin 13* (2).

Guild, Sonny (1978). A Meaningful Expression of Unity. *Christian Chronicle 35* (4), 8.

——— (1996). *A Model for Enhancing Interpersonal Relationships Within Mission Teams.* Unpublished doctoral thesis, Abilene Christian University.

Hackett, Berkeley (1978). Spotlight on Kenya. *Christian Chronicle 35* (4), 1.

——— (1978). Urban African Mission Work. *Christian Chronicle 35* (4), 8.

Hobby, Georgia (1916, 1988). *Give Us This Bread.* Winona, MS: J. C. Choate.

Horne, Donna (1986). *Meanwhile Back in the Jungle: Tanganyika Tales.* Winona, MS: J. C. Choate.

Hood, Maurice (1989)._Please Doctor: A Christian Surgeon in Iboland.* Dallas, TX: Gospel Teachers Publications.

——— (nd). *Don't Be A Sick Missionary, A Guide To Spiritual, Mental and Physical Health in The Mission Field.*

Johnson, Greg (1989). The Church Participating in Development. *Kenya Church of Christ Brakenhurst Men's Meeting 1989*, pp. 33-56. Unpublished manuscript, Cascade College.

Jones, Rex R. (1971). *A Strategy for Ethiopia*. Unpublished masters thesis, Fuller Theological Seminary, School of World Mission.

Kee, W. Paul (1991). *Retention Among the Nso' of Cameroun : A Case Study*. Unpublished master's thesis, Harding University Graduate School of Religion.

Kehl, Kevin L (1993). *A Review of Jewish and Nandi Levirate Customs: Understanding Some Problems Facing Christian Widows Among the Nandi*. Guided Research Paper, Harding University Graduate School of Religion.

Kennamer, David (1978). Why Retire to the Mission Field? *Christian Chronicle 35* (4), 6.

Kenya Mission Team (1980). *Church Planting, Watering and Increasing in Kenya*, ed. B. J. Humble. Austin, TX: Firm Foundation.

Kipsigis Team. (1981). *God's Increase Among the Kipsigis*. Privately published.

Kisumu Team (1979, 1985). *Back to the Bible: A Study of the Pattern of New Testament Christianity*. Kisumu, Kenya.

Labnow, K. & Granberg, S. E. (1992). *Kanisa la Kristo: An Overview of the Kenya Church of Christ*. Unpublished booklet, Cascade College.

Lawyer, Zelma Wood (1943). *I Married a Missionary*. Abilene, TX: ACC Press.

Malone, Jenny Kay (1998). *A New Look at an Old Genre: Apologetic Discourse in Africa*. Unpublished masters thesis, Abilene Christian University,.

McCaleb, J. M. (1930). *On the Trail of the Missionaries*. Nashville, TN: Gospel Advocate.

Merritt, Dow (1980). *The Dew Breakers*. Winona, MS: J. C. Choate.

Merritt, Avanell (1978). Educating Children on the Kenya Mission Field. *Christian Chronicle 35* (4), 5.

Merritt, Hilton (1976). *A Study of Change in Circumcision Rituals among the Abaluyia of Bungoma and Kakamega Districts of Kenya.* Unpublished doctoral thesis, University of Nairobi.

———— (1980). Ten Years Later. *Mission Strategy Bulletin 7* (4).

Merritt, Leila (1983). So you are Going Home. *Mission Strategy Bulletin 11* (2).

Miller, Matt (2000). *A Truth Encounter Between Hosea and Kabiye Traditional Beliefs of Causality.* Guided Research Paper, Harding University Graduate School of Religion.

Mitchell, Dennis (1971). *Biblical Hermeneutics as Applied to a Mission Setting.* Unpublished masters thesis, Abilene Christian College.

Mitchell, Donna (1995). *Among the People of the Sun- Our Years in Africa.* Irving, TX: J. C. Choate.

Moore, James R. (1978). Simon the Sorcerer. *Christian Chronicle 35* (4), 4.

Nicks, Bill & Gerry (1997). *Short Stories of West Africa Long Remembered.* Winona, MS: J. C. Choate Publications.

Noell, Marcia (1986). Single Women on the Mission Field. *Mission Strategy Bulletin 14* (1).

Parker, Anthony B. (1992). *The Doctrine of Revelation in African Christian Theology.* Unpublished masters thesis, Abilene Christian University.

Priest, Doug Jr. (1989). *The Problem of Animal Sacrifice Among Maasai Christians.* Unpublished doctoral thesis, Fuller Theological Seminary, School of World Mission.

———— (1990). *Doing theology with the Maasai*. Pasadena, CA: William Carey.

Randall, Max Ward (1970). *Profile for Victory: New Proposals for Missions in Zambia*. Pasadena, CA: William Carey Library.

Reed, Grady W. (1973) *Church Growth in Southern Zambia, Volume 3*. Privately published.

———— (1981). Be Careful Little Hands What You Do. *Mission Strategy Bulletin 8* (4).

Reppart, James David (1982). *Church Growth Variables of the English Speaking churches of Christ of Cameroun with Proposals for the Future*. Unpublished masters thesis, Abilene Christian University.

Ries, Bryan J.1(999). *Toward a Contextualized Theology of Kabiye Spiritual Warfare Based on Ephesians 6:10-18*. Unpublished master's thesis, Harding University Graduate School of Religion.

Rowe, Myrtle (1968). *Silhouettes of Life*. Abilene, TX: Quality Printing.

Schug, Howard L. & Sewell, Jesse P. (1947). *The Harvest Field*. Athens, AL: Bible School Bookstore.

Shewmaker, Sam. (1975) *Church Growth in Southern Zambia, Volume 4*. Privately published.

———— (ed). *Drumbeat: The Africans Claiming Africa Newsletter*.

———— (ed.) (1993). Africans Claiming Africa Conference, 1992, Embu, Kenya.

———— (ed.) (1999). Africans Claiming Africa: Living the Vision.

Shewmaker, Stan (1969). *A Study of the Growth of the Church of Christ Among the Tonga Tribe of Zambia*. Unpublished masters thesis, Fuller Theological Seminary, School of World Mission.

—— (1970). *Tonga Christianity.* Pasadena, CA: William Carey Library.

—— (1971). *Church growth in Butonga: Surveying the Church of Christ in southern Zambia.* Unpublished manuscript, Harding University, Searcy, Arkansas.

—— (1973). New Approaches to Mission (Tonga, Zambia). In A. R. Tippett (Ed.) *God Man and Church Growth.* Pasadena, CA: William Carey Library.

—— (1976). Identification. In G. Gurganus (Ed.), *Guidelines For World Evangelism,* pp. 57-80. Abilene, TX: Biblical Research Press.

Short, W. N. (ed.) (1944-1960). *Glimpses of Africa.* Kalomo: Northern Rhodesia.

—— (ed.) (1974). *Rays of Light.* Bulawayo: Southern Rhodesia.

Steeves, Guy W. (1990). *Contextualizing the Atonement for the Sukuma Tribe of Tanzania.* Unpublished thesis, Abilene Christian University.

Stephens, Diane (1978). Homemaking in Africa. *Christian Chronicle 35* (4), 6.

Stephens, Larry (1987). The Independent Leader. In *Advancing The Kingdom: Church Growth Through Leadership Development,* pp. 67-76. Unpublished manuscript, Cascade College.

Tankersley, Oneal (1991). *In His Footsteps.* Eldoret, Kenya.

Tarbet, Gaston (1978). Utilizing Young Adults as Apprentices in Kenya. *Christian Chronicle 35* (4), 9.

—— (1980). KENYA: One Nation But Many Different Peoples. *Mission Strategy Bulletin 9* (1).

—— (1991). World Survey Chart–1991. *Journal of Applied Missiology 2* (1) [on-line] http://www.bible.acu.edu/missions/Journals/jam/vol_02_1/wrldsur1.htm.

Tate, Van (1970). *Patterns of Church Growth in Nairobi.* Unpublished masters thesis. Fuller Theological Seminary, Pasadena, CA.

———— (1973). *Kangemi: The Impact of Rapid Culture Change on Community and Family.* Unpublished doctoral thesis. University of Nairobi, Nairobi, Kenya.

———— (1978). Historical Sketch of the Church of Christ in Kenya. *Christian Chronicle 35* (4), 1f.

————. (1987). *Commentary on the New Testament in Simple English.* Searcy, AR: Resources Publications.

Van Rheenen, Gailyn (1974). *A Comparative Study of Church Planting in Uganda.* Unpublished masters thesis, Abilene Christian College.

———— (1976). Leadership Training Among the Kipsigis of Kenya. *Mission Strategy Bulletin 4* (1).

———— (1976). *Church Planting in Uganda.* Pasadena, CA: William Carey Library.

———— (1984). A Balance between Maturing Churches and Training Leaders. *Mission Strategy Bulletin 11* (4).

———— (1985). Vernacular or Trade Language. *Mission Strategy Bulletin 12* (3).

———— (1991) *Communicating Christ in Animistic Contexts.* Grand Rapids: Baker.

———— (1993). *Biblically Anchored Missions.* Austin, TX: Firm Foundation.

———— (1996). *Missions: Biblical Foundations and Contemporary Strategies.* Grand Rapids, MI: Zondervan.

Vogt, Tod K. (1996). Jesus and the Demons in the Gospel of Mark. *Journal of Applied Missiology* 7 (2) [on-line] http://www.bible.acu.edu/missions/Journals/jam/vol_07_2/markdmon.htm.

Walker, Wimon (1985). *Utilizing Traditional Beliefs About Spirits in Teaching Africans about the Holy Spirit.* Unpublished thesis, Abilene Christian University.

Walker, Rosalinda (1992). We are Family. *Journal of Applied Missiology 3* (2) [on-line] http://www.bible.acu.edu/missions/Journals/jam/vol_03_1/fldsel.htm.

Watson, Joe (1989). *The African Drums.* Winona, MS. J.C. Choate Publications.

Webb, Charles (1992). *Putting out the Fleece: The Missionary Life of J. C. and Joyce Shewmaker.* Unpublished manuscript.

Wheeler, P. R. (nd). *An African Safari.*

White, Ronald K. (1984). *An American Church Develops an African Missions Program.* Guided Research Paper, Harding University Graduate School of Religion.

Woodhall, Chester Ian (1979). *A Study of How Churches Grow in Zambia.* Unpublished masters thesis, Abilene Christian University.